MASS OBSERVING THE
CORONATION OF CHARLES III

The Mass-Observation Critical Series

The Mass-Observation Critical Series pairs innovative interdisciplinary scholarship with rich archival materials from the original Mass-Observation movement and the current Mass Observation Project. Launched in 1937, the Mass-Observation movement aimed to study the everyday life of ordinary Britons. The Mass Observation Project continues to document and archive the everyday lives, thoughts and attitudes of ordinary Britons to this day. Mass-Observation, as a whole, is an innovative research organization, a social movement, and an archival project that spans much of the twentieth and early twenty-first centuries.

The series makes Mass-Observation's rich primary sources accessible to a wide range of academics and students across multiple disciplines, as well as to the general reading public. Books in the series include re-issues of important original Mass-Observation publications, edited and introduced by leading scholars in the field, and thematically-oriented anthologies of Mass-Observation material. The series also facilitates cutting-edge research by established and new scholars using Mass-Observation resources to present fresh perspectives on everyday life, popular culture and politics, visual culture, emotions, and other relevant topics.

Series Editors:

Jennifer J. Purcell is Professor of History at Saint Michael's College in Vermont, USA. She is the author of several books and articles on Mass Observation and the BBC, including *Domestic Soldiers* (2010), *Mass-Observation: Text, Context and Analysis of the Pioneering Pamphlet and Movement* (2023) and *Reflections on British Royalty: Mass Observation and the Monarchy, 1937–2022* (2024). She is also the author of *Mother of the BBC: Mabel Constanduros and the Development of Light Entertainment on the BBC, 1925–1957* (2020).

Benjamin Jones is Associate Professsor of Modern British History at the University of East Anglia in Norwich, UK. He is the author of *The Working Class in Mid-Twentieth-Century England: Community, Identity and Social Memory* (2012) and co-editor (with Lucy Curzon) of *The Historical Contexts and Contemporary Uses of Mass Observation: 1930s to the Present* (2025). His latest research on football casuals, fanzines and the emotional politics of rave and acid house was published in *Modern British History* and *Contemporary British History* in 2023 and 2024.

Lucy D. Curzon is Professor of Modern and Contemporary Art History at the University of Alabama, USA. She is the author of *Mass-Observation and Visual Culture: Depicting Everyday Lives in Britan* (2017), which was awarded the Historians of British Art Book Prize for a single-authored book with a subject after 1800. With Benjamin Jones, she is the co-editor of and a contributing author to *The Historical Contexts and Contemporary Uses of Mass Observation: 1930s to the Present* (2025). She has previously published work on contemporary queer portrait painting and photography, Second World War British women war artists, the Ashington Group, and Humphrey Spender.

Editorial Board:

Fiona Courage, Director of the Mass Observation Archive and Deputy Director of Library, Culture and Heritage, University of Sussex, UK

Claire Langhamer, Director of the Institute of Historical Research and Professor of Modern History, University of London, UK

Jeremy MacClancy, Professor Emeritus of Social Anthropology, Oxford Brookes University, UK

Kimberly Mair, Associate Professor of Sociology, University of Lethbridge, Canada

Rebecca Searle, Principal Lecturer in the School of Humanities and Social Sciences, University of Brighton, UK

Matthew Taunton, Associate Professor in the School of Literature, Drama and Creative Writing, University of East Anglia, UK

Published Titles:

The Biopolitics of Care in Second World War Britain, Kimberly Mair (2022)
Mass Observers Making Meaning, James Hinton (2022)
Mass-Observation, edited by Jennifer J. Purcell (2023)
Everyday Life in the Covid-19 Pandemic: Mass Observation's 12th May Diaries, edited by Nick Clarke (2024)
Reflections on British Royalty, edited by Jennifer J. Purcell and Fiona Courage (2024)
The Historical Contexts and Contemporary Uses of Mass Observation: 1930s to the Present, edited by Lucy D. Curzon and Benjamin Jones (2025)
Mass Observing the Coronation of Charles III: Monarchy, Spectacle and Experience, edited by Jennifer J. Purcell and Lucy D. Curzon with Fiona Courage (2026)

MASS OBSERVING THE CORONATION OF CHARLES III

Monarchy, Spectacle and Experience

Edited by
Jennifer J. Purcell and Lucy D. Curzon with Fiona Courage

BLOOMSBURY ACADEMIC
NEW YORK • LONDON • OXFORD • NEW DELHI • SYDNEY

BLOOMSBURY ACADEMIC

Bloomsbury Publishing Plc, 50 Bedford Square, London, WC1B 3DP, UK
Bloomsbury Publishing Inc, 1359 Broadway, New York, NY 10018, USA
Bloomsbury Publishing Ireland, 29 Earlsfort Terrace, Dublin 2, D02 AY28, Ireland

BLOOMSBURY, BLOOMSBURY ACADEMIC and the Diana logo are trademarks of
Bloomsbury Publishing Plc

First published in Great Britain 2026

Copyright © Jennifer J. Purcell and Lucy D. Curzon with Fiona Courage 2026

Jennifer J. Purcell, Lucy D. Curzon and Fiona Courage have asserted their right under the
Copyright, Designs and Patents Act, 1988, to be identified as Editors of this work.

For legal purposes the Acknowledgements on p. xi constitute an extension of this
copyright page.

Cover image: photograph © Lucy D. Curzon

All rights reserved. No part of this publication may be: i) reproduced or transmitted in
any form, electronic or mechanical, including photocopying, recording or by means of
any information storage or retrieval system without prior permission in writing from the
publishers; or ii) used or reproduced in any way for the training, development or operation
of artificial intelligence (AI) technologies, including generative AI technologies. The rights
holders expressly reserve this publication from the text and data mining exception as per
Article 4(3) of the Digital Single Market Directive (EU) 2019/790.

Bloomsbury Publishing Plc does not have any control over, or responsibility for, any third-
party websites referred to or in this book. All internet addresses given in this book were
correct at the time of going to press. The author and publisher regret any inconvenience
caused if addresses have changed or sites have ceased to exist, but can accept no
responsibility for any such changes.

A catalogue record for this book is available from the British Library.

A catalog record for this book is available from the Library of Congress.

ISBN: HB: 978-1-3504-4178-1
PB: 978-1-3504-4177-4
ePDF: 978-1-3504-4179-8
eBook: 978-1-3504-4176-7

Typeset by Deanta Global Publishing Services, Chennai, India
Printed and bound in Great Britain

For product safety related questions contact productsafety@bloomsbury.com.

To find out more about our authors and books visit www.bloomsbury.com and
sign up for our newsletters.

CONTENTS

List of figures	ix
Acknowledgements	xi
Notes on contributors	xii

INTRODUCTION: MAY THE 6TH: MASS OBSERVING THE
CORONATION OF CHARLES III   1
Jennifer J. Purcell and Lucy D. Curzon with Dorothy Sheridan

Part I
OBSERVATIONS I   12

1 TALES WE TELL OURSELVES: THE ENDURANCE OF BRITISH
   MONARCHY IN THE TWENTY-FIRST CENTURY   31
   Jennifer J. Purcell

Part II
OBSERVATIONS II   56

2 VISUALIZING CORONATION   77
   Lucy D. Curzon and Jennifer J. Purcell

Part III
OBSERVATIONS III   102

3 'TIMID, BOOKISH, AND UNPRODUCTIVE'?: MASS OBSERVATION,
   MONARCHY AND ACADEMIA   119
   Lucy D. Curzon

Part IV
4 MAJESTY, MAGIC AND MASS-OBSERVATION   133
   Martin Francis
5 CHARLES III'S ROYAL BODY: SOME REFLECTIONS   137
   Paul R. Deslandes
6 OBSERVING THE CORONATION FROM WALES   141
   Nick Hubble

7	ANOTHER CORONATION Janet Wolff	145
8	RAIN, REVELS AND REBELLION: THE PEOPLE'S CORONATION 1937 AND 2023 Claire Langhamer and Lucy Noakes	149
9	ROYAL FAMILIES Lucy D. Curzon	153
10	CARLOS III E CAMILA: NOTES FROM A VERY SMALL ISLAND Catherine Ellis	157
11	RUMOUR AND THE CORONATION RITUAL Kimberly Mair	161
12	'CORONATION ORGIES' AND A 'TERRIBLY WHITE BALCONY': EMOTION AND RACE IN THE CORONATION OF KING CHARLES III Khaleda Brophy-Harmer	165
13	'LIGHTING UP THE NATION'?: SOUNDING MULTICULTURAL BRITAIN AND THE COMMONWEALTH AT THE CORONATION CONCERT Trevor R. Nelson and Christina Baade	169

OBSERVATIONS IV   173

Appendix: Spring 2023 MO Directive   183
Notes   187
Selected Bibliography   207
Index   214

FIGURES

1	'Royal Graffiti': Queen's Silver Jubilee marker on London pavement	36
2	'Royal Graffiti' at the Keep, home of the Mass Observation Archive	37
3	Mixed decorations with mug detail, Lewes, East Sussex ('People say she acted like she didn't give a f*ck . . . It wasn't an act')	80
4	Shop decoration, Chichester, West Sussex	80
5	Bill's Restaurant, coronation marketing, Soho, Central London	81
6	'The crowning moments in your family story', London Underground, Central London	82
7	Royal faces, Lewes, East Sussex	83
8	Blank royal faces, Lewes, East Sussex	83
9	Man in hat sits on chair	84
10	Duchy Organic limited edition shortbread	85
11	Coronation cakes, Brentford, West London	85
12	Prince of Wales, no decorations, Brixton, South London	86
13	Throne in Victoria Rail Station, Central London	86
14	Union Jacks in Piccadilly (looking towards Green Park), Central London	87
15	Piccadilly Circus (looking towards Coventry Street), no decorations, Central London	87
16	Open as usual, Thames Embankment, Central London	88
17	Media preparations, Westminster Abbey, Central London	88
18	Rotary commemorative poster (note: Charles's eyes are scratched out), Chichester Rail Station, West Sussex	89
19	Windrush Statue, Trafalgar Square, Central London	90
20	Commemorative royal sign, London Underground, Central London	90
21	Decorations in Soho, London	91
22	British campers on the Mall, Central London	91
23	Campers on the Mall take pictures in hopes of capturing very important people, Central London	92
24	Postbox topper, Salisbury, Wiltshire	92
25	Canadians on the Mall, Central London	93
26	Americans on the Mall, Central London	93
27	Protest posters (opposite 10 Downing Street), Whitehall, Central London	94
28	'The King Is Coming', outside Westminster Abbey, announcing a 'special chapel meeting' at Westminster Baptist Chapel, Central London	94
29	Repent, Houses of Parliament, Whitehall, Central London	95

30 a, b, c	Union Jack fashion, Hyde Park Central London	96
31 a, b	Diana Walk on the Mall and outside coronation barricades, Central London	96
32 a, b	Boating Lawn (first image at approximately 9.00 am and second image at approximately 10.30 am), Hyde Park, Central London	97
33	Morris dancers, Eccleshall, Staffordshire	98
34	Flag on pavement, Hyde Park, Central London	99
35 a, b	1953 postcard, courtesy of Janet Wolff	146
36 a, b	1953 family photographs, courtesy of Janet Wolff	147

ACKNOWLEDGEMENTS

The editors would like to thank Mass Observers and all contributors to this volume. We also wish to thank and acknowledge Jessica Scantlebury, Jacinta Mallon, Kirsty Pattrick, Suzanne Rose, Ellie Turner-Kilburn and the entire team at the Mass Observation Archive for all of their assistance with this project. We especially want to acknowledge the invaluable insights and continued support of Dorothy Sheridan. Lucy Curzon wishes to acknowledge support from the University of Alabama's Department of Art and Art History and the College of Arts and Sciences. Jennifer Purcell would like to thank Anthony Bassignani, Laura Crain and all the librarians at Saint Michael's College, and Braden Dwinell for his assistance with social media research and express gratitude to Saint Michael's College for their ongoing support of her research.

We are grateful to the Trustees of the Mass Observation Archive for permission to reproduce original Mass Observation materials.

CONTRIBUTORS

Christina Baade is Professor in the Department of Communication Studies and Media Arts at McMaster University in Ontario, Canada. Her publications include her award-winning book, *Victory through Harmony: The BBC and Popular Music in World War II*, and three co-edited collections: *Music and the Broadcast Experience*, *Music in World War II*, and *Beyoncé in the World*.

Khaleda Brophy-Harmer specializes in histories of 'race' and whiteness in contemporary British history. Her publication, 'An "Anthropology of Whites": Race, Diversity and Mass Observation', considers the role of racial identities in the construction of MO material, and asks how we might use it in discussions of 'race' and ethnicity in Britain. Her doctoral research, 'Understanding Performances of Whiteness in England through Mass Observation Directives, 1990–2000', works across disciplines to consider the role of emotion and memory in productions of 'race' in 1990s England (funded by the UKRI Economic and Social Research Council South Coast Doctoral Training Partnership).

Fiona Courage is Deputy University Librarian and Director of the Mass Observation Archive at the University of Sussex, UK. Her publications include 'Mass Observing Sport' in *Recording Leisure Lives: Sports, Spectacles and Spectators in 20th-Century Britain* (with Jessica Scantlebury, 2013), 'Recipes for Co-production with Children and Young People' in *Time, Technology, and Documentation in the Digital Age* (with Liam Berriman and Kate Howland, 2018), and *Reflections on British Royalty: Mass Observation and the Monarchy, 1937–2022* (with Jennifer J. Purcell, 2024).

Lucy D. Curzon is Professor of Modern and Contemporary Art History at the University of Alabama, USA. She is the author of *Mass-Observation and Visual Culture: Depicting Everyday Lives in Britain* (2017), which was awarded the Historians of British Art Book Prize for a single-authored book with a subject after 1800. With Ben Jones, she co-edited *The Historical Contexts and Contemporary Uses of Mass Observation: 1930s to the Present* (2025). She has previously published work on contemporary queer portrait painting and photography, British women war artists, the Ashington Group and Humphrey Spender.

Paul R. Deslandes is Professor of History and Associate Dean for Student Success in the College of Arts and Sciences at the University of Vermont, USA. He has written widely on gender and sexuality and British visual culture and is the author, most recently, of *The Culture of Male Beauty in Britain: From the First Photographs to David Beckham* (2021). He is also the author of *Oxbridge Men: British Masculinity and the Undergraduate Experience, 1850–1920* (2015) and *Notorious London: A City Tour* (2021). His current work focuses on architecture and cultural exchanges between Britain and the United States in the nineteenth and twentieth centuries.

Catherine Ellis is Associate Professor in the Department of History at Toronto Metropolitan University, Canada. Her research focuses on post-1945 Britain, particularly the history of the Labour Party and the impact of youth culture and young voters on British politics. Her work has appeared in journals such as *Contemporary British History, Journal of Political Ideologies*, and *Journal of British Studies*, as well as the *Oxford Dictionary of National Biography* and edited volumes, including *The Palgrave Handbook on Rethinking Colonial Commemorations* (2023).

Martin Francis is Professor of War and History at the University of Sussex, UK, where he regularly incorporates Mass Observation materials into his classes on the 1953 Coronation, 1940s cinema, the history of beauty and fashion, approaches to historical methodology, and the history of emotions. He has published widely on British history in the 1940s and 1950s, and his most recent monograph is *Empire, Celebrity and Excess: King Farouk of Egypt and British Culture, 1936–1965* (2022). He is currently writing an 'intimate history' of Britain's Second World War senior military commanders.

Nick Hubble is Professor of Modern and Contemporary English at Brunel University London, UK. They are the author of *Mass-Observation and Everyday Life: Culture, History, Theory* (2006) and *The Proletarian Answer to the Modernist Question* (2017), and one of the series editors of Bloomsbury Academic's 'British Fiction: The Decades Series'.

Claire Langhamer is Director of the Institute of Historical Research and Professor of Modern History at the University of London, UK. She works on feeling and experience and has published on children's writing, courtship, happiness, 'home', emotional politics and women's leisure. Her most recent books are *Class of 37* (with Hester Barron, 2021), *Total War: An Emotional History* (edited with Lucy Noakes and Claudia Siebrecht, 2020) and *The English in Love: The Intimate Story of an Emotional Revolution* (2013).

Kimberly Mair is Associate Professor of Sociology at the University of Lethbridge, Alberta, Canada. She is the author of the books *Guerrilla Aesthetics: Art, Memory, and the West German Urban Guerrilla* (2016) and *The Biopolitics of Care in Second World War Britain* (2022).

Trevor R. Nelson is Assistant Professor of Musicology at Wichita State University, Kansas, USA. His research centres on the post-Second World War British Commonwealth and how music informed globally minded Britishness. His writing has appeared in *Twentieth-Century Music, Ethnomusicology Review, Notes,* and *NABMSA Reviews,* and he is working on a monograph which considers music as a form of educational media that teachers and broadcasters used to reform British identity in the wake of imperial decline. He completed his PhD in musicology at the Eastman School of Music – University of Rochester.

Lucy Noakes is Rab Butler Chair of Modern History at the University of Essex, UK, and President of the Royal Historical Society. She is a historian of war and memory, with a particular interest in emotions in and after wartime, and the experience and memory of civilians at war. She is a trustee of the Mass Observation Archive and has been fascinated by the material collected by the Archive and what it tells us about 'ordinary people' ever since she was an undergraduate at the University of Sussex. Her most recent book is *Dying for the Nation: Death, Grief and Bereavement in Second World War Britain* (2020), which won the Social History Society book prize for 2022.

Jennifer J. Purcell is Professor of History at Saint Michael's College in Vermont, USA. Using Mass-Observation diaries and directives, her first book, *Domestic Soldiers* (2010), seeks to understand the day-to-day lives of six women on the home front during the Second World War. She is also the author of *Mother of the BBC: Mabel Constanduros and the Development of Light Entertainment on the BBC, 1925–1957* (2020) and editor of *Mass-Observation: Text, Context and Analysis of the Pioneering Pamphlet and Movement* (2023) and *Reflections on British Royalty: Mass Observation and the Monarchy, 1937–2022* (with Fiona Courage, 2024).

Janet Wolff is Professor Emerita of Cultural Sociology at the University of Manchester, UK. Earlier, she taught at the University of Leeds, UK; the University of Rochester, USA; and Columbia University, USA. Her books include *The Social Production of Art* (1981/1993), *Aesthetics and the Sociology of Art* (1983/1993), *Feminine Sentences* (1990), *Resident Alien* (1995), *AngloModern* (2003), and *The Aesthetics of Uncertainty* (2008). Recent edited volumes are: *Traces, Memory and the Holocaust in the Writings of W. G. Sebald* (with Jean-Marc Dreyfus, 2012), *Writing Otherwise* (with Jackie Stacey, 2016), *Culture in Manchester* (with Mike Savage, 2013), *The Photographs of Zygmunt Bauman* (with Peter Beilharz, 2023) and *The Simons of Manchester* (with John Ayshford et al., 2024). Her most recent monograph, *Austerity Baby* (2017), combines memoir, family history, transatlantic reflections and visual imagery. She is currently completing a book on Germans in Manchester.

INTRODUCTION

MAY THE 6TH: MASS OBSERVING THE CORONATION OF CHARLES III

Jennifer J. Purcell and Lucy D. Curzon with Dorothy Sheridan

Throughout its history, Mass Observation has shown an interest in documenting royal spectacle and ceremony, scandal and crisis. The Abdication Crisis, which saw Edward VIII abdicate the throne in order to marry twice-divorced American Wallis Simpson, and the reaction of the British populace and the British press to it, helped to stir the organization to life in late 1936. The founders of Mass-Observation articulated their theories regarding the study of British society over the next few months in *The New Statesman* and other journals, and in a pamphlet published by Penguin in June 1937.[1] During the first few months of that year, a volunteer panel of Mass Observers was created, which, by Coronation Day on 12 May, counted seventy-seven in its number. Starting in February, Observers recorded their activities (called Day Surveys) on the twelfth of each month. In this way, the ordinary rhythms of life could be compared to an ostensibly extraordinary event in national life. The experiences, or observations, of Coronation Day in 1937, as well as the earlier Day Surveys, formed the core of 'the first published example of the [Mass-Observation] method in action', *May the Twelfth: Mass-Observation Day-Surveys 1937 by over Two Hundred Observers*.[2] Focusing on another Coronation Day eighty-six years later, this volume is inspired by Mass-Observation's original inquiry into the relationship between the British people and royal spectacle, thus capturing an in-depth view of British society and culture in 2023.

Inspired by the anthropological work of co-founder Tom Harrisson in the New Hebrides (now Vanuatu), M-O sought to create an 'anthropology of ourselves' and was particularly curious about British responses to the symbolic nature of royalty and ritual in modern society. Harrisson's counterpart and co-founder, Charles Madge (who would later become chair of sociology at the University of Birmingham), was driven by an interest in 'how, and how far, the individual is linked up with society and its institutions'.[3] In order to understand this, Madge imagined the 'social area of the observer' radiating outwards from the individual and one's closest social relations in Area 1, to strangers and 'chance acquaintances' with whom one might come in contact in Area 2, and finally Area 3, which comprised 'people and institutions whose pressure and contact was less direct and personal', but were nonetheless influential in the construction of one's 'social consciousness'.[4] Madge situated celebrities, royalty and the media, as well as 'ancestors, literary and mythological figures' in Area 3. That the media played a central role in this process could be seen in the decision to place Humphrey Jennings's 'documentary-style' interpretation of news reports anticipating George VI's Coronation in the first third of *May the Twelfth* – before Observers' accounts of the day. As historian of Mass Observation, James Hinton has noted, *May the Twelfth* represented an 'inconclusive deployment' of Madge's theory of social areas,[5] yet it nonetheless provides the reader with intriguing and voluminous grist for consideration of the relationship between self and society, the role of the media in mediating social consciousness, and the place of monarchy in mid-twentieth-century Britain.

While much of the work done by the organization after 1937 veered away from royals and public engagement with the monarchy, M-O continued to document Observers' attitudes towards and activities around royalty during major events and scandals. M-O issued Directives (or qualitative questionnaires) when Princess Elizabeth married Prince Philip in 1947 and in the wake of the Townsend Affair in 1955. M-O captured overheard conversations ('indirects') when the Duke of Windsor resigned his post as Governor of the Bahamas in March 1945 and when rumours circulated that he might return to Britain later that year in internal memos called File Reports.[6] Interested in the impact of television on public engagement with royal spectacle and ritual, M-O staff geared up to replicate the 1937 survey in anticipation of the Coronation of Elizabeth II in 1953. The scale of this operation far eclipsed the original but was never fully published; only a fraction of its findings appeared in a short chapter in Tom Harrisson's *Britain Revisited* in 1961, in which he reflected on the common themes and questions found in both M-O studies of coronation. 'Many of the controversial issues of 1937 were raised and battled over again in 1953', Harrisson wrote. Comparing the two events, he noted that Observers questioned the costs of coronation and its over-commercialization. Concerns about access to the processions and representation in the Coronation service were also raised. Comments were made about decorations and the distribution of souvenirs by local councils, while concerns regarding the religious significance of the ceremony and whether or not people acted appropriately on the day ('are people just out to enjoy themselves?') were also evident.[7]

Despite a shift in the organization's mission towards consumer market research, Leonard Harris ran a public opinion survey on the monarchy under the auspices of M-O in the mid-1960s. It was published in 1966 as *Long to Reign over Us? The Status of the Royal Family in the Sixties*. Before his untimely death in 1976, Tom Harrisson considered following up *Living through the Blitz* with a volume on royalty. In preparation for the Queen's Silver Jubilee in 1977, royal biographer Philip Ziegler took up Harrisson's mantle and reconstituted a small Mass-Observation panel and published its findings in *The Crown and the People*. After a pause in activity, Mass-Observation was brought back to life in 1981, in what was eventually called the Mass Observation Project (MOP). This was partly in response to another royal event: the wedding of Prince Charles and Lady Diana Spencer. Since then, Observers have responded to Directives on other major royal weddings (since 1981), Queen Elizabeth II's *annus horribilis*, and the deaths of several major royals (Diana, the Queen Mother and the Queen).[8] The first coronation in seventy years presented the opportunity to revisit and reconsider many of the themes brought up in previous Directives focusing on royalty.

May the 6th

Comparisons between 1953 and 2023 were made quite frequently across the media and in Observer accounts of Charles III's Coronation. Those who remembered the previous coronation cast a nostalgic glow on 1953, looking back fondly on childhood memories of excitement, street parties and souvenirs, the summiting of Mt. Everest, and feelings of excitement as a new age dawned with a young and vibrant queen. One 89-year-old woman speaking to the BBC recalled the crowds camping out to watch the 1953 Coronation procession in the rain as, 'cold, wet, tired but very happy'.[9] But the Mass Observers provide more varied answers and tend to complicate this narrative somewhat. This includes an 83-year-old male from East Yorkshire, who did not have fond memories of 1953:

> I was thirteen and looked forward to playing cricket with friends on THE DAY. Inevitably it rained. It didn't stop all day. I endured twelve hours incarcerated in a suburban front room in company with several adults, plates of sandwiches and a 12-inch flickering black-and-white television set. I hated every boring second. And then my friends and I had to endure it all again in colour on film at school. To add insult to injury, a short while later came the film of the Royal Tour of the Commonwealth – more school punishment. Deference ruled – Royals could walk on water.

Much as other commentators on the subject did, on the broader national level, this Observer noted 1953 as standing in contrast to 2023. In addition to the scaling of Mt. Everest, 1953 was about sports glories like the Derby win of the Queen's horse, England's first Ashes victory since the Bodyline tour of 1932–3 and Stan Matthews' legendary performance in the FA Cup. 'We had a young queen in 1953 and her youth encouraged a national feeling of optimism after years of post-war drabness', he concluded. For him, Charles III was old and Queen Camilla was of 'dubious popularity', royal scandal and drama diminished any allure the monarchy may have once had.[10]

Of course, youthful memories and the passage of time tend to soften the day-to-day realities of past lives. Eight years after the Second World War, rationing of some items was still in place. London and other cities and towns were still digging out of the Blitz – evidence of which was stark along the procession route: viewing stands were constructed on bomb sites and the blitzed-out Carlton Club was still visible on Pall Mall, for example.[11] New technologies and a vibrant royal family were set against global anxieties about decolonization, the Korean War, the emergence of the Cold War and nuclear warfare. Musing on post-war Britain, *The New York Times* special correspondent C. L. Sulzberger reported to his American readers the lengths to which Britons were imagining (and hoping for) a New

Elizabethan Age despite its wartime experience, and, he stressed, the loss of status vis-à-vis the US. Britain was, he stated confidently, no longer the 'superpower' it once was. London was no longer the centre of global finance; even the British Navy paled in comparison to the American Navy. Despite 'realities', 'there is little doubt', Sulzberger commented,

> that the emotional wave of self-confidence based on neo-Elizabethanism has intruded deep into the public consciousness . . . The Briton is an optimist, and perhaps it is for this reason that he so often has succeeded, by what he himself terms 'muddling through', in surmounting bleaker crises than any now upon the immediate horizon.[12]

But optimism was rare in Britain in 2023.[13] Facing crises and anxieties framed by Brexit, Covid-19 and a revolving door of inept Tory leaders lurching from crisis to crisis, as well as global economic dislocation and heightened tensions in Ukraine and Palestine, Britain in 2023 seemed exhausted and bitter; the New Elizabethan Age had given way to 'Broken Britain'.

A closer coronation comparison might be best drawn between 1937 and 2023. As with 2023, George VI's Coronation took place in the midst of economic hardship and wider concerns about the rise of fascisms and the far-right, as well as political violence, across Europe and the UK. At the time, George VI was an untested, generally unpopular king. As Prince of Wales, his brother, Edward VIII, had cultivated a likeable, modern and populist public profile which made him wildly popular. Harrisson explained, 'Edward VIII had gained the reputation of people's champion against poverty and officialdom . . . Thus, there was a double loss to face – of tradition and new-style leader at once'.[14] Some Mass Observers in 1937 mentioned that they or others they knew refused to celebrate or listen to the wireless broadcast, and freely admitted that they would have been excited about the day had it been Edward VIII's Coronation.

With the cost of living crisis casting a pall over the proceedings, Observers in 2023 similarly felt less enthusiastic about the Coronation of Charles III. Some contrasted Charles's age with that of his mother and wondered whether there would have been more enthusiasm if William was to be crowned. Most Observers seemed less critical of Charles and Camilla in 2023 than they were after their marriage in 2005, at which time Observer opinion was strenuously against the notion that Charles may one day become king, let alone that Camilla might one day replace Diana as queen.[15] Some holdouts remained in 2023, disgusted by the notion of crowning two divorcees, wishing that Charles had ceded the throne, or still angry over the mistreatment of Diana. One 67-year-old female from Wales titled her observation, 'WASN'T THERE, DON'T HAVE A TELLY, SO NOT MUCH INTERESTED'. Much of this Observer's writing recounted her memories of the day Princess Diana died, and her assessment of the day – perhaps unsurprisingly – was 'It should have been Diana'.[16] Most Observers, however, said their opinions had changed about Charles, Diana and Camilla and were in favour of Charles becoming king. This 80-year-old female from Milton Keynes wrote,

I must confess that once upon a time I didn't relish the thought of Charles becoming king and rather hoped it would skip to William (who I still think will be an excellent king). But my views have softened as has Charles himself. He no longer seems as aggressive in his views as he was. Despite myself I put this down to Camilla's influence. She has been very good for him. I wasn't happy about her being crowned queen either, but I think she's earned her place now. She really hasn't put a foot wrong since they married, but has remained true to herself.[17]

Time and careful image 'rebranding' since the early 2000s has helped smooth out raw emotions and bend public opinion in favour of Charles and Camilla.[18] If these efforts to rehabilitate Charles and Camilla as individuals have been successful, there nonetheless seems, in 2023, more existential questioning about the value of the monarchy in the twenty-first century in Observer writing than was seen in 1937 or 1953.

Thinking with the Mass Observers

Mass Observation's studies were never about documenting royalty or royal life, but rather, the lens has always been trained on the ways that the British relate to royalty and participate in (or protest) royal events, how they think and feel about the Royal Family and the institution of the monarchy, and more generally, 'the complicated place of the monarchy in national life'.[19] The social experience of national events and institutions lay at the heart of MO's original and successive inquiries into monarchy. These studies, as with all other Mass Observation work, reach beyond the monarchy and provide insights into changes and continuities central to modern British society.

Observers' reflections on and documentation of their experiences offer space to contemplate the ways that individuals negotiate the boundaries between the personal and the public worlds around them. Observer writing suggests how media forms and media discourses wind their way through everyday experience and thought; it opens windows upon active and ongoing identity construction, the evolutionary processes of opinion formation, shifts in knowledge and feeling and the subtle crisscrossing of porous boundaries between self and society. Mass Observation's qualitative methods enable deeper insights into British attitudes and outlooks, everyday lived experiences, identity construction and engagement with national institutions than does quantitative opinion polling seeking to find answers in percentages and percentage changes. While these polls are necessary bellwether measures, Mass Observation responses allow one to go beneath the trends and consider why the surface of opinion might shift or remain stable. Observer writing is deep and rich with contradictions, questions, anxieties, surprises, ambivalences, certainties, emotion and reason, highlighting the messiness of experience and the tenuous nature of opinion and identity. It also illuminates 'social consciousness' and the constant negotiations between and across the three social areas Madge imagined in the 1930s. Further, the collection and preservation of Observer writing since 1937 enables longitudinal studies lacking in modern opinion polling, especially as regards British attitudes towards royalty, since careful and sustained polling on the monarchy dates back only to the 1980s.[20]

Mass Observation Directives that ask Observers to consider national institutions and events, such as the monarchy and coronations, allow researchers of MO access into negotiations of thought and emotions surrounding institutions and individuals which might, on the surface, seem distanced, aloof or overpowering. Observer writing on these subjects often underscores the proximities of these forces, suggesting that perhaps Madge's concentric circles of social areas were too strongly drawn and confident. Instead, Observer writing often demonstrates how intimate Area 3 may feel in the lives of individuals. Observers who remember the exact details and emotions surrounding Diana's death nearly thirty years later remind us of this intimacy. Regarding royalty in this way points to important factors in the endurance of monarchy in modern Britain.

Alongside *May the Twelfth*, the MO collection *Reflections on British Royalty*, and archival sources, readers can consider continuities and changes to these questions over time. In turn, we can think with Mass Observers across the three MO coronation studies about the ways people engage with the monarchy: how the emergence of popular media has changed popular experiences of the monarchy, how different media (radio, television, social media) have shaped our relationship with (and attitudes towards) the royals and the monarchy over time. Across these three studies, Observers have given us insight into the experiences of coronation from street-level or community-level. Equally, Observers have written about the experiences of new media: radio in 1937, television in 1953 and social media in 2023, which help us understand the mediatization of monarchy across space and time. Insight into the tenor of British attitudes towards royals and the institution of monarchy is also evident. In his assessment of the 1937 *May the Twelfth* study, James Hinton argued that:

> MO found not the regimented hysteria of the Nazi rally but the same quirky individualism and the same comforting capacity to domesticate and gently laugh at the pretentions of power ... that Orwell was later to celebrate in ... *The Lion and the Unicorn*.[21]

It is worth considering the extent to which this assessment still holds true, and asking how much the ability to criticize the monarchy, sometimes scathingly, works into enduring notions of national identity. As in 1937 and 1953, this 2023 study of Charles III's Coronation affords opportunities to contemplate existential questions about the place of monarchy in Britain and British society: its endurance, its relevance and its potential future. Equally, Observer writing allow us to broaden the lens outwards, giving us insights into British culture and society far beyond the specific topics of royalty and the monarchy.

It should not be surprising, given the expansiveness of Mass Observation's approach and the wealth of information it creates, that MO materials have proved a boon to historians, sociologists, anthropologists and other scholars – particularly after the founding of the Mass Observation Archive at the University of Sussex in

1976. Scholars have used these materials to chart the impact of the Second World War, Thatcherism, inflation, industrial action, social and romantic relationships, ageing, education and the AIDS crisis, among many other topics. And while Observer responses form the backbone of Mass Observation collections, these observations are not the only ones relevant to understanding monarchy, war, epidemics or the project of Mass Observation itself. Indeed, if we consider Mass Observation more holistically – 'as a [continuous] set of practices, people and ideas' – then those who use Mass Observation data, for example, are an essential part of the observation process.[22]

In 2023, Observers watched Charles III's Coronation unfold before them and sent their reflections about it, in the form of Directive responses, to the Mass Observation Archive. This was the second stage of the 'conversation', of course, since it was the archive staff who devised the Coronation Directive in the first place. Staff also made preliminary observations, before Observers ever received the Directive, including how to formulate questions in such a way that Observers engaged meaningfully with them, rather than responded with a mere 'yes' or 'no'. Upon receiving the completed Directive responses, the archivists, in turn, performed yet another kind of observing – the kind of assessment involved with cataloguing and preserving these written materials safely and efficiently. Finally, as the researchers who visited the archive, we undertook still more of the observation process. Like many other investigators who use MO materials, we recorded patterns, themes and data trends. We also highlighted singular or individual responses for the unique insights they reveal.

It must be emphasized, however, that the relationship between the Observers who write and those (researchers, archivists, etc.) who use their insights is not a case of the former being surveilled by the latter unawares. Rather, as Dorothy Sheridan has argued, Observers respond to Directives and send materials to the archive with the specific intention of having their materials read.[23] Observers are fully aware, in other words, that their narratives are catalogued for a future audience of investigators.[24] Lucy Robinson suggests that the Observers are, in fact, conscious of themselves as historical actors. They regularly 'evaluate which events they think will be remembered in the history books . . . They worry about whether they are giving the right sort of answers. [Mass Observation] . . . is, after all, an "archive of feeling" and that includes feelings about the archive'.[25] Given this reciprocity, Robinson rightly suggests that scholars and archivists cannot assume that they control or shape the information contained within the archive. Instead, they must work 'with, rather than on, everyday voices thinking about the joint composure of narratives and the blurred lines between analysts and their objects of study'.[26]

In this volume, therefore, we have asked scholars, many of whom routinely use the Mass Observation Archive as part of their research practice, to provide observations about the Coronation of Charles III. In so doing, our intention is to highlight the collaborative nature of the archive (and Mass Observation overall). In asking scholars to write about the same topic *and* to do so at the same time as the panel of Observers, the sometimes-problematic gaps between the two bodies are significantly reduced. For example, Observers may feel a sense of distance between themselves and the 'readers of the future' who assess or otherwise use their work. The anxiety evident in Robinson's quote above is a good example of how this sensibility impacts Observer writing. But in the instance of this volume, the Observers and the researchers are speaking at the same time. Moreover, these scholars do not have the advantage of hindsight in mining Directive responses from years if not decades before. Instead, scholars and Observers address the issue at hand *together*. Observer accounts are interwoven in sections throughout the present volume, juxtaposed alongside one another and placed in conversation with and against the academic essays and reflections contained within, fundamentally destabilizing and repositioning academic voice and analysis. In doing so, we challenge the reader to find meaning within and between Observer accounts on the one hand and Observer and academic accounts on the other, thereby inviting opportunities for original insights and new vistas of inquiry. And this seems much more in line with the 'science of ourselves' initially hailed by Madge, Harrisson and Jennings in 1937.

Like all Mass Observation work, this study is primarily about documenting British life and society at a particular moment in time. As with the twentieth-century coronation studies, this twenty-first century volume engages the individual (whoever they might be – part of the Observer panel, researcher or reader) within the national and asks us to reflect on broader questions of identity and belonging. Observation and reflection, in short, lie at the heart of this collection. We have supplemented archival documents with essays meant to stimulate, broaden and deepen thought about contemporary British society and culture.

Note on the current study

In anticipation of Charles III's Coronation, Mass Observation issued a Directive to Observers in spring 2023. The Directive consisted of three parts, with a bank of qualitative questions or considerations for each.[27] As always, there were no constraints or requirements for the length of writing, and Observers could choose to answer any or all of the questions in any way they saw fit. Most typed their answers and emailed them to the organization, while some sent their handwritten or typed responses through the post; a handful supplemented their responses with line drawings, photographs, programmes of community activities or printed copies of internet content. A Coronation Day Survey was handed out in a few communities in southern England and as part of MO initiatives engaging with prison populations. In the week before the Coronation Ceremony, the editors observed home and shop decorations in several high streets in the south of England, including Lewes, Brighton, Chichester and Salisbury. The editors also observed activities in and around central London during the Coronation weekend, keeping in touch with the MO Archive through the social media app, WhatsApp.

Observer writing is interspersed in four sections throughout this volume. In these sections, all grammatical, typographical, and spelling errors have been retained in order to preserve the original tone and spirit of the observations. At the end of each individual observation, readers will find a series of letters and/or numbers in bold text. Where indicated, gender and age are listed first followed by the Mass Observation Archive's unique identifier for that Observer. Observations written in response to the Day Survey do not include Observer numbers. Mobile observer records are identified by INV (or investigator).

Finally, as with previous publications in this series, some contributors have chosen to retain the original hyphenated spelling of Mass-Observation, while others have dropped the hyphen, and still others use both spellings depending upon the era of the movement under discussion.

Part I

Observations I

27 April

Asda has Union Jacks hanging over the mezzanine level. Far more low-key than this time last year, when every lamp-post in the carpark had a flag tied to it. Unfortunately, whoever was in charge of lamp-post flags only managed to hang them as high as their own height, leaving the flags flapping at half-mast. This was eerily prescient, given Her Majesty's demise in September.

I check out a coronation caterpillar celebration cake. It's a regular caterpillar cake wearing a rice-paper crown and cloak. Horrifying. And not worth the money – for £7 I want it to have Charles' face.

Whilst getting the dinner ready, last year's street Jubilee Whatsapp Group pings into life. The man from No 7 asks, 'Is there anything planned for the Coronation?' It's tempting to reply, 'Yeah, a big parade in central London', but I don't dare. It's also tempting to reply, 'Bit late now, if you wanted a street party you could've set the ball rolling weeks ago yourself'. I think he's being cheeky to ask, and is possibly assuming someone else has already got things in hand. I reply with a, 'No plans, we're a bit busy at the moment, hope all are well, Best wishes'. Hope that isn't too blunt.

One other couple replies to say they are busy with their church that weekend. No one else responds at all . . .

30 April

. . . During my weekly phone call to my parents, Mum says that the couple across the road have invited them round to watch the Coronation on the TV, and she's really looking forward to it. She surprises me by saying she won't be swearing allegiance to the King though as she thinks it's a bit much. She's usually quite a Royalist.

Dad recalls watching the last Coronation. He was 11. The family got invited to watch it on their friends' new television set, and then he remembered going with his sister to a children's party at a community hall. He says it rained heavily, and he was transfixed at the sight of the Queen of Tonga getting drenched in an open-topped carriage, as if it was perfectly normal.

In the evening, we watch The Windsors Coronation Special on Channel 4. Very irreverent and funny, especially Princess Anne in a pant-suit from M&S, and the planned scaled-back Coronation in a hotel function room in Slough . . .

I think the country, on the whole, embraced the coronation of King Charles III. Shops had special coronation marketing displays – my favourite was Ableworld's King's Coronation Offer on mobility scooters (now only

£1699), *perhaps a comment on Charles and Camilla's ages? Red, white and blue appeared everywhere, and a large number of people enjoyed extra time off work. Although the ceremony was ridiculously archaic (Spurs of Chivalry? Really?), it was enjoyable and showed how the British excel at pageantry and excessive grandeur (who wouldn't want a gold coach? Although I must say that I was disappointed that it wasn't pulled by unicorns).*

Perhaps we just like an excuse for a party. On the Friday, the school where I work held a Family Picnic to celebrate the coronation. Parents joined their children to sit at tables on the front playground and eat their picnic lunch brought from home (although children entitled to free school meals could order a packed lunch [with Union flag] from the kitchen). The pupils had made bunting to decorate the playground, the headteacher wore a Union flag waistcoat, and children careered around the playground in high spirits. All great fun until 1.30 pm when the torrential rain started.

6 May – The Great Day Itself

My friend J and I decided to mark the coronation by pigging out on afternoon tea (albeit served at noon) at the British Ironwork Centre by Oswestry. They had advertised a royal celebration afternoon tea for £25 a head, serving King Charles's apparent favourites of cucumber sandwiches, Battenberg, fruit cake and Coronation Quiche (cheese, spinach, broad beans and tarragon). The very generous portions were served with a bowl of thick-cut fries and a glass of Pimms. All very delicious – although I expect the fare at the Palace was a little grander and the table probably not decorated with coronation red, white and blue paper napkins. And they may not have had balloons. I did wear a plastic tiara for the occasion – but then found out later that Charles had banned them (just as well I hadn't been invited to the Abbey then).

Our tables were set up on the balcony in front of a TV screen showing the BBC's coronation special. I think the Ironwork Centre was originally expecting more people to book because the promised 'big screen' was probably only about 40 inches – but the lack of people worked in our favour because the four tables were inside in the dry and not in a tent in the pouring rain. We watched the TV from when the King arrived at the Abbey until he left – then we wandered around the sculptures and shops at the Ironwork Centre for a bit, trying to ignore the small choir singing in the rain.

Penny Mordaunt, bearing the sword of state, was admirable (despite being a Tory); and I felt for all the participants who had to carry the precious and symbolic items ('Don't drop the crown, don't drop the crown, don't drop the crown!'). I also marvelled at their bladder capacity/control – amazing!
F61, E7722

3 May

On train to Southampton. One flag in backyard. Prominently displayed for trains. Some bunting on the inside of a garden greenhouse.

50s female at Chichester Cathedral, excited for coronation. 'I think he'll be a good king', and cites his concern for the environment all those years back – 50 years, even when he was laughed at. 'He said we should save the world.' 'Not happy about' Camilla initially, but has warmed to her over time. 'She's a support to him.'

G., 60s white female, thinks people will be interested on the day. Her feelings about royalty are ambivalent. She's from a royal-supporting family, but has since questioned the cost. Still, what are the options? Doesn't want an American President.

4 flags in a row in private gardens on west side of E. Worthing, 1 flag of St. George on east side, between E. Worthing and Lancing.

4 May

L., 50s white male, republican. Asked how to abolish the monarchy. L. says you don't need to do anything. Just remove them. We don't need a head of state.

First camper on the Mall: 50s white male from Bolton. Came to Queen's funeral, but not able to see anything. Decided to camp out this time. Got here Tuesday (May 2). Was told by police that campers would not be moved despite media reporting that they would be. White woman, also 50s, on hearing man was from Bolton, mentions Wanderers' Football team. She tells him that she once dated a footballer from the team. The conversation moves on to football, no more coronation talk.

Two white women (sisters) late 50s/early 60s. Camping for their mother who can't because of health. One woman (40s) staying until mum comes, then she'll leave. She says people just walk up and ask them questions and take pictures. They say I am 'one of the nicer ones' because I asked them if I could talk to them. They 'feel like public property'. Woman (40s) says she can 'take it or leave it', but admits she's 'getting into it'. Thinks monarchy is a 'unifier', but the money spent is problematic.

Two white women in their 40s from Yeovil and Somerset and third from Kent. Male 10-yo hiding in tent playing video games. Came on Wednesday (3 May). Very jovial. They all met at the Platinum jubilee, camped together for the funeral and came together for coronation. One woman says she initially thought William should be King, but now she believes 'it's right' that Charles should be King. 'William will have his time.' All nod assent. Woman from Kent says she didn't like Camilla initially. 'Diana was our Queen of Hearts. She'll always be our Queen of Hearts', but because there's so much hatred in the world, it's time to forgive. She saw Camilla in Scotland and thought she wasn't as severe as the media make her out to be. They all agreed that the media made Camilla look bad. On the subject of Meghan, they all agree that she stole Harry and was a gold digger and a loose woman.

Canadians, 1 70 yo white woman and 2 white women 40s. One 40 yo woman very vocal about the monarchy and how important it was to keep it for the sake of the community of the Commonwealth. She loves that she (as a Canadian) is a part of a larger community. She points out the Brits and Aussies next to her. The meaning of the monarchy, she says, is that community. Older woman doesn't like the British disdain for the monarchy. Other 40 yo woman said 'if you lose it [the monarchy], who are you? You'll lose your culture, you'll have someone else's culture'.

Group of Canadians and one American. White woman in 40s, white male in 40s (Canadians). White woman in 40s with 17 yo white son, who is a royal blogger (from San Fran). Son became interested in royalty binge-watching The Crown. Mom flew him out and is here to support him. She wants to focus on 'the positivity of the royalty'. Canadian and American women say they didn't like the poor journalism surrounding Harry and Meghan. Canadians were also at the funeral. They say one female police officer cried seeing everyone in the crowd crying.

5 May

Brixton center not very decorated, with the exception of some chain stores/ restaurants, and even at that very subdued. Even the Prince of Wales pub undecorated. One black man, in his 60s, sitting next to the tube entrance, selling coronation-themed items and Union Jacks.

Black woman 20s. 'It's just another day', and she'll be working during the Coronation, 'you have to work, you know'. On the monarchy, 'disgusting, the cost'.

6 May

Stopped at first viewing area in Hyde Park and speak to two security guards – one male Algerian 50s and another male Nigerian 20s. Nigerian says coronation doesn't really matter to him explaining that he had his own traditions and implied that colonial relationship complicated it for him. He said the coronation was good work: double pay, and hoped to work a 13-hour day. Algerian says to me in confidence, while another security guard comes up to speak to Nigerian, that I should talk to people who are waiting for the ceremony to start because I would get 'better answers'. Inv said she is interested in all viewpoints. Algerian explains that his country has a lot of resources and money, but it was only for a few. Elections were corrupt and politicians keep resources from the people. Nigerian hears tale end of the conversation, when Algerian stated 'they only care for your vote'. 'Who? The Prime Minister?' the Nigerian says. 'No – my country', says Algerian. 'Where you from, Mate?' asks Nigerian. The two swap information and fist-bump at the fact that they're both from Africa.

Nigerian explains that elections are also corrupt in his country: '10 year olds are allowed to vote, so long as they vote for the right person.' Algerian tells Inv that the UK may be a small country, but it has more jobs and more than at home and a better life here. Nigerian says all he wants is a job so he can take care of his family. Algerian agreed. Algerian in country for 19 years, Nigerian 7. **INV, JP**

The coronation of King Charles was an interesting day for me. I had asked my kids, one age nearly 19 the other 12 the day after the coronation, whether or not they wanted to get involved in any of the local events. They didn't, which was kind of unfortunate since, as I had told them it was a moment in history. The general feeling in our town was one of mixed emotions and a range of people who wanted to celebrate at one end, and showing no interest at the other. So in that respect it demonstrates to me the difference between the current, modern understanding of the monarchy compared to that at the time of Elizabeth II's coronation.

As my kids didn't want to celebrate it or show much interest in events at all, I spent the night before with my partner at his pub. We went to bed quite late and woke just after 10 the next morning. So we missed the beginning of the televised celebrations. We started watching the BBC on iPlayer just around 11.30 at the point the King was completing the vows/formalities required. We then watch the Queen Consort being crowned, and the rest of the celebrations whilst also serving people in the pub. We expected it would either be a quiet day, or a busy day. We had a quiet one. In fact when I nipped out to the shop and to speak to my kids who were with their grandmother, it was really quiet. Either people were watching the events on the TV or they were otherwise occupied. **B6900**

I am so excited about the Corrie! What a historic event, I don't expect I'll get to see another. Charles is not beloved like his mother was, but I do like him. He has a nice warmth. The build-up has been off-putting with all the Harry and Meghan stuff, I am sick of them both. Then you hear the Corrie will be very toned down, only an hour long, not much pomp etc. I want the glitz and glamour! I want to revel in the fantasy! I want to see the amazing jewels and witness something spectacular! Times are tough at the moment – I want something to cheer my heart. I know other people think it's crass to display such wealth, but I say go for it! We all know they are rich anyway. We should make the most of our assets – this is what the Armed Forces are for if they are not fighting. I can't wait! The sight of them coming down the Mall will be unbelievable. That for me, is the real Britain, not all these awful politicians!

I am going to be watching at home on Saturday. My brother will be with me. He works in a shop and they were going to open but now have realised their folly and are going to be shut. Otherwise I would have watched alone. So I'm thankful. I will get up really early, I don't want to miss anything. I love the reporting beforehand when people are lining the route! It's all too exciting. I am going to make special food – scones with jam and cream, delicate sandwiches and possibly a quiche. It will take me through to about 3 pm I believe, when the balcony appearances will have been done.

There is going to be a party on the green in my little village. I'd rather watch at home so I don't miss anything and I can have my own food, which I do prefer.

4 May 2023: Getting dead, dead excited now. I've just come in to watch the BBC news channel and get a bit of the building atmosphere in London. I'm getting butterflies now! It's such a nice escape from politics, the Ukraine War and all the other nasty stuff we've had lately. I also follow along with a forum called Tattle Life, they have a Meghan and Harry thread I read quite a lot. They discuss all the stuff Harry and Meghan get up to and hold them to account a bit. I will probably read that live during the Coro. I have got my scone recipe out today and I need to prepare for tomorrow when I will make the scones and quiche, and possibly the dainty sandwiches later in the evening . . . not sure as I don't want them to be ruined by Saturday.

5 May 2023: Really excited. It's so good for people like me to have something like this to enjoy – I've recently lost my parents and I'm very lonely. Things like the Coro and the World Cup and Eurovision make me feel a connection to other people and it makes the days go by easier . . . It's very stormy out which is a shame. I think the Red Arrows might be cancelled – such a pity. Half of me wishes I was in London for it, the atmosphere looks great. But seeing it all unfold is so special too . . .

6 May 2023: Absolutely overawed by today. It has been amazing. I'm too tired now so I will write my full debrief tomorrow.

7 May 2023: Well the Coronation yesterday was simply wonderful. A bit different to what I was expecting – poor Charles and Camilla looked utterly terrified for much of it. Also the procession afterwards was very short and it seemed over far too soon at 2.30. They could have done a few more balcony appearances throughout the evening – the Queen did six. William was just wonderful, Kate was excellent and so beautiful – iconic. Harry I found a pathetic figure. He looked really scruffy and had a really stupid grin on his face. Andrew looked totally haunted. Anne, Edward and Sophie are just a bit boring for me. Loved that Anne's feather covered Harry!

The ceremony itself was fabulously done. It was highly charged with so many emotions and the Archbishop of Canterbury did an excellent job as the calm anchor in the middle of it all. I loved the Grecian chanting. The ancient book. The moment of the crowning. All so special. Great to see Prince George 'mucking in' as one of the boys. That is what Harry is depriving his kids of. I loved when Charles was holding the items of regalia with that most special crown on. It was simply jaw-dropping indeed, just as one of the bishops had predicted beforehand. I found the tension quite unbearable when Charles was making the oaths during the first bit. It almost seemed too much for him. It was raw – electric! It was the most scintillating, spine-tingling thing I have ever seen. We are not used to seeing real, raw, palpable emotion on TV – everything is so bland and rehearsed and performative – false in other words. What we saw Charles go through was as fundamental and earth shattering as it is possible to ever see. Honestly, it was. It was extraordinary. It was the kind of thing one can only dream about from books like Harry Potter. Zadok the Priest was an outstanding moment. The choral performances were all perfection. The music pressed on every button in you. The Queen's funeral, for all its high pomp, was rather robotic somehow, whereas this was deeply human and transformative; to see an exhausted looking man with his reticence and humility, burdened with the destiny of his birthright, emerge from the ancient ceremony, not only a king but The King, who will be known as such throughout the world.

I do think Charles's age has been a big factor in the ceremony being toned down and having a rather muted, sombre tone to it. He looks like he is feeling his age, so does Camilla. It must be so hard to have to do all this so late on in life. He can reign for two decades at best. Not like his mother who must have felt she had unlimited time in her favour.

9 May 2023: The Coronation Concert was last night. I thought it was so bad!! It was tacky and very . . . woke. It was more woke than Meghan and Harry – maybe the whole thing was to prove them wrong. Charles seemed to really enjoy it. William's speech was good. But after that we had an eco lecture, argh!! While the whole audience wore light up wristbands which would have caused huge damage to the environment when they are made and they don't decay like organic matter would. What a disgrace.

Today has been dreadful for me – alcoholic family member caused a huge disturbance at 2 am last night. Feel sick with worry. It's ruined the whole Coronation weekend unfortunately.

10 May 2023: I wonder if Charles was behind Justin Welby's speech in the House of Lords? It's got him written all over it.

11 May 2023: I like that there has been quite a few appearances by the Royals – nice to see them pulling their weight. They used to just let the Queen do everything. As long as they keep quiet in politics, quit the eco lectures and stop the woke nonsense, I think they can do okay. The House of Windsor shall survive. I'm thrilled I bore witness to a Coronation, which has always seemed so mythical. What a jolly nice weekend it was. **F37, B5342**

The Coronation was the subject of a blog by an economist I read, who was a lot clearer on the monarchy's wealth than I'd seen before. In my head, all Crown lands were held in trust by the state, who then paid a stipend; which is correct, but fails to include land and property held privately, for instance in the Duchy of Lancaster. I also hadn't realised Charles had not paid any inheritance tax on, for instance, his priceless art collection, or on all the swans he now owns. The economist gave the cost for the Coronation as £100million, paid for by the public, which, if anything near correct, does seem quite offensive. Particularly given, again according to this economist, Charles had suggested we celebrate his enhattening by volunteering at our local foodbank.

If true, the foodbank suggestion is an interesting one, because it highlights the weird position the monarchy is in. Clearly Charles is aware of foodbanks, and has a sense that the need they represent is in some way bad. Potentially he has a sense that, as King, he has a sort of noblesse oblige to his subjects – that on some level, the point of a king is to protect those who owe him fealty as justification for that fealty. That relation between monarch and subject is clearly political – it is bound up in considerations of distribution. But Charles can't criticise the policies of the democratically elected government which led to his subjects needing to rely on foodbanks. That would be a political intervention, and thus out of bounds. Maybe he's worried about the optics of criticising a government for starving his subjects while he is wearing a hat made of gold, but the optics of saying 'celebrate my golden-hat day by feeding the poor while I ride around London in a golden carriage' are probably worse. Is it cowardice at that point? Role-playing 'father of the people' by shaming the government into treating the weakest in society with some degree of dignity feels like an easy position for his PR team to defend, which would be a relief for them given their usual responsibilities. I don't know. If this is his idea of playing a role in public life though, I don't think much of it. **M37, J5734**

It was quite an exciting prospect – having a coronation as neither myself, my husband, children or grandchildren had ever been to one/experienced one before. This was a once in a life-time event and we determined to mark it.

I made ribbon wreaths for both my front door and that of my Daughter-in-Law and son. They were having a street party, so they also had the flags, bunting, tablecloths, and cups. Our village had celebrated the Queen's Jubilee the year before and so there was just a picnic up at the other end of the village for the King's Coronation.

The Yarn Bombers had decorated the tops of the post boxes, utilising the toppers from the Jubilee, and just adapting them for the coronation theme.

Overall, I think that it was much quieter than the Jubilee, the weather was rubbish, but it brightened up in the afternoon for the picnic, which was well attended. We went to the allotment, as the event was mainly for families and for people who did not get the chance to go to the street party the year before for the Jubilee.

I watched the event on the TV and felt that I was watching history being made as this was the first time that it was televised in colour, and you really *felt that you were there, taking part. I am not sure that it mattered that it was more low-key – I think that the Jubilee the year before was more celebratory as the Queen had achieved a great feat and this was probably in the King's mind, along with the austerity and poverty that was more evident with the fuel crisis etc.* **F64, B8020**

When I think of the coronation the words that come to mind are outrageous, revolting, disgraceful, inappropriate and out of touch. I cannot imagine the mindset of a government or monarchy who believes it is right to spend between £100 to £200 millions of taxpayer's money on this medieval spectacle. The Monarchy is worth billions. This should be public money to be spent on the people for the people and I do not mean those in power.

There are people in this country who will die because they cannot get access to health care or a place to sleep, there are people daily who are going hungry and cannot afford nutritious food. There are people whose education is so poor that they will never achieve their true potential. There are people who cannot afford to pay their bills. The suffering in this country due to the deliberate Tory polices causing inequalities is unforgivable. And here we have a new monarch who accepts the right to be King.

It just blows my mind that anyone can think that this is okay. Why are people supporting this absolute nonsense. Why are protesters being locked up. I am scared that we are no longer able to protest.

The local elections show that people are sick of the Tories, but we need a radical rethink and a society that is fit for everyone to live in.

I don't know what to do to stop feeling so angry and the injustice and inequality. I have no faith in our political system at all and especially not in a system that still has a monarchy.

I did not watch any of the coronation, I spent the day avoiding it and any coverage. I have only read articles about the cost of the event. If this were a Netflix film, it would be like some dystopian future where millionaires do not care about the lives of the many. This is archaic.

I feel very much Not in My Name for both the Tory Government and the king and royal family. I have been told that as we live in a democracy that I must accept the outcome of an election. If the election were democratic and truly democratic such as the best and fairest form of proportional representation, fair boundaries, fair access to voting, education about the voting process and its history, access to ID for all and compulsory voting from 16 then I may just accept it. As it stands, this is not a democracy and the idea that we still have a Royal Family is the most shocking of all.

It was ridiculous to have another bank holiday for the king's Coronation, that would have been costly in itself. This event should not have been allowed to happen. The Queen dying should have meant the laying down of the royal family and all wealth be for the people, invested for long-term good, a source of income for the NHS and social care. **F58, J2891**

Being situated 2 miles out to sea on the Isle of Portland, I look out of my window and to see out whole prison swathed in cloud and rain, I wonder if the Coronation's aerial fly past will happen. All of the major tv channels seem dedicated to today's events and, having checked for a voicemail from my son on my in-cell phone, settle to enjoy the forthcoming celebrations. Having served in Her Majesty's Armed Forces, I've always been a staunch royalist and today nothing will spoil King Charles' Coronation. Alongside my coffee I have a bar of fruit and nut chocolate as a celebratory breakfast.

As I watch the numerous regiments, units and corps assemble it's a bittersweet feeling of national pride but envy at not being there to be part of this unforgettable event. Seeing the smiles and emotions of the 1,000s that gather along the Mall is truly amazing and it makes me wonder why there are those that seek to remove the King and Monarchy.

I see their applause increase as the Royal coach travels these 1.3 miles to the Abbey, how I love all of the pomp and ceremony I think back to my school days when I fell in love with Tudors' and Stuarts' history and admire the stunning beauty of this historic event. How amazing it would be to be sat with the honoured audience as their majesties begin the ceremony.

An officer shouts along our corridor that it's lunch time and I hurriedly go down to . . : to collect my meal – a cheese bap, mini choc-chip cookies and an apple.

I'm glued to the tv, I've even chosen to ignore the freedom of my morning's association period to become a small insignificant part of proceedings. Wow, I love this almost heraldic chivalry, Penny Mordaunt looks stunning and in a bizarre way would fit into my mental image of what a Tudor courtier would look like.

Ceremony complete I now channel hop to see what other programmes are on. I'm a grand-prix (F1) fan and switch between the return to Buckingham Palace and the E-Prix racing from Monaco.

Frustratingly, although HMP the Verne claims it's diverse and inclusive, there's little evidence of today's historic event within any department, room or corridor apart from mine where I've made and painted my own window bunting, crown and CR.

As many of us have single rooms (cells) we can effectively isolate ourselves and its probable that among our among our population of 600 that others are doing as I am, watching events alone but to all intents and purposes, it's just another Saturday in prison. **M50s, HMP The Verne**

I love history so I was very interested to watch the Coronation. However, I think that I was the only person among my present work colleagues who was intending to watch it – there were quite a few comments in advance about it being a waste of money, or people said they had no interest in the monarchy. When we went back to work after the weekend, one person commented that parts of it felt like a Shakespeare play, but he was the only person who mentioned having seen any of it. I watched the BBC1 coverage from about 8am until about 3.30pm.

There definitely were bits which felt like a Shakespeare play – seeing Charles kneeling in his undershirt felt like a very medieval image. And when he was sitting in the Coronation chair wearing his gold robe and holding the orb and sceptre, he looked like the painting of Richard II in exactly the same pose (which now hangs in Westminster Abbey and is the earliest known portrait of an English monarch, from 1390). I find the sense of the length of historical tradition very moving. Other things I found interesting or notable were: the 12th century anointing spoon being the oldest remaining part of the regalia; and the choir singing 'Vivat! Vivat Regina Camilla!' and 'Rex Carolus' as they entered, with such precise diction. Previously I only knew this phrase as the title of a play about Elizabeth I – I didn't realise it was something used in the Coronation service.

My parents and sister also watched it but I haven't discussed with any other friends whether they did or not. At the Queen's funeral a lot of my stage manager friends were fascinated by the amount or organisation and rehearsal behind the events, if nothing else. I definitely felt the same watching the Coronation, especially the procession afterwards and how it was all so coordinated to the same music. **F47, S6976**

As of now (19th April) I have zero knowledge of what's happening for the coronation. I'll probably see a bit of it on TV because it'll be unavoidable but I won't be planning my day around it. It'll probably be a big deal in East Belfast where I live because it's a chance for them to shout about their Britishness. It doesn't feel like as big a deal as the Queen's coronation would have because Charles is so old it's not going to be another long reign. We'll be doing this again in a couple of decades. I don't mind Charles, I think he's probably the best of them but I think these days we're very aware that it's a problematic institution as a whole. The pomp and spectacle are a bit of entertainment but I don't know that people take it very seriously anymore. It's not even that special to witness it, which most people throughout history would never have got to do, because everyone in the world can witness it now. It's just a TV show. You can even watch it on catch up. I think the most interesting part of it would be what it means to Charles and how he's feeling about it all but you'll never know that. I doubt he'll be following Harry to the Memoir shelves.

Coronation Day – 6th May 2023

I've been weeding all morning but it's 10.20 am now and I've just sat down and turned the telly on. Am also, of course, whatsapping friends about how ridiculous the whole thing is. As with the Queen's funeral, everyone's very 'I'm not a monarchist but I'll watch the ceremony'. It's just a big spectacle, I suppose. Though, as my mum pointed out last night, it must be pretty galling for people who can't afford to feed their kids to watch a literal gold coach process through the streets accompanied by £150 million worth of security. Although she's just bitter because she hates Camilla.

I also sowed some wildflower seeds this morning. Not for any symbolic reason, I just happened to have time today, but Charles likes wildflower meadows so I'm calling the little patch Coronation Meadow just to be funny.

They've just started off in the coach and I do feel oddly emotional about it. Not that it means anything to me personally in a patriotic sense but it's a very momentous thing for any human to experience, I can't help wondering how Charles is feeling right now. How many people ever get to know what that's like. And Camilla. At least Charles grew up knowing he'd be King. It must be completely mental for her. Everyone in the crowd is watching through their phone screens, they might as well have watched on telly. As if there won't be enough footage of this.

Crowning someone this old feels faintly ridiculous but maybe that's just ageist. My friend said, 'it feels like these once in a lifetime events come along every 18 months now'. They do make a massive fuss out of everything.

I think people are a bit unfair about Camilla. If Charles had been allowed, he'd have married her in the beginning, he only married Diana because he wasn't allowed to marry the woman he loved. They're finally reunited, I think that's nice. It was a bit crap for everyone involved. And why shouldn't she be Queen? Every King's wife has been Queen. And there have probably been Kings and Queens before who were married to someone else first.

Harry's arrived. No Megan, don't blame her. Anne's arrived in fantastic robes and hat. I love Anne, she's so butch and horsey. I really think she doesn't give a shit what anyone thinks of her.

I think Andrew's there too. Ick. His poor family too. Though, God knows what Charles might have got up to, I'm sure they'd put more effort into protecting his reputation than Andrew's. I'd like to think Charles is not an asshole but you'd never know. He does like gardening though so I'm giving him the benefit of the doubt.

I like Camilla's dress. Charles's robe looks cosy. It's basically a fancy oudie. Which is what I'm wearing because I'm cutting back on the heating bills.

I think Camilla looks nervous but Charles looks quite relaxed. When he said, 'I come not to be served but to serve', I honestly welled up a bit. He seemed to mean it.

My friend says there's a lady in a union jack dress in her street.

All the kids got trowels and wildflower seeds in school and they made crowns, they're all into it. My nephew is very excited about the whole thing. My mum remembers the Queen's coronation, I suppose they'll remember it forever...

I did buy some Fry's Chocolate Creams and they had 'Coronation' on the packet for no reason whatsoever. I thought that would do as a celebration...

Twitter is awesome today and includes such gems as 'Can't believe they are going to make a MAN queen. This woke nonsense has gone too far'. And 'Buckingham Palace is unoccupied right now. It is time'. . . . Twitter is being very irreverent. 'This could have been an email' was my favourite. I've been retweeting but I feel a bit guilty actually. It's so easy to take pot-shots at a big institution but they're also people. This is the entire purpose of Charles's existence and he didn't get a say in it. And how many of us would do any better in his position? How many of us recognise our own privilege?

They're arresting protesters. Which I don't agree with at all. But again, I'd feel bad for Charles as a person if he was on his way to be crowned with people holding up signs that basically say we don't want you. I really don't think he has much of a choice about it.

Well, I hope he'll do good things, especially for the environment. He seems the only one of the royal family who actually might care about the environment. If he could fund decarbonizing the global economy, that would be great! Probably he'll just launch a wildflower meadow initiative and distribute seeds . . .

Had a baked potato. They've left the cathedral and got in the gold coach. They're saying the gold coach is the sort of thing you see in fairy tales. It's also the sort of thing you see in countries with massive wealth inequality but whatever. It's pretty impressive, historically speaking.

They're marching now. It's slightly disconcerting, as a person from Belfast, to see so many union jacks in one place. I love that Anne's riding instead of being in a coach.

The commentators are talking about how good natured the crowd are and how they only need a few police officers. No mention of how the rest of the police are busy arresting protesters.

Actually it is a bit sickening to see them all retreat back into their castle in their gold coach, knowing how hard some people have it.

It's all over. The flyover was cut short because of the weather. My dad will be disappointed. He's always liked Charles because he flies and likes nature. My parents are at their neighbour's house for a party so my mum could well be drunk by now and arguing with people about Camilla. The weather has improved so I might go out for a walk. **F45, M6082**

I've written before about having anti-monarchist leanings yet also having a compulsion to observe the Royals and all the antics, spats and ceremonies that accompany them wherever they go. Someone has to ponder on the sheer bonkersness of their lives in the midst of all the royal gushing that's going on at the moment. So I will be watching the coronation on TV while my husband, B, is out having a nice long walk (weather permitting) and trying to ignore it all. But I won't be taking part in any events. The thought of a street party – no, no, no! . . .

As to the scale of the event, 'small scale' obviously has a different meaning to the Royals than it does to ordinary folk. Even though in their eyes it's been shrunk to tiny proportions, it will still involve an enormous venue, thousands of guests, sackloads of bling and blanket TV coverage because, despite all the belt-tightening, the rest of the world still has to be impressed. We've already been told exactly how many priceless jewels encrust those hideous crowns, orbs and sceptres, what precious robes will drape the royally anointed bodies and which gilded coach is new and comfy and which is old and rickety. I think we're meant to gasp at the beauty of it all but my God, that ancient bumpy Cinderella coach is the last word in vulgarity. It's a good thing horses don't know the meaning of embarrassment.

And who's paying for it (£250 million allegedly)? None other than the taxpayer! That's you and me, in a time when nurses are being denied the pay rises they deserve. Is this fair? If Charles and Camilla think that 'the people' want this level of spectacle, they should have set up a Go Fund Me page, asked their fans to contribute what they could, then made up the shortfall from their own pockets. Sorted.

And on top of all this, it's just been announced that we are being invited to join in a timed, unified swearing of allegiance to our King. What? Allegiance? It's not as if Charles is riding into battle, leading his army against the pesky French and saying, 'Come on now chaps and chapesses, you are behind me, aren't you?' It's a pity there's going to be no way of counting how many allegiances were sworn from living rooms and pubs across the land, especially as a poll has just found that two thirds of the population 'don't care' about the coronation at all.

I must include something wonderful that's come out of all this lunacy though Channel 4's The Windsors: Coronation Special. I'm a big fan of The Windsors and this one off was sheer joy what with Anne swallowing the Koh I Noor diamond to prevent Camilla nicking it; Pippa, lacking an invitation, injecting Sophie Wessex in the neck so that she could impersonate her (successfully, as nobody noticed), and Camilla/Cruella slaughtering the corgis in order to get the only fur she was going to be allowed for the ceremony. But my favourite moment went to Beatrice (or was it Eugenie who can tell the difference?) for uttering the words, 'York's a real place? I thought it was made up, like Narnia or Wales'.

So, on 6th May I'll be pouring myself a drink, cracking open a fresh tube of Pringles and pigging out on the whole ridiculous Royal shenanigans . . . until I get fed up of the obsequious TV commentary and switch off. I can't wait to see if the Stone of Scone gets stolen the night before and is whizzed back to Scotland in a plain white transit van. If anybody at all speaks to Harry. If Andrew starts to cry when he realises he's been seated behind a pillar. It's all going to be marvellous. **F66, J7420**

Watched the whole procession – smiling when I spotted a face or two at the Abbey or on parade. To be honest, I was pleased the King had a great ceremony. I recall the few words he once said to me . . . at Colours Party and Officers' Mess photo, he stood me as a kind person. **M52, HMP Isle of Wight**

Our two children had coronation tea parties at school and nursery on the Friday. They wore red, white and blue clothes. On Saturday we went to the library for Lego Club and took home some coronation colouring and activities and bookmarks. At home I watched the ceremony with our children. Lots of Christianity in the service and we felt nervous for the moment Justin put the crown on the King without it falling off. Justin is known well by our local church friends so there is an element of knowing that he is a normal human being rather than someone very senior and unapproachable.

My husband avoided the ceremony because he believes that leadership should be voted in, rather than given senior positions by birth. We agree to disagree especially as British politics has not been looking after the economy or cost of living. **F44**

I watched most of the Coronation, seduced by the spectacle, precision, talent, discipline and history.

    My very young self just remembered 1953 on a small black and white TV
    I loved the COLOUR this time
    The hats and dresses, uniforms and clerical regalia.
    The horses.
    BUT too much GOD
    TOO much military and too much church, and too much maleness.

Our little community had a Street party for the Queen's Silver Jubilee, but not for King Charles 3 Coronation. I felt it too soon after Queen Elizabeth 2 death, while understanding it had to be. **F78, A5854**

I won't be watching the coronation but I'm glad it's happening. I think there is value in tradition and in ritual. I think it doesn't matter what it is, but the fact that something is done and repeated I think imbues it with meaning, I think the imagery of it provides a language that allows us to speak of things that would normally be very hard. I think of this imagery and ritual as a sort of container as well, a place to hold emotion, an outlet maybe. I think it's important to have a shared language in this way, I think we've lost a lot of this over the years. These things can give a sense of community which is useful. I am interested in history as well, and the history of the crown, and so I like to see and hear about the tradition behind it and I like the link to the past. Perhaps if I lived alone I would watch, however I know my kids won't be into watching it and so we'll likely take the opportunity to be out for the day. It's nice to have an extra day off but it would feel a waste to spend it watching the TV. We try and make the most of holidays and other days off by doing things as a family. **H7993**

Saturday 6th May

Spent the day enjoying a 9 mile walk up Harkerside in the Yorkshire Dales with my partner and a friend who shares anti-monarchist sentiments. Beautiful sunny day and a lovely walk with sightings of Ring Ouzels and the sound of Cuckoos across the valleys.

Sunday 7th May

Hunkered down at home – reading, gardening and not putting on the TV or Radio.

Monday 8th May

Accompanied my partner to the nature reserve where he works as he was leading a 5am Dawn Chorus walk which I joined. Spent the rest of the day at the reserve -walking, birdwatching, reading and even fitting in a small nap in the Visitor Centre during the afternoon . . .
   Rest of week
   No TV news, no newspapers.
   Result
   Coronation successfully avoided. **F52, F4813**

I went to the Hayward Gallery on the almost empty South Bank and then to Borough Market – which was filled with tourists who seemed to be in London without interest of the coronation. Bizarre! But I have successfully not seen any of it on any platform. So I remain happy. No one but my Mum was interested. **M52**

I think Queen Elizabeth was so well liked and respected because she was seen as belonging to another age, she conducted herself well and was a constant in many people's lives simply because she has been queen longer than many people have been on this earth. The royal family are a relic of the past we could do very well without. I doubt very much that Charles will command the same respect.
   I cannot believe in these hard and trying times that as a nation we had to contribute so much money to this event. The money would be have been much better spent supporting our ailing NHS, or on building affordable homes. Such pomp and ceremony in my opinion shows that the royals do not understand the lives of ordinary people, or the real hardships faced by many in Britain today, with ever increasing numbers of people being made homeless, some end-

ing up living on the streets and many more families having to depend on food banks. There is so much hardship at the moment it's outrageous that a family with so much personal wealth is funded by us the tax payers.

If Charles was that keen to be crowned king, it may have been more appropriate if it was a private ceremony attended only by his very close family. It would appear that the scaled down ceremony was double the cost of the late queen's Coronation, even though we were informed two thousand people were invited to attend, compared to eight thousand who were invited to the late queen's Coronation. In my opinion there should have been a referendum to gauge just how the public really feel about the continuation of this archaic institution and whether it should have been privately funded. As a survey conducted on 13 April 2023 by YouGov indicated that far less people actually cared about the coronation, of those surveyed only 9% cared, while 29% did not care at all. Personally I did not want Charles' now wife, previously his mistress to be crowned queen. **F76, R7226**

I was a bit ambivalent about the Coronation in the weeks before it took place. As news of the various stages of preparation trickled through via the news media (such as a special screen being ordered for the anointing to take place in private, and embroidery of the robes etc.), it all sounded terribly irrelevant and expensive. I decided to try and understand the process better by watching the previous 1953 coronation on YouTube, one rainy weekend afternoon. I think this helped me to be better informed about the structure of the service and the reasons behind its different components, and also about the people, Crown jewels and costumes involved. Without having done that, I think I'd have found the Coronation service quite bizarre and rather long-winded.

I had been working at home in the morning and listening to the music from Westminster Abbey before the service on Radio 3. Just as the Coronation service itself began, my husband kindly drove me into Gawthorpe village, to see if anything was taking place; but as anticipated, the bunting was for the May Queen celebration the following week, not because of any event taking place for the Coronation itself. We then drove into Leeds, to watch part of the Coronation on the big outdoor screen set up in Millennium Square in the city centre.

Why did we drive into Leeds, instead of into Wakefield which is nearer where we live? Well, I'd already checked online and seen that no events were planned for the centre of Wakefield other than a broadcast of the service inside the local public library. We found this quite a surprising contrast with how Wakefield had responded to the Jubilee the previous year, when there had been a civic event in the city centre, including a live DJ, union flag deckchairs, and entertainment for children.

When we arrived at the Millennium Square in Leeds, there was a crowd of – at a guess – two to three hundred people, sitting on temporary tiered seating, and on coloured public art seating in front. There was also a catering van offering hot drinks and food next to the tiered seating, and a couple of armed policemen keeping an eye on things. The people were a mix of student-age groups & individuals (my husband observed that he thought many were overseas students, due to the variety of ethnicities present), older grey-haired people mostly alone or in couples, and families with children. People were also coming and going all the time, walking through and taking in the scene for a few minutes before going on their way. People chatted quietly among their own groups, but cheered (and booed) and applauded at the moment when the crown was placed on the King's head. Other than at that moment, the atmosphere was quiet and relaxed, rather than noisy and enthusiastic. The people weren't joyous flag-waving royalists, they were more interested in sitting quietly and witnessing history. It seemed rather low-key, and the crowd rather smaller than the space allowed or the preparations suggested had been expected . . .

I am ambivalent about the Royal Family. I think we should have a national conversation about whether it's time for an elected non-executive head of state, one that the British people can replace if necessary. I think it's time there was more transparency surrounding the influence individual Royals have over central elected government; and about the Royal income and how it is spent. I'd welcome more transparency around the Crown Estate and the Duchies of Lancaster and Cornwall, about how they are run, how they treat their staff, local communities and tenants and about what they own and spend. At the very least, I would like to see a greater implementation of environmentally-friendly management, and greater investment in 'green' businesses and initiatives. While they continue to exist, they ought to do good with what they have. **F48, E7936**

I'd been listening to the pre-Coronation coverage on my radio in the kitchen, but when Mum arrived we switched on the television just in time to see members of the royal family arriving at Westminster Abbey. I thought the Princess of Wales looked so beautiful and stately – as if she'd been born to it. It's so easy to imagine her being Queen one day. The Queen seemed a bit nervous and awkward in contrast, although I know it must have been a very intense day for her. I saw that when images were posted by the royal family on Instagram afterwards, there were so many (an overwhelming number of) negative comments along the lines of 'not my Queen'. . . . **F36, O7697**

Although it's true that these rituals create community and patriotism in the population, I think they are in poor taste. I think it's a generational difference of opinion – my parents and grandma (although not royalist or particularly patriotic) watched the coronation together to witness history, whereas myself and my friends thought the whole thing to be ridiculous.

Most people my age are perhaps too aware of the economic and political environment we are inheriting. To spend so much money on the coronation *of an outdated system of rule with such clear ties to racism, colonialism, paedophilia, misogyny etc. etc., when the British population is experiencing a housing crisis, low wages in a time of inflation, racial tensions and increasing violence is frankly bizarre. It shows an ignorance to real people and problems to disappear into the pomp and practice of ritual that has no place in the modern world. The importance of the royal family and its rituals is reminiscent of a past time, not the modern issues and realities my generation are experiencing. We are not reminiscent of a 'golden' age of the royal family – to us they are just privileged people, above the law for no reason and incapable of evolution. I did not watch it, I just enjoyed memes of it on the internet later. It was frankly quite embarrassing.* **K8117**

Yes we can do ceremony well but can't run a national rail or bus service adequately. **F70, M6763**

Chapter 1

TALES WE TELL OURSELVES

THE ENDURANCE OF BRITISH MONARCHY IN THE TWENTY-FIRST CENTURY

Jennifer J. Purcell

We stood in the pouring rain, watching as more and more people pushed their way into the ever-decreasing spaces between tangles of couples, friends and families in front of a massive screen in Hyde Park. Hoping to secure a place near Buckingham Palace, we set out early in the morning (but not obscenely early – around 7.00 am) through Hyde Park, but were kettled back via the streets of Mayfair once Green Park had reached capacity. In the crowds that turned back, a few showed up in fancy dress: one group straight out of the turn of the (twentieth) century, wearing boaters and bowlers. Girl guides gave out Union Jack flags. Along the way, some stopped to snap photos and selfies in front of festive patriotic displays.

When we first arrived at the Boat House Lawn viewing site – about an hour before Charles III's Coronation procession started – the green lawn was still visible, punctuated only by a few groups of people lounging on blankets or coats as they hunkered under umbrellas. The atmosphere was easy and festive. We watched carefree toddlers wheel happily across the grass and listened to laughter as it wafted through the air. A few people queued for ice cream at a stand along the Serpentine; two young men strolled leisurely by, dressed head to foot in Union Jack suits. The pre-ceremony broadcast played on a jumbotron some thirty yards away, beaming messages of good wishes to the King from politicians and celebrities knitted together by videos of Prince Charles engaged in an array of charitable activities – with emphasis especially on his environmental activism.

As the crowd grew, three Old Age Pensioners (OAPs) plonked their packable lawn chairs down in front of a family with two young children who had been settled long before. Rain poured. All available space filled in; the green of the lawn was replaced by a patchwork of umbrellas, cheap flags and ponchos. As the procession broadcast started, people near the screen stood up, creating a wave as successive rows got up to see the show. Behind us, cries of 'sit down, sit down' erupted. The shouts became angrier and more insistent: 'Get down!' There wasn't much those in the middle could do, so they continued to stand. A group of Spanish tourists were incensed. 'Put your umbrella down', one shouted repeatedly at me as he tried to impress his girlfriend with this act of chivalry. Unable to see, and tired of the abuse hurled from behind, we pushed our way out of the crowd towards the ice cream stand and its burgeoning queue. Once out of the crush of people, just by the park pathway, we could see the screen perfectly.

We wandered to the Cockpit viewing area just to the west and caught the rest of the ceremony standing along the pathway. A St John's Ambulance brigade cleared the path as they patrolled the park. One very enthusiastic woman in her thirties danced, sang and conducted to 'Zadok the Priest'. A cheer burst forth from a crowd gathered at a viewing area across the Serpentine, then another from a different direction. Our broadcast of the crowning was delayed a few seconds more, followed by a rather anaemic cheer from our compatriots. Some stayed to watch Camilla's crowning moment, but most left once Charles was suited up in his kingly kit and handed his orb and sceptre.

Why had thousands stood in the rain, packed into irritable knots peeking through umbrellas for a royal glimpse – a familiar royal face, some shiny crown? – straining their ears to hear the ceremony, when they could have quite comfortably watched the whole thing on television elsewhere with a far better chance of actually seeing and hearing *something*? I found myself wondering this repeatedly that morning as I longed for a cosy, dry pub far away from the fray. For me, it was 'for science': I was a Mass Observer – but what of the others? The crowd gathered in Hyde Park was not homogenous, nor did it think or move as a singularity. It was comprised of Londoners, Brits and members of Commonwealth countries; in this age of global tourism, the crowd's composition also extended far beyond the Commonwealth. And the reasons for attending this Coronation ran the gamut from genuine support for the British monarchy, to witnessing a spectacle or historic event, to recording the event or protesting it, to sheer boredom and, of course, the human propensity to gravitate towards a crowd (just as moths enjoy their flame).

Regardless of the reasons for being there, the crowds assembled in the streets of Westminster and London were good for the monarchy, underscoring at least some assent. None of us had to show up for this occasion and pack ourselves along procession routes or into viewing areas.[1]

Watching the proceedings on a big screen in Hyde Park is truly of the late twentieth/early twenty-first century, and the crowds stuffed into the several viewing locations across St. James, Green and Hyde Parks were a product of the fact that the procession route had been shortened drastically from the five-mile-long route followed by George VI and Elizabeth II to the meagre 1.3 miles between Buckingham Palace and Westminster Abbey chosen by Charles III. Aside from the trappings of our modern lives – the jumbotron and massive speakers, yellow security guard vests and folks fumbling with their mobiles – this was an experience not unlike past coronations.

London has always been the hub for all manner of royal events. Traditionally, a monarch's power hinged on the support of London. London crowds have barred the gates to unwanted (potential) monarchs, witnessed triumphal entrances and lined royal procession routes for centuries. For Henry VII's Coronation, some among the crowds witnessing Elizabeth of York's procession to the Abbey fought one another – some to the death – for a piece of the ray cloth which lined the route.[2] (There were reports of scuffles among the umbrella-ed crowds in 2023 because those umbrellas blocked views of the procession route.[3]) In his diary, Samuel Pepys recalled people hanging out of windows to witness Charles II's Coronation procession.[4] In both 1937 and 1953, Mass Observers recorded crowds on the procession route who delighted in trying to figure out which royal figure(s) might be riding in a royal coach – all the while listening to the BBC's radio commentary through loudspeakers erected along the streets.[5]

For a ha'penny, a lucky individual might escape the bustling processional crowds and buy a seat inside the Abbey at Edward II's Coronation; inflation bumped the price to a crown for Charles II in 1661 and as much as ten guineas at the opening of the Hanoverian age.[6] When Charles II entered the City in advance of his Coronation, he was met by London crowds who welcomed him with cheers and tableaux meant to remind him of the tenets of good kingship.[7] With the procession party behind closed doors in the Abbey, London crowds were treated to a number of amusements, such as the ascent of a hot-air balloon in Green Park and boat races in Hyde Park for the Coronation of George IV in 1821.[8] Firework displays were staged in Hyde Park for all three of the nineteenth-century coronations.[9]

Londoners haven't always been in a celebratory mood: those who stood outside Westminster Abbey at William the Conqueror's Coronation were reportedly silent.[10] London crowds attacked Matilda and her supporters during her pre-coronation banquet, running them out of the City and sending support to her rival, Stephen, who was held captive in Winchester.[11] And while crowds came out in support of George IV's jilted Queen Caroline, they failed to show up for the King: according to *The Times*, many prime seats along the procession route of the unpopular monarch went unsold.[12]

Beyond London, communities have marked and celebrated the accession of monarchs and their coronations for centuries, with fetes, fireworks displays, plays and processions of their own. Medieval and early modern 'Royal Progresses were accompanied by much popular fun and ingenious displays and contrivances, as well as by obeisances and savage punishment of transgressors'; Elizabeth I's Coronation Procession in London and across England featured 'tableaux and festivities putting the pallid ceremonials of her Windsor successors to shame'.[13] Local celebrations marking royal moments didn't need the august presence of the monarch. Early modern coronations were observed across England with bonfires, gun salutes, music, processions and libations.[14] Elizabethan and Stuart societies annually celebrated 'Crownation day', the date of a monarch's accession, with 'bonfires, bells, candles, services, music, hospitality, beer, and bread'.[15] Memories of popular monarchs competed with current rulers as some chose to celebrate the Crownation of Elizabeth I but refused to attend ceremonies marking Charles I's Coronation.[16] Public dinners and processions were popular ways to mark coronations across the country and beyond.[17] Residents of poor houses across London were treated to special coronation feasts or presented with special coronation allowances of a few shillings.[18] In 1937, the British Consul General held a special thanksgiving service at Trinity Church in New York City, while other groups organized their own events, such as the dinner and broadcast of George VI's Coronation at the Ritz-Carlton put on by the Daughters of the British Empire.[19] Mass Observers in 1937 and 1953 reported on local community celebrations that could have come out of any century, including ox-roasting, fetes, music, dancing, church services and amusements for children.[20]

Street and window decorations and illuminations have long featured in the marking of coronations. *The Times* reported on the decorations on view across the capital for Victoria in 1838, such as the Grand Cross Hotel's 'very superb radiated star in brilliant gas; likewise, a transparency of the usual emblems of England, introducing a likeness of Her Majesty'. In another display further down the Strand, WH Smith's featured 'a magnificent star of the Order of the Garter in brilliant gas'.[21] Since 1937, Observers have also reported and commented on street and shop decorations laid out in advance of a coronation.[22] One Observer in 1953 noted a rather shabby decoration in the shopwindow of a local engineering works:

> A model of the Coronation procession made from unsuitable coloured cardboard, which through not being strong enough, bends in several places. In front of the model at the letters EIIR worked in small, square metal nuts. These would be improved if they did not include several which are going rusty. This display is an eyesore.[23]

One 82-year-old Observer in 2023 was 'amazed and disgusted' at what she believed was a lack of flags and decorations to mark Charles III's Coronation, so much so that when she noticed a well-decorated shopwindow display in a hairdressers', she opened the door and complimented them on it.[24] Politically conservative towns tended to take their window-dressing seriously, while those with tendencies to the left or mixed constituencies either couldn't be bothered or offered light-hearted displays.[25]

On 11 September 2022, towns and cities across the country acknowledged the accession of Charles III in public ceremonies, like the one at King's Lynn Town Hall. Local dignitaries in full civic dress and regalia stood on a dais in front of locals as the mayor of West Norfolk borough read out the proclamation of accession. The crowd responded with three cheers and sang the national anthem.[26] Similar public proclamations took place across the country and Commonwealth, from Birmingham to Papua New Guinea to New Brunswick, Canada. The New Brunswick proclamation included prayer, playing of the national anthem, toasting the King and a twenty-one-gun salute. Wolastoqey elder, Imelda Perley, said of the event, at which she performed a traditional blessing, 'When anything historical happens, that's what we call the braiding of sweetgrass. It's coming together with our different traditions and bringing them together in the sacredness of being New Brunswickers, being related, and being here together'.[27]

Planning, organizing and staging royal events – coronations, 'Crownations', celebrations of the monarch's birthday, and jubilees – brings the monarchy into the experience of the everyday. Long before the fetes and processions take place, committees are set up and meet regularly to organize events; subscriptions are solicited in support of these activities; purchases made and contracts signed; decorations, order of events and procession participants decided upon.

Those not involved in planning, or tapped for subscriptions, pass by flags and bunting – or lifesize cutouts and digital displays of royals (as in 2023) – during the course of their day-to-day activities. Royal ceremonies and celebrations are reinforced by this 'banal monarchism', or, 'the ways in which a positive view of the monarchy is insinuated into the everyday lives of its subjects'.[28] Historian Andrzej Olechnowicz borrows this concept from sociologist Michael Billig's notion of 'banal nationalism'. Everyday 'flagging' of the nation is, very often, also the 'flagging' of the monarchy. Many reminders of the British nation are marked by the monarchy: the crown is ubiquitous in British life – more so than the Union Jack.[29] The most obvious of monarchical 'flags' are coins, stamps and postboxes. Postboxes are everyday artefacts which act as permanent reminders of a deeper past connected through royal ciphers that date the space they occupy. More recently, postboxes have become objects for further engagement with royalty as knitted postbox toppers can be found popping up across the country in anticipation of royal events.[30]

It would be hard to miss the iconic red postboxes that dot the built environment, but the nation and monarchy are woven even more seamlessly into the fabric of everyday life: royal warrants mark consumer products and services with a seal of royal approval, plaques and named features commemorate either the presence of a monarch or a royal celebration. In Brentford, the Strand on the Green Association spent nine years lobbying for, and eventually unveiling, an accessible pathway under Kew Bridge named (and signposted) in honour of Queen Elizabeth II, on the occasion of her Platinum Jubilee.[31] Walking the pavements of London, one might notice plaques that commemorate the 1977 Silver Jubilee Walkway. We barely register the ubiquitous 'royal graffiti' signifying 'the Queen (or some other royal) was here', such as the one at the Keep – where Mass Observation's archives are kept – which is elegantly etched upon a beautiful slate plaque, 'This building was opened by HER MAJESTY THE QUEEN accompanied by HRH THE DUKE OF EDINBURGH on 31 October 2013'. On the day of the Big Lunch – a day after the Coronation – representatives of Ealing Council unveiled a commemorative plaque marking Charles III's Coronation inside the town hall and gave a 'loyal toast'.[32] Outside, on the pavement, is a plaque commemorating Elizabeth II's Platinum Jubilee.

Media and the experience of coronation

While the day-to-day banal markers of the British monarchy and nation are carried in pockets and experienced in the built environment, the media plays a critical role in reinforcing this connection. The rise of nationalism, Benedict Anderson argued, was aided by the construction of an 'imagined community' nurtured by the advent

Figure 1 'Royal Grafitti': Queen's Silver Jubilee marker on London pavement.

of 'print-capitalism' which 'made it possible for rapidly growing numbers of people to think about themselves, and relate themselves to others, in profoundly new ways'.[33]

In the eighteenth century, as official censorship loosened and more newspapers began to circulate in London and regionally, expressions of both criticism and support of monarchy could be found in print. Constitutional monarchy and the British imagined community were thus worked out within a media culture that allowed criticism of royalty, as seen most vividly in 'the "efflorescence" of visual satire' during the Georgian period.[34] With the burgeoning of print media and the rise in literacy in the nineteenth century, the monarchy became increasingly experienced through the media. John Plunkett argues that this was particularly true under Queen Victoria and Prince Albert: 'The roles they created were inseparable from the modernity of their lives existing as royal news, disseminated as never before by prints, periodicals and newspapers.'[35] This relationship has grown apace throughout the twentieth and twenty-first centuries, with the introduction and proliferation of a wide variety of media through which the monarchy is experienced.

Despite a number of new media forms introduced in the late nineteenth and twentieth centuries, print dominated the mediation of the monarchy until very

Figure 2 'Royal Graffitti' at the Keep, home of the Mass Observation Archive.

recently. Over the twentieth and twenty-first centuries, the media landscape has become more and more layered and diverse. Each new media form – newsreels, radio, television, internet, social media – coexists with already existing forms, simultaneously supplementing and competing with one another for consumer attention. Each media form offers novel ways for the public to engage with royalty, and the layering of different media experiences can both deepen and broaden a sense of connection with and knowledge of royalty. This accretion of media-specific presentations has increasingly imbued the monarchy with humanity and ordinariness. As Edward Owens has argued, audience responses to media presentations of royals and royal events in the mid-twentieth century 'reveal that members of the public . . . forged empathetic relationships with the main protagonists of the House of Windsor . . . [and] increasingly identif[ied] with the private lives and feelings of the royal family'.[36]

With the emergence of new media forms, the monarchy seeks new ways to connect with the public. Victoria and Albert's family were photographed in 'sober' dress in a domestic setting, engaging middle-class sensibilities of the nineteenth century and contributing to a more familiar, intimate and 'inclusive style of monarchy'.[37] The popularization of radio brought royals to the microphone in the 1920s, with George V successfully connecting with his audience through an 'emotional register' marked by the usage of 'personal pronouns and family references' in his speeches.[38] Radio also gave listeners the opportunity to assess royal character and personality.³⁹ Photographs in magazines and newspapers, newsreels and television further animated royalty for the British public. Despite mixed reviews, the use of *cinéma vérité* in shooting the 1969 documentary, *The Royal Family*, captured the royals more naturally and casually than ever before. While the visual impact of seeing them in their natural environment was striking, the soundtrack was equally revolutionary as it enabled the public to hear the non-scripted, 'informal dialogue of the family off-duty' for the first time.⁴⁰

If poorly managed, however lifting the veil on royal life could damage notions of moral stewardship and the sense of mystique and difference which the monarchy needs to maintain its position in British society. The public airing of royal divorce scandals in the 1990s is a case in point: while these scandals destroyed the chimera of royal moral leadership, these revelations could also be brokered into moments of connection and identification as the public recognized the royal dramas as human ones not dissimilar to their own.⁴¹ Poor image management might lead to the ridiculous, as in the case of the hour-long 1987 gameshow *It's a Royal Knockout* featuring the Duke and Duchess of York, Prince Edward and Princess Anne competing alongside various celebrities in a tournament of 'overwhelming silliness'.⁴² That this attempt at outright celebrity-style attention-seeking failed underscores the delineation between royalty and celebrity: a more modern, inclusive monarchy *allows* the public *limited access* behind the veil, but it must not throw the curtains wide open and play-act for the public.

Image management and wise public performance alone cannot account for the continued endurance of the British monarchy. Parsing the boundaries of royalty and celebrity can help make sense of the persistence and popularity of the British monarchy, despite royal scandal and malfeasance. As opposed to ordinary celebrity, 'a person . . . known for [their] well-knownness'⁴³ in Daniel Boorstin's famous phrase, royalty has a permanence and performs a symbolic function against which no celebrity can hope to compete. In a 1955 critique of the Royal Family and public 'adulation' of them, Malcolm Muggeridge explained:

> The film star soon passes into oblivion. She has her moment and then it is all over. And even her moment depends on being able to do superlatively well whatever the public expects of her. Members of the royal family are in an entirely different situation. Their role is to symbolise the unity of a nation; to provide an element of continuity in a necessarily changing society.⁴⁴

The royal relationship with the public is transmitted from generation to generation, gained simply through the act of royal conception; even stories of brushes with royalty can be treasured and transmitted across generations (that time Nan met the Queen).⁴⁵ As Billig observed, 'No other figures are guaranteed a lifetime of celebrity from birth, and this permanence of royal fame means that "our" lives run in parallel to theirs in a reassuring continuity'.⁴⁶ As Observers reflected upon the theme of coronation, some compared their lives to that of Charles, as did this 75-year-old male: 'Charles 3rd was born the same year as me, 1948, that simple fact has made me compare my life with his, as we age.'⁴⁷ This phenomenon of lives lived in parallel was most clearly on display during the emotional processing of the Queen's death in September 2022, when many recalled personal milestones experienced over the course of her long reign.[48]

Still, royals *are* celebrities. Much as your garden-variety celebrity, our experiences of royalty are primarily mediated by the press; our para-social relationships with them crafted by an 'imagined intimacy fostered by the media'.[49] As celebrities, royals offer compelling popular distractions, but the drama, the glamour, the soap opera and the glitz of it all are just that – distractions that lead us away from deeper, more existential reasons for the allure of monarchy. As Tom Nairn argued, the 'Monarchy dwells in a category all its own . . . The Royal glamour has appropriated and used the world of celebrity, not vice versa'.[50] Royal drama and 'appropriation' of celebrity, he added, can 'eclipse' the institution from close public scrutiny.[51] Monarchy is not 'an abstraction disguised as an institution', as has been recently argued, but rather the royals – their public/private lives and scandals – are convenient diversions that keep effective criticism and useful questions about the very real institution of the monarchy at bay.[52] As was made clear during the spring 2024 disappearance and photoshopping of the Princess Kate scandal ('Kate Gate'), royals must be seen and seen to be genuine (or, at least not overly disingenuous). Real damage can be dealt to the institution when the veil of celebrity falls away (or gives way to infamy) through royal absence, deceit or wrongdoing. The Kate Gate social/media clamour for royal bodies and the frisson of potentially exposing the royals as evil conspirators in an imagined metaworld *Game of Thrones* drama ended in shame-faced apologies by social/media for having ruthlessly pried the truth out of a suffering family trying to come to terms with a cancer diagnosis. The (revealed) drama of the Wales's health crisis thus phased the otherness of celebrity/royalty into something entirely recognizable, understandable, and ultimately, ordinary and utterly human – strengthening the para-social bond with 'ordinary' non-royals and bringing out numerous champions for respectful distance and privacy: 'this is not just an institution, it is a family', one royal correspondent scolded.[53] 'A family on the throne is an interesting idea', Walter Bagehot mused somewhat cynically in the nineteenth century, pointing out the power of mass emotion in propping up a constitutional monarchy as against a republic: 'So long as the human heart is strong and the human reason weak, Royalty will be strong because it appeals to diffused feeling, and Republics weak because they appeal to the understanding.'[54]

It is not helpful to imagine that the public has no agency and that the monarchy is nonsensical, nonexistent or irrelevant. If we want to understand the staying power of the British monarchy, it is better to wrestle with the emotional register of royalty and the reality that, 'popular Royalism is visibly *not* passive and mindless. It has something positive about it – an apparently inexhaustible electric charge'.[55] This positive charge is fundamentally animated and sustained by the continual emotional evocation of monarchy in the national story and identity.

On myth and monarchy

Myth is a narrative imbued with meaning that plays an important role in identity formation.[56] For existential psychologist Rollo May, myths are absolutely essential to the human condition.[57] Myths, he argued, aid in the construction of both personal and communal identity, they connect us to place and self, and are thus critical to belonging and well-being.[58] 'Our powerful hunger for myth is a hunger for community', May believed; 'The person without a myth is a person without a home ... To be a member of one's community is to share in its myths.'[59] This posits myth as fundamentally exclusionary: though those on the outside can consume myths, only those on the inside can possess 'our myths'.[60] Given that national identities are also exclusionary in this way, thinking about national identity formation – and stability – through myth can be helpful in understanding the construction and maintenance of 'imagined communities'. To reframe May, the nation without myth is a home without a people – or a place without purpose.

Considering British monarchy through the lens of myth offers a frame that meaningfully connects the Crown and the nation with identity. To deploy the term 'myth' is usually meant to diminish something as untrue, irrational or wrong-headed. This is not my intention here; instead, I want to acknowledge the function or 'social validity' of monarchy in everyday British life and society.[61] Using myth in this way highlights the deep emotional power of the narratives of nation built around, and intertwined with, monarchy such that arguments for republicanism or dismantling monarchy – even the mere *suggestion* of its end – can imperil personal and national identities. As Michael Billig observed in his study of attitudes towards the British Royal Family,

> Remove monarchy and you remove the very thing which distinguishes this country from other countries: England/Britain would cease to be like England/Britain. Such a future should be avoided, even in the imagination: to imagine the imagined community without its special element would be to de-imagine it.[62]

The persistent linking of monarchy and nation together enacts a sense of timelessness which binds the two in mythical union such that one cannot/should not exist without the other. Without the monarchy, Britain would cease to be Britain, the refrain goes; it would be something else – usually, the imagination runs to America or France, two impossible alternatives to countenance. If the monarchy slimmed down or stopped its glamorous performances and ceremonies, it would be other: Scandinavian or Dutch. The monarchy is uniquely, and enviably, some would argue, British. One 61-year-old female from Kent put it this way after the death of Queen Elizabeth II:

> On a constitutional level I would really not like the alternative of a republic – I feel we have a kind of safeguard in having a constitutional monarch sitting above the parliamentary system ... We have something that other countries do not

have and possibly envy. We should celebrate this as for me it is an indelible part of our culture.[63]

Pushing too hard for the dismantling of monarchy has traditionally resulted in spirited backlash or punishment. Even during a moment of heightened republican political sentiment in the nineteenth century, Charles Dilke nearly destroyed his nascent political career when he dared to imagine the nation without the monarchy.[64] In December 1936, ILP member for Glasgow, James Maxton, argued in Parliament that the Abdication Crisis offered an opportunity to rebuild Britain as a republic, thus ending the monarchy and the system of class privilege that it represented. The discussion that ensued saw a handful of ILP members stand in support of Maxton, but the two who stood to counter it, Sir Austen Chamberlain and Home Secretary Sir John Simon, articulated the myth and the boundaries upon which it could be engaged. A republic was no better than a monarchy, Simon asserted, but British monarchy was the product of British 'genius' and 'far greater than the life or experiences of any individual. If institutions were not greater than our frailty or the inscrutable promptings of an individual human heart, orderly development would be impossible'. Chamberlain noted that his West Birmingham constituents suffered in 'poor streets and mean houses', still, he argued, they supported the King, because they believed the 'Monarchy [was] their safeguard' and 'the first servant of the nation'.[65] Only five voted against the continuance of a bill that affirmed the transfer of the Crown to the Duke of York, who would become George VI. The lack of debate regarding the institution during the reading of the Abdication Bill is striking. It was enough to remind the members that the monarchy was more than any one of them. It was their 'genius' and their inheritance; it was their national myth. As Thomas Mann observed about the workings of myths, 'For it is, always is, however much we say it was. Thus speaks the myth, which is only the garment of mystery'.[66]

Ceremony and regalia: The 'throat-catching "Thousand Years"' of monarchy and nation

The rituals and ceremonies of the British monarchy endow the institution with the mythical mystery that shrouds it, much like a celebrity, from critics delving too deeply into the nature of its core. Of the Coronation Rite, historian Roy Strong wrote, 'Such rituals should not be lightly dismissed as so much insubstantial pageantry. They are powerful icons in which a society enshrines its identity and its continuity'.[67] 'What the pageantry . . . does', Nairn noted, 'is elevate [the monarchy] into the throat-catching "Thousand Years" of Orb and Sceptre, in order to stabilize and sweeten the present and define a people into the future'.[68] Indeed, the act of coronation, George V believed, was 'a gathering up of the treasures of the past and a preparing of the path of the future'.[69] Tales of these rituals, and their trappings, steeped in a storied past (even if invented and modern as David

Cannadine reminds us[70]), elevate into public consciousness the deeply-entwined roots of monarchy and nation.

Ceremonial rites are deeply emotional moments meant to mark significance, both for the event itself and for the actors involved. Rituals are specialized and mythologized to heighten mystery and exceptional otherness. In the case of the British monarchy, the public is granted access to *just* enough knowledge and insight into these rituals to perceive – and feel – the mystery of the institution and its relevance to the national past, present and future. This power is demonstrated in one viewer's comment on *The Guardian's* YouTube coverage of the Lord Chamberlain breaking the Wand of Office upon the lowering of the Queen's coffin:

> I've never been a big fan of the Royal family but after today seeing the Queen[']s funeral it was absolutely mesmerising and I feel totally different now on how I feel about the Royal family, its made me realise that the history is very important to this country and she will never be forgotten for her service, RIP her Majesty and long live our new King.[71]

The performance of monarchy through these rituals, enacted by many servants of the institution and explained in hushed tones by media commentators to mesmerized audiences, signals the supposed timelessness and otherness of royalty while simultaneously pointing up the inextricable link between monarchy and nation.

During the eight months between the Queen's death and the Coronation of Charles III, the media educated the public on the 'Thousand Years of Orb and Sceptre', telling and re-telling the story of coronation, linking it to the national past, present and future and signposting the significance of each moment in the ancient rite. *The Mail Online* offered a primer typical of this instruction:

> During the ancient Ceremony, the Sovereign is 'anointed, blessed and consecrated' by the Archbishop of Canterbury.
>
> Many will witness for the first time a new monarch take thee [sic] oath to 'maintain and preserve inviolably the settlement of the Church of England, and the doctrine worship, discipline, and government thereof, as the law established in England'.
>
> Having been sanctified, the sovereign will then be presented with a jewelled sword and the golden spurs – the symbol of chivalry – and the armills – golden bracelets of sincerity and wisdom.
>
> He will put on the Robe Royal of gold cloth and will be presented with the orb, the coronation ring on the fourth finger of his right hand, the sceptre and the rod.
>
> Then Charles, sitting in King Edward's Chair which was made in 1300 and has been used by every monarch since 1626, will be crowned by the Archbishop with St Edward's Crown, with the congregation shouting out 'God Save the King'.[72]

Such lessons on royal rituals remind readers of a supposedly timeless nation rooted in monarchical majesty, and thus underscores the ways that monarchy 'anchors us to the past . . . and provide[s] continuity and . . . stability'.[73] According to these (media) guides that teach royal rituals and link monarchy to nation, it is the longevity of the institution that signals its legitimacy: the 700-year-old throne, the medieval symbols of chivalry and wisdom, the links to the eleventh-century king, St. Edward. This last connection is meant to draw monarchical legitimacy back to ancient, Anglo-Saxon England, before the Norman invaders whose Westminster Abbey (built by Edward the Confessor) has been the site of coronations since William I (the media refrain went), and to underscore the religiosity at the heart of English/British kingship. This type of reporting creates a sense of 'Messianic time, a simultaneity of past and future in an instantaneous present'.[74] The regalia and the monarchical stories link past and present, and project into the future, such that 'it is impossible to establish by reason in the horizontal dimension', the connection between monarchy and nation except through 'Divine Providence, which alone is able to devise such a plan of history and supply the key to its understanding . . . the here and now is no longer a mere link in an earthly chain of events, it is *simultaneously* something which has always been, and will be fulfilled in the future'.[75]

The sacral element of the Coronation Rite, and thus, the power of 'Divine Providence' in this process, is drawn out in *The Mail Online* article through discussion of the anointing and blessing from the Archbishop of Canterbury, as well as the oath to defend the faith(s). The article then explains each of the six elements of the service: the Recognition, Coronation Oath, Anointing, Investiture (including Crowning), Enthronement and Homage. This brief explanation notes, for example, the origins of the Recognition in the supposedly democratic Anglo-Saxon witan and draws attention to the antiquity of the regalia and plate of the ceremony, such as the fourteenth-century silver-gilt anointing spoon. Beyond linking the nation to a timeless and significant past, articles like this generate and feed interest in the monarchy and Royal Family (alongside added commentary on 'working royals' and their roles in the upcoming ritual), heighten anticipation for the events and fuel desire to witness history in the making, while also providing good copy for the media outlets which distribute them.

As the commentor on *The Guardian* video coverage of the breaking of the Queen's Wand of Office quoted above demonstrates, these lessons in royal history and mystery underscore a sense of a unique, and significant, national community in monarchy. In the frenzied atmosphere to report royal news and stories during the eight-month wait for coronation, the media taught the public about a unique national past, which included side-long glances at the nation's failed experiment in republican government in the seventeenth century (the regalia which survived Cromwellian/republican destruction, the nation's renewed embrace of royalty through the updated/replicated regalia for the enthronement of another Charles in 1661), thus also subtly reminding the nation of its embarrassing, never to be revisited, republican experiment. Meanwhile, global media were careful to note that these grand royal rituals are the last in what was once a large field of European royal majesty, thus setting Britain apart from its Continental counterparts and deepening the power of the Windsor's royal performance which carried not just the standard of British, but also European, monarchical legacy (and history) into the present and future – a living heritage re-enactment for the world to witness the glory of European civilization.[76] The repeated recitation in the media of these stories educates the public (both British and global) into a national myth of British identity inextricably bound up in a monarchical past, present and future.

Good King Charles: Hagiography and the apotheosis of a king

From the moment of the Queen's death in 2022 right through to Charles III's Coronation ceremony eight months later, the public was incessantly instructed on these histories of monarchy/nation. The Queen's long reign was reviewed and remembered, intertwined into national and personal narratives, often in hagiographic tones of respect and awe. Positive image-making surrounding Prince Charles and Camilla, which had been in the works for at least a decade prior to the Queen's death,[77] was now stepped up, and the new King was increasingly presented to the public as one worthy of reverence (on a level similar to the Queen's) through narratives that elevated his charitable activities, his environmentalism and his love of family; meanwhile, Queen (Consort) Camilla appeared naturally at his right hand, the faithful and loving (and longtime) support and companion. Diana was largely written out of the narrative, save her role in producing an heir and spare for her prince.

Queen Elizabeth's parting gift, and master stroke, to this process of elevation, came during the Platinum Jubilee when she made known her 'sincere wish' that Camilla be recognized as 'Queen Consort'[78] – a particularly wily sleight-of-hand, which seemed, at the time, a limiting concession to a public generally unaware that past queens (through marriage) have also been called 'Queen Consort', a term typically shortened to 'Queen', thus enabling a rather smooth transition to 'Queen' Camilla.[79] As *The Guardian* noted when the invitation issued in April 2023 proclaimed her 'Queen Camilla', 'It marks the incredible journey of Camilla over more than five decades, from secret romantic involvement to official partner and finally wife of the king – and which will end with her formally being crowned queen alongside the new king'.[80]

Documentaries aired in Britain during the week before the Coronation presented the King to his people. *Prince* Charles would have needed no such introduction: his story was already quite familiar. But *King* Charles III could no longer be the incredibly flawed prince of the 1990s, who featured in Tampongate and ruined Princess Di's life. The Coronation was to be his apotheosis, and through the rites of that ceremony, he would be (mystically) elevated from mere human to national symbol.

The documentaries emphasized a challenging childhood (in strikingly similar emotional tones as the second season of *The Crown*) that ultimately fortified him to weather criticism for being a crank-environmentalist before environmentalism was cool and to establish the Prince's Trust charity despite pushback from government ministers. In one such documentary, actor David Oyelowo praises the Trust, and Prince Charles specifically, for the support given to him during the early stages of his hugely successful career; while CEO of the Trust, Dame Martina Milburn, underscored the tireless work Prince Charles did for the nation: 'I think what motivates the King is a real desire to make life better for people, and to make society better, to make community better.'[81]

The through-line narrative of these documentaries can be summed up nicely in the many children's books dedicated to teaching the new King Charles story to young people, dotting the shelves of WH Smith (three for two offer) and other booksellers in the week leading up to the Coronation. In the 'Little People, Big Dreams' series, the twenty-eight-page long *King Charles,* which topped the UK top 50 in book sales,[82] recounted how young Charles bonded with his grandmother while his parents were busy at work, how he was sent away to boarding school, where he 'felt quite alone'. Later, he spent time studying in Wales so he could 'be a good prince for the Welsh'; the Welsh, the narrative continues, were not appreciative and protested his presence. About halfway through the volume is a two-page spread of rolling countryside complete with sheep (of course), mountains in the distance, and Charles in the foreground 'falling in love with Wales' and vowing to protect the environment. The book then shifts to his military duty and the establishment of the Prince's Trust. Another two-page spread depicts the balcony at Buckingham Palace from which the Prince and his 'fairy-tale princess', alongside the Royal Family, wave to the reader. Turn the page, and in two sentences, Charles and Diana are divorced, Diana dies, and everyone is very sad. No need to despair, though, for on the next page, we find Charles planting trees alongside his 'closest friend for thirty-five years', Camilla. Next, Charles steps more fully into the role of senior royal (a big help to his mother). On the final page, a sweet little boy sits enthroned with orb and crown and dressed in a robe far too large for him, who hopes he will 'not . . . let anyone down'.[83]

Conversations in the week prior to the Coronation demonstrated that, at least for some, this narrative had been well-learned. A docent at Chichester Cathedral said she believed Charles would be a 'good king' and praised him for 'saving the world' despite all those who laughed at him fifty years ago for his environmentalism. Though she did not initially like Camilla, the docent had warmed to her over the years because she was 'such a support' to Charles.[84] Campers assembled along the Mall in the days before the Coronation had also absorbed the narrative. Three women who had become friends at the Queen's Platinum Jubilee celebrations and had camped out together for the Queen's funeral procession confessed their initial dislike of Camilla but reported that they had also come around to her, reconciled to the idea that Charles would become king and would not be skipped over in favour of William, as they had once hoped. One of the women said emphatically that 'Diana was our Queen of Hearts, she'll always be our Queen of Hearts', but there was too much hatred in the world and it was time to stop digging at Camilla. (No such forgiveness was saved for Meghan, who was described in highly unfavourable terms!)[85]

Similar rehabilitations occur in the world of celebrity: witness the rise, fall and redemption of modern celebrities such as Robert Downey Jr. and Hugh Grant.[86] But the hagiography of Charles articulated in the media, and worked into the hearts and minds of at least some members of the public represented more than mere redemption; this was a collective elevation transforming prince to king during the eight months of accession.

Three important elevations occurred during that time, lifting Charles to the heights of a sovereign: the emotional public ritual that accepted the hagiographic narrative of Good King Charles (and Queen – not Consort – Camilla), a shift in the way the media approached the man who had just become king, and the final mystical apotheosis performed through the Rites of Coronation. Only the first two elevations featured in the remaking of the abovementioned celebrities' public image. The final transformation underscores the difference between royalty and celebrity: flawed prince became virtuous king, 'the living representative of an institution', transcending anything possible through mere celebrity.[87]

Through these stages of elevation, we witnessed the making of 'royal duality', the modern re-imagining of the medieval concept of the King's two bodies: the corporeal and the immortal, the flawed and the transcendent Divine Monarch.[88] Shedding power over the eighteenth and nineteenth centuries, the monarch increasingly became seen as the 'embodiment of a . . . more plural society', an embodiment, Roy Strong explains, 'contrived' to make the monarch represent 'a whole list of antithetical qualities. A king was royal yet he was also republican, permanent yet transitory, sacred yet mortal . . . [thus] enabling [the monarchy] to respond to virtually any political or social circumstance'.[89] To critical observers, this is a mere parlour trick to be laughed at, derided and dismissed as putting one over on the gullible (women, working classes, Tories, the over-sixties, the uneducated, historians of the monarchy – depending on your viewpoint). Yet, Strong argued, these new notions of monarchy exerted a 'psychological [power] over its people . . . often far from rational and certainly inexplicable. That psychological pull is still there in the twenty-first century reflecting a deep and, at the same time, unfathomable public need'.[90]

'Pathetic . . . stubborn little boycotts': Social media, ambivalence and change

Does Roy Strong's assertion in 2005 that the monarchy serves an 'unfathomable public need' hold up twenty years later? Alongside lessons on monarchy and nation discussed earlier, the accession of Charles III also brought with it far more public discourse about the long-term viability, relevance and value of the monarchy than during any other accession period in modern history. The British media canvassed a number of stories about failing links between monarchy and Commonwealth, lukewarm opinion polls, political opposition and the antics of the most-publicized republican pressure group, Republic UK. Reporting on the breakup of the Commonwealth's links to the monarchy underscored anxieties about the loss of traditionally-white Commonwealth countries, Australia and

Canada, and assumptions that the majority of non-white Commonwealth countries were inevitably lost to the cause. Despite polling numbers that demonstrated a majority of Britons supported retaining the monarchy,[91] press coverage depicted an embattled institution and articulated concern over a long-term softening of support. *Express Online* reported that the CEO of the National Centre for Social Research believed that popular support could dip below 50 per cent over the next decade, which would be 'catastrophic for the monarchy'.[92] Active opposition, according to the media, could be found in elements of the Labour Party who pressured leader Keir Starmer to call for a referendum on the institution, Scottish National Party (SNP) opposition and pressure group Republic UK.[93] Still, it was reported with some relief, even republicans stated their opposition to monarchy was one of principle since they largely agreed that monarchy works.[94]

Moving away from traditional media reporting, social media platforms offer spaces to express all manner of opinions about royal events, royals and the institution of monarchy. Platforms such as X (formerly Twitter) and Reddit provide fora to publicly declare one's support of royal individuals or the institution or to express anti-monarchist sentiment and work to convince the public that the royals are not to be trusted. For instance, the Reddit community, r/AbolishTheMonarchy, boasts 57,000 members (in the top 2 per cent of communities) and provides:

> A space to contest popular monarchist myths/narratives that rationalize their continued existence. We cannot have class consciousness in a population that identifies with royals and even loves their subjugation by a hereditary monarchy. Ceremonial or not, they need to go.[95]

On this 'Myth Debunking' site, users upload media stories as evidence of royal malfeasance. The top pinned post for the 'Get to know King Charles III Megathread' is a list of news articles organized by the following categories: 'Selling cash for access and sham philanthropy', 'secret influence and lobbying the government', 'financial misconduct', 'close contacts with paedophiles', and 'Misc. abusive/weird behaviour'. Users, who are by default anonymous, post news stories according to the theme and discuss British republicanism. Yet the information is not always credible: some of the articles posted as evidence are associated with less-than-above-board websites, and 'Reggie-bot', an automated bot assigned by the moderator (user HMElizabethII) of the site, regularly posts news articles. The site and the moderator link to other Reddit communities, such as r/Britain – a site for all things Britain – and users, such as Republic_Campaign (Graham Smith, CEO of Republic, publicly links his name to this account). r/Britain allows commentary with rules against imperialist or monarchist 'bootlicking', the intentional spreading of disinformation, and bias ('no classism, ableism, homophobia, racism, religious discrimination, sexism, transphobia, xenophobia').[96]

Meanwhile, r/RoyalFamily boasts 65,000 members, and touts itself as 'A non-pro or anti-monarchist community to discuss the British royal family'. Users tend to ask questions about the British monarchy, such as 'what will happen to Camilla once Charles passes?' and 'Who dictates or enforces royal protocol in the royal family?' Like r/Britain, rules include no discriminatory or hateful language, but also ask that users refrain from 'comment[ing] with the intent to push an agenda, soapbox, sealion, or argue in bad faith'.[97] Unabashedly monarchist is r/monarchism, with 48,000 members. This site states that it exists, 'For the proliferation, reestablishment, and defence of monarchy. This is a forum for those who think monarchy is a noble and viable alternative to the crude and materialistic mob mentality of republicanism'.[98] Its users post articles and polls about monarchies around the globe, such as those in Belgium and Jordan, and those who want to create or restore monarchy in their countries, such as user 'cath_monarchist', who expressed hope for the 're-establishment of the monarchy in Brazil'.[99]

On X, official royal hashtags compete with organizers against the monarchy and royal watchers. Some of the leading anti-monarchist or republican X handles are @RepublicStaff, with 90.9k followers and Campaign to Abolish the Monarchy, @nomoremonarchs, with 20.5k followers. A myriad of royal watchers compete for small and large audiences, mostly between 1k and 15k, some of whom are critical of the Royal Family's racism, and especially their handling of Harry and Meghan, like Julieth, @troubleshade, who posts pictures and positive perspectives on the couple to its 14.9k followers. Official X accounts for the Royal Family (@RoyalFamily) and the Prince and Princess of Wales (@KensingtonRoyal) report 5.6m and 3m followers, respectively.[100] These accounts are generally managed to create a positive image of the royals by posting royal happenings, images and messages to the public, many of whom respond with their own comments. For instance, over 36k responded to the Princess's video message regarding her cancer diagnosis on 22 March 2024. While many of the responses are prayers, words of support or chastisement of press hounding, some include conspiracy theories, such as American user 'UltraMAGAAuntieX', who pushed the conspiracy that Kate's appearance was AI-generated or photoshopped or those who posted arguments that Kate's cancer was linked to Covid vaccines.[101] A massive number of content producers exist in the social media space, and, as this user reminds us, many of them are not British; further, since users are often anonymous, some vocal critics may be state actors intent on sowing social division and instability.

Social media divides and amplifies opinions on either side of the question. The rise of the 'autonomous individual, unmoored both from the bonds of media producers and from other members of the media audience', has fractured imagined communities that print media and broadcast technology of the twentieth century often cultivated.[102] Opinion and information silos proliferate across social media, creating communities and subcommunities, fragmented groups which provide social interaction that can obtrude flexible thinking and conversations outside of these communities. How these processes will impact levels of popular support for the monarchy is yet to be seen.

The stories mentioned above point to a softening of interest in younger demographics, which could be linked to younger generations' use of social media, but could equally be a product of perennial angst and rebellion of younger generations. Results of the British Social Attitudes Survey (BSA) demonstrate that the generational gap seems to remain across time, with attitudes shifting as individuals age. In 1994, BSA polling found that 'only 22% of those born in the 1960s felt that it was "very important" to have a monarchy', while in September 2022, this generation's attitude had become more favourable towards the monarchy with 38 per cent expressing this view.[103]

Reporting of poll numbers often focuses on the extremes: those in support of the monarchy or those against it. Yet, the more important figure may be the numbers in the middle, which suggest a great deal of apathy or unwillingness to change. While a March 2024 YouGov survey showed that those who believed the monarchy was 'Good for Britain' numbered at 51 per cent, a further 28 per cent believed that the institution was 'Neither good nor bad'. Those who responded to this latter category may be unwilling to change, thus 79 per cent may actually be supportive of retaining the monarchy.[104] This tracks with an IPSOS MORI poll in September 2023 which did not allow respondents to choose a neutral position. In it, 66 per cent were 'in favour of the monarchy', while 25 per cent were 'in favor of a republic', and 9 per cent didn't know.[105] Even if one ticks the 'anti-monarchist' box, they could still be quite 'prepared to tolerate the institution', like one 65-year-old female Observer from the south coast.[106]

Significantly, a majority of those polled in Britain were reluctant to put the abolition of the monarchy to a referendum in May 2023: 52 per cent were against the idea, while a sizeable minority (31 per cent) were in favour of putting a vote to the people (17 per cent were undecided).[107] Observer writing in this book articulates a constellation of criticism, anger, embarrassment and impatience alongside support, excitement and pride, as well as ambivalence about the institution. Many Observers responding to the 2023 Coronation Directive worried over the costs of Charles III's Coronation and the Royal Family amid a cost of living crisis and believed the monarchy should be retained but reformed. Certainly, many now seem far more willing than at any other time in modern history to critically consider the relevance of monarchy and its future, and that could bode ill for the royals and their supporters.

Another important indicator of support for the continuance of Britain as a monarchy is the extent to which the myth of monarchy and nation remains relevant to British national identity. Citing polls in the 1990s and early 2000s, historian Andrzej Olechnowicz argued that the 'claim that the monarchy is a national symbol . . . needs careful consideration'.[108] Recent polling does not seem to have plumbed this link, but the rise in nationalism since 2016 in the UK, and across the globe, may have reversed turn-of-the-twenty-first-century trends, reinvigorating more traditional forms of national identity. As has been argued here, the myth seems durable at least across mainstream media and banal monarchism remains a powerful, if often silent, force linking nation and monarchy physically and psychologically.

While a sizeable minority of Observers articulated a desire to abolish the institution, many who expressed this hope nonetheless understood monarchy and nation as tightly interwoven. This consideration created tension for some, who, like the following Observer, found it difficult to square republican leanings with the monarchy/nation myth:

> I would like to start by saying that I have some republican beliefs, but appreciate that the Royal Family are a massive part of Britain's national identity and provides a clear link with the history of our country – factors that cannot be overlooked or flippantly dismissed – so, I am quite conflicted about the whole situation.[109]

Another Observer positively linked monarchy/nation and personal identity:

> I accept that money has to be spent and don't kid yourself that it will be any cheaper if we have a republic other than a monarchy. It won't be. It might even be worse. GB has a very proud history, and this is the time to celebrate that. It is bound to be quite different to what happened in 1953. We are a small nation which, in the great scheme of things, isn't that important. But I'm proud of my country (Patriotic, not Nationalist) and I value the history which exists here. We often get things wrong, but we get an awful lot right as well.[110]

Yet another Observer demonstrated collective national ownership of the monarchy in her remarks about 'our King and queen', even if they were a 'crumpled twice-married elderly couple'.[111] The power of the myth of monarchy and nation may well be found in this form of backhanded ownership of the royals.

Some Observers linked ambivalence and inaction with British identity. One 47-year-old female from Devon spent the day avoiding Charles III's Coronation. Upon writing her response, she 'reflect[ed] that I have trully [sic] lived out a very traditional set of British values today: grumbling rather than rioting, dealing with things I don't like by ignoring them and hoping they go away and walking in the rain. If only I could have managed some queuing as well'.[112] The national narrative may well be about grousing and inaction, coupled with a nagging feeling that the monarchy may *actually* be as significant as everyone says it is. This 32-year-old married female from Norwich wrote, 'It's all so pathetic, this coronation, all the money that's being spent on it', but went on to confess, 'And yet there's something pathetic about my stubborn little boycott. Because isn't there still a part of me that wonders if I am missing out on this great historical moment? But I think that's what they want us to think'.[113] Commenting on decorations in her district, this Observer fantasized about scrawling protest graffiti on a bare brick wall lined with bunting:

> All week I've been imagining what could be written across it in chalk. The cost of the coronation? Upwards of 100 million. A figure so huge I struggle to gauge its weight. The figure Charles has inherited from the Queen, none of which he will pay inheritance tax on after a law change in 1993? 15.2 Billion. Or something simpler and 'calmer'? Coronate the people.[114]

A comment made by her partner that the local press might report the incident, 'put me off'. 'That and the energy required to enact the fantasy', she continued,

'What good would it do?'[115] The threat of exposure may well dampen one's desire to graffiti a wall, but social media provides the wall, the chalk and the anonymity for many who may feel the same as this Observer, enabling alternate narratives to take root and potentially grow into something tangible and emotionally viable to compete with the monarchy's hold on national identity. On the other hand, scrawling criticism about the monarchy across the social media wall may let off just enough steam to lead to continued apathy.

Feelings of failure and incompetence which colour ambivalent or frustrated Observer accounts cast a decidedly bleak shadow on Britain in the 2020s. In the past, ineptitude of leadership and those doomed to deal with its consequences might be cast ironically as a redeeming aspect of British identity, as in Tennyson's 'Charge of the Light Brigade'. Now, in the context of Brexit and recent Tory disasters, Broken Britain – with its failing infrastructure, flagging economy and hollowed-out NHS – has shorn ineptitude of any sense of ironic British gallantry and left in its wake bitter exhaustion. For those who imagine the monarchy to ride above politics, monarchy might well be the one remaining saving grace; but to those who see monarchy and Tories inextricably yoked together, the institution is as bankrupt as Broken Britain.

Since the accession of Victoria, republican spirit in Britain has rarely reached above 1/3 of the population.[116] Recently, a mixture of anxiety and hope regarding the abolition of the monarchy has been evident in reporting on the institution, but still opinion polls suggest that this statistic remains durable. In an August 2024 YouGov poll, 32 per cent of those polled had either a 'fairly negative' or 'very negative' view of the monarchy, while 59 per cent reported a 'fairly positive' or 'very positive' attitude.[117] While generational differences may tip the balance, regional disparities are also significant – especially among the Scottish, who are split over support for an elected head of state (43 per cent) and the monarchy (41 per cent).[118] Social media and its potential to erode the national 'imagined community' constructed and aided by the traditional media may yet damage the monarchy irreparably. And general malaise or apathy about the institution, evident in a rather unimpressed overall attitude towards the 2023 Coronation,[119] might enable the institution to endure, but equally, it could lead to a population that can't be bothered to fight for the British monachy's continued existence.

Still, change would require action and that seems quite a challenge if the national narrative includes the continual relevance of monarchy to the nation's identity and history and, equally, the notion that change – especially regarding the monarchy – is impossible or undesirable. Considering the well-oiled institutional machine (and all the stakeholders standing by their prescribed levers of that machine) that hummed into action on 8 September 2022 and smoothly elevated Charles to king the moment his mother breathed her last, the battle is an uphill one.

National mythologizing and connection: Braiding sweetgrass

Summing up her thoughts about the Coronation on ITV's coverage of the day, actor Adjoa Andoh commented, 'We've gone from the rich diversity of the Abbey to a terribly white balcony. I'm very struck by that.' Her observation sparked a firestorm of affected outrage and handwringing from a number of right-leaning pundits who feared that it was no longer acceptable to be white in Britain. Her brief comment stirred up over 8,300 complaints to media regulator Ofcom, which ultimately decided not to pursue action in order to protect the freedom of expression in the UK.[120] In the fog of outrage documented on YouTube when one searches 'Adjoa Andoh terribly white', mention is made of Andoh's Ghanese roots as if that somehow disbarred her from speaking on the subject of coronation or, indeed, from the right to imagine herself within the 'we' of Britishness. Those who present as white rarely have to offer credentials to participate in the national British narrative or to imagine themselves as British, to answer the question of 'where are you from?' multiple times ('no, really, where are you from?').

Andoh was born in Bristol and grew up in the Cotswolds, her father left Ghana because he refused to toe the line as a journalist in a dictatorial regime, and her great-uncle lost an arm in the Second World War.[121] In an interview about her directing the Shakespearean play *Richard II* at the Globe, Andoh stated her intention to 'reclaim the flag of St. George' because she told the interviewer:

> My great-uncle lost his arm in the Second World War, fighting for this country. Ghana was a country of Empire, my grandfather was a surveyor who surveyed the land for the Commonwealth back in the 1930s. My family had been educated in Ghana on the lines of a British public school system – that's the history that they were taught. The Empire has made this country what it is in terms of everything: slavery, post-slavery, colonisation, raw materials, people's land, their history, their language, their everything has been taken by Empire and used to fuel the industrial revolution in this country. That's just on the Ghanaian side. On the English side of my family I've got farm labourers and merchant seamen and a great grandfather who fought in the Boer war. My connections to this country are deep. I was born in this country, I was raised in this country, I have a right to claim that flag.[122]

The fact that Andoh was present at ITV's coverage of the Coronation looked like an invitation to claim the flag as her own, to participate in the national narrative, but the lie was told by the outburst of outrage when she dared to articulate her sense of nation. Andoh saw in the ceremony, in some small measure, a reflection of herself. As she would later say, in an apology meant to stem the outrage for her claiming a part of the flag, Andoh pointed to the 'loving prayer' the King made during the service, 'reflecting his wide embrace of the rich diverse peoples celebrating his coronation'. 'There was no intention to upset anyone', she continued. 'I continue to celebrate the king, who created the Prince's Trust [charity], loves the arts, cares for all faiths and for the future of our environment, as he has done for many decades. It's an exciting moment in our history.'[123] Employing 'our' in this statement, Andoh once again, tenaciously, claimed Charles III's Coronation and the flag as her own.

Media-created imagined community more often than not cultivates a narrow, exclusionary sense of nation, marking out the boundaries between 'us' and 'them' along faultlines which are legion, including (but not limited to) race, class, gender, lineage, sexual orientation, ethnicity and religion. But as Andoh reminds us, the myths of self can, and do, traverse across and between the boundaries of imagined community articulated in the media and in dominant narratives of nation. Nineteenth-century theorist of nationalism, Ernst Renan wrote that 'The nation is a soul, a spiritual principle. [It] consists of two things. One is the common legacy of rich memories from the past. The other is the present consensus, the will to live together'. Because nations (and Empires) are so often wrought through violence, oppression and injustice, that consensus, Renan believed, rests upon, "*L'oubli*, the act of forgetting . . . one might even say historical falsehood."[124] To that end, Renan believed that serious historical inquiry might ultimately jeopardize national unity. Instead, it seems to me, knowing the past, honouring and remembering the multiple experiences, traumas, traditions, cultures and identities that constitute themselves within a nation points towards a better future for nations, if they are to exist. (Renan suggested that nations were not timeless and there was no reason they should endure).[125]

Perhaps the way forward is best described by Wolastoqey Elder Imelda Perley's aforementioned explanation of braiding the sweetgrass as part of New Brunswick's Proclamation of King Charles III: 'It's coming together with our different traditions and bringing them together in the sacredness of being . . . related, and being here together.' Traditionally, the act of braiding sweetgrass is an act of connection. 'The sweetest way', to braid sweetgrass, writes Robin Wall Kimmerer,

> is to have someone else hold the end so that you pull gently against each other, all the while leaning in, head to head, chatting and laughing, watching each other's hands . . . linked by sweetgrass, there is a reciprocity between you, linked by sweetgrass, the holder as vital as the braider.[126]

It seems an ideal time to reimagine and rearticulate the national myth, the story Britons tell themselves, and which brings them together by braiding the sweetgrass of a modern, multinational, multicultural, multiethnic and vibrant Britain.

Part II

Observations II

Ah, the coronation. The biggest, most ridiculous waste of money, pomp and circumstance of the year – right behind all the Tory donor COVID contracts. I can hardly believe that the UK is going forward with this self-indulgent piece of flummery in 2023, for goodness sake, and at a time when health workers, educators and numerous other professional groups are on strike due to the cost of living crisis. Why are we spending billions that the country apparently doesn't have, for some billionaires to cos-play medieval pageantry for the day/weekend? I am furious about the costs, but also about the slavish sycophancy that this country pays to the royals – as with the Queens funeral, I never feel more un-British that when there is a royal event. It makes me sick.

Needless to say, I am going away as far as possible for the entire weekend – travelling up to Scotland and an island at that with two friends to go walking. I'm hoping Scotland is one of the more republican parts of the UK, and by doing a 50 km walking trail I should be far enough away from the media. To date, and luckily, there appears to be far less media attention than I feared, particularly given the absurd hoopla of the Queen's funeral, and it has been quite easy to avoid. In fact, until this prompt came through, I had almost forgotten about the coronation . . . **F41, H7048**

I am not a royalist and deeply disagree with many aspects of royal life, so fair to say I didn't watch the ceremony or have any involvement with it whatsoever!

I'm also not very patriotic, maybe because of being brought up in a very Irish household but having said that, my grandmother was from a privileged Irish background and was pro the royal family. I'd say my mother is also more pro than anti but I didn't follow suit! At lot of which is to do with the shocking imbalance in this country between the rich and poor, with a gap that is forever widening.

Considering the huge cost of the Coronation and knowing many people are struggling to pay bills or eat properly, it seems farcical to me . . .

Personally, I think these ceremonies and rituals are very interesting historically but are outdated and should be consigned to the history books. Some estimates suggest that the Queen's coronation in 1953 would in todays money equate to a cost of around 50 million. Yet Charles III's coronation would be more in the region of 100 million due to the hugely different times and security costs for not just the main two royals but all those who attended from world leaders to fellow royals.

As a friend of mine said, 'I'd rather see five new hospitals being built than see an absurdly wealthy man riding along in a gold coach!' **M52, M5198**

I'm actually looking forward to the Coronation, and if anything, am slightly disappointed that its being pared back and stream lined. Whilst I completely understand the reasons for it, the cost particularly in the current economic climate etc. This sort of pomp and pageantry is what Britain does so well, the Queens funeral being an example, and I almost feel a bit cheated we're not doing to get the full bells and whistles for what is such a rare occurrence. Admittedly, with the King being in his 70s, its more than likely that I will see another one in my lifetime, so perhaps this is also part of the reasoning for it being simplified as we may be doing it again in 20 years or so, rather than the 70 its been since the last.

I also understand that times have changed, Britain isn't a pro-monarchy as it was at the time of the last Coronation, and also in 1953, the country wasn't long past the war and rationing and it was seen as a celebration and the marking of an era, more so than today.

I will be watching on the day, more because it's a historical event than for love of the monarchy. We are planning to have a small party on the Sunday, both sets of parents, my partners sister and family just to mark the occasion and all get together. I'll put the bunting up (still in the box from last years Platinum Jubilee) but its more a reason to get everyone together. I know the town where I live is taking part in The Big Lunch event on the Sunday, and is putting on music and entertainment in the towns main park for people to take along a picnic too. I believe local scouts are doing a barbeque for everyone at the park. **F46, E7024**

No one in our hamlet was doing anything for the coronation. My daughter's school had a picnic and mufti day and badge to commemorate it. Our friend gave the children a mug to keep for the future.

We went to my father-in-laws... in Cheshire to watch it together. I made smoked salmon, coronation quiche, and chicken and salad, and strawberries and cream and asparagus and champagne. The coronation quiche was awful.

I made it all so I could watch it from start to finish and I absolutely loved it. It was quite Disneyesque which was excellent and so interesting all the bizarre objects and processes. I loved the music and the inclusivity of it- to an extent. I did love the celebrity who said it was very white! That did make me laugh. It was high pageantry for our benefit and it was wonderful. I thought the king and queen carried out their roles brilliantly can you imagine doing all that at 73 when you are winding down. I thought William and Kate and the children performed very well. It made me feel very proud and very British. **F48, M3055**

We had a street party here years ago but this will not happen now because all the English people have moved out. Our neighbours are now Greek, Somali, Lithuanian, Rumanian, African – and that's the ones I know of. Their English is poor and they will not celebrate our royal family. Out of the 12 houses ... we are one of 3 who will put bunting up.

Today is Friday 28th April. During the week one of our neighbours did put up bunting with the King's face on. Today I went outside to put wire up and the other neighbour was doing hers at the same time. I helped her and she gave me a flag which I put in a flower pot. When I came in my husband offered to buy me a wooden jigsaw of Buckingham Palace as there was a discount this weekend so we ordered it. Its total cost is just over £31 including delivery. It is from Wentworth jigsaws and the special cut out 'whimsie' shapes will more than likely include the profile of Charles' head and the coronation date. It has cheered me up as I have not had a very good day so far . . .

1st May. Another neighbour has put flags up and there are some in the next street.

Our neighbour says a black nurse at the hospital was complaining and saying he's not her king. My friend (the neighbour) said you're in this country so he is your king. I do not know if the nurse claims to be Black British or not. She does however work in Queen's hospital and is presumably happy for doing so. **F69, C5991**

I have always been interested in pageantry, ceremony, history and royalty. That aspect of British culture has fascinated me for a long time and probably began in 1953.

I never imagined that I would live to see a second coronation and I feel sure I will not see a third. But, who knows? British support for the monarchy being what it is, there are many who feel that Charles III will be the last king of this country. King in the sense of being a ceremonial head of state by virtue of heredity. Some republicans are calling for the head of state to be elected (a prospect that fills me with dismay given what I have seen of the other examples, such as Macron, Putin, Berlusconi . . .).

I watched a programme broadcast by BBC television about how the ceremonial tunics are being made for the coronation. Presented by Patrick Grant (a Savile Row tailor and fashion designer), the programme looked at the company making ceremonial tunics for participating military and adding the new cipher to the costumes being worn . . . This was a fascinating insight in to the preparations. It brought all the historically interesting aspects of this ancient ritual . . . I do not claim to be a monarchist and yet I was fascinated by what happened during the coronation. The ancient ritual enacted that day appealed to me as one who loves history . . .

I spent the whole day watching the television. I looked for local events but found nothing taking place in my immediate neighbourhood that was of any interest to me. Websites listed a variety of big screens, in the city, on which people could watch the broadcast. My own television screen is quite big and so I saw this as not being of interest to me . . . **M73, L6048**

Ironically it happens to be Coronation Day as I'm writing my contribution, so I am well placed to comment. I'm extremely excited to watch the procession and the ceremony. My children are 7 and 5 and I hope they will enjoy watching the proceedings too as this marks a day in history for our country. Not so many people these days have seen a Coronation. I think in my family the only people to have lived through a Coronation before is my mother-in-law in 1952 when the Queen was crowned. I very much doubt she watched it on television though. It was the first Coronation to be televised but not everybody could afford a television back then. I doubt very much that my mother-in-law had one. I know she was given a cup from school to commemorate the day and she still has it to this day in her hall.

I hear the King has scaled down his coronation considerably compared to that of his mother, The late Queen. I think this is very sensible and forward thinking of him. The King is by nature quite a frugal person whenever he can be, and I would expect he will want the coronation to focus more on the spiritual elements than the showier parts. I feel he is judging the mood of the nation correctly. I hear that communities are being encouraged to enjoy a 'greener coronation' for the king to minimise the impact on the environment. I think that is marvellous and about time too. I've noticed in the media that local councils are suggesting people use reusable or biodegradable decorations, including potted flowers which can be planted out afterwards; use sustainable transport, encouraging guests to travel on public transport, walk or cycle; serve food made from local and seasonal ingredients; and reducing waste, by choosing reusable utensils over single use plastic ones, and providing recycling and food waste bins. Whether or not this will be taken into account and borne out remains to be seen but I remain hopeful. The design for the king's Coronation invitations were released a few weeks back and it was reported that the logo and the invitations have again all pointed to the King's lifelong environmental interests, the invitations are recycled paper, there's the Green Man that features at the bottom of the invitation and lots of floral references.

Something that we have noticed that we haven't been pleased to hear is a lot of anti-monarchist sentiment. Liverpool is a particularly republican city, and I am a monarchist so quite often feel a little outnumbered in my own city. My husband says that he has noticed more and more programmes on the BBC discussing whether we should still have a monarchy, can we sustain it? what the future of the monarchy could mean for Britain etc whereas I know the opposing view often accuses the BBC of reporting solely pro monarchist reports. My husband works in a particularly pro republican office, and he says that he often feels shouted down by colleagues. He himself would be happy to engage in a healthy debate on the subject and to see both sides but often feels that the republicans literally shout too loudly.

As previously mentioned, we are going to my aunt and uncle's Coronation Garden party this evening. Just a small gathering really of friends and family. From my aunt and uncle's point of view I'm not sure that it is an excuse for them to throw a party or they genuinely support the king but I'm happy to celebrate regardless and I wish the king a long and happy reign. **F37, A5426**

I am not taking an active part on the celebrations. Charles became king when his mother died, so what's all this ceremony about except another opportunity for the Church of England to exert its authority. Why is the coronation ceremony held in a church at all? The Anglican Church has far more power than it should be entitled to as it represents a very small segment of the population. I was so relieved that the suggested 'pledge of allegiance' to the King was ditched at the last minute. I certainly had no intention of saying it.

I think the Monarchy costs us a lot of money, despite their enormous private untaxed wealth, and there are far too many people in the extended family who ought to be out earning a living. The monarchy accumulated its undisclosed wealth through empire, colonialism and the slave trade. I don't have any objections to the individual or role of the Monarch, but I think they should be financially self-supporting, and open about the extent of their inherited property and income, which should be taxed. I believe the Danish queen can be seen riding around on a bike. I approve . . .

I think the new king understands and believes in a lot of the environmental issues that concern me, and he has done, is doing, some really good things in that regard. I also think he wants to modernise, but there is a lot of inertia in the system to stop him being able to. I've thought a lot about whether an elected head of state would be better, but I have very little faith in elections. The fact that, according to some authors, 76% of our MPs are millionaires just goes to show that the electoral system doesn't produce a representative body. They don't represent us or me in particular, at all, and many of the social and financial policies they create, and attitudes they express are really abhorrent to anyone with a social conscience. Rich people have a way of getting themselves, with the help of their friends and relatives, into positions of power. Removing the monarchy wouldn't change that, or change the existence of the aristocracy. Just think – we could end up with King Boris Johnson, our own version of Donald Trump!

P.S. After the event: I was horrified to see the police cracking down on peaceful protest. This isn't Hong Kong. We supposedly have the right to express our views in peaceful protest. Any government that tries to stifle peaceful protest is asking for bigger trouble. I was delighted to see the Conservative party getting a thorough kicking at the local elections, hidden almost from general sight by timing them the day before the coronation. **H8036**

I had very mixed feelings about the Coronation.

I'm an anti-royalist. I don't believe people should be given positions of power and privilege just because they were born into a certain family. I should therefore like to see the monarchy abolished. A popular conception is that they work hard. So do lots of other people but they don't have chauffeured cars to take them to work, a designer wardrobe, a palace or two to live in, no worries about paying the bills, no childcare problems in the school holidays and no coming home to household chores, washing cooking and cleaning. They get the best tickets in the house at the theatre, see exhibitions before the hoi polloi get in and travel the world. It must be a very hard life. I'm up for it if there's a vacancy.

But I'm a realist. I know the royal family are popular here and abroad and they attract tourists, although, come to think of it, I've never seen statistics to prove this. I'm also a sucker for ceremony and history.

I did watch the Coronation as I had a pile of ironing to do and there was nothing else much on TV. And if I'm honest it was an historic spectacle I may never see again. I enjoyed the music especially. I was glad Chaz had pared down the ceremony and therefore the expense although it looked pretty full on to me. The best part of the whole day was the continual text messaging I shared with my sister P. We commented on everything from Penny Mordant's outfit (we liked) and Kate's (which we didn't). **K8158**

I think it's right that the Coronation should be a less lavish affair than the Queen's was. I do enjoy pageantry, but in the present financial climate, it would be at least irresponsible to spend huge sums of money for it. I know many people think that even a scaled-down version is unwise. I do think that the trappings of monarchy such as this set a tone for our country and bring in money from tourism. I will certainly watch the event on television, and I expect to enjoy it.

It amused me to read today that Charles is 'recycling' two of the several chairs/thrones used in the ceremony, in the spirit of sustainability. I suppose it shows some sort of willing, but it took two months to refurbish them, so hardly saving money! Bit of a joke! . . .

I'm fine with there being an extra bank holiday – I think it's appropriate. I didn't know pubs were staying open late, but that seems a bit unnecessary, given the extended opening hours we have these days. I hadn't been aware of the Big Help Out initiative at all! It sounds like a good idea. What I don't approve of, which has only just been announced, is that Camilla will be given the title of Queen. It goes against what the late Queen wished and specified. Given her (and Charles') history, Queen consort was enough I think. **F72, D6836**

Left entirely to my own devices I wouldn't have paid much attention to the Coronation. Not that I'm hostile to the Royal Family, even if I do have serious doubts about the institution of monarchy; in fact I'm rather fond of the man I still can't stop referring to as 'Prince Charles'. It's more that I've never been fond of elaborate and/or extended ritual . . . King Charles became King the second his late mother breathed her last; it's not as though somehow or other he wasn't really King until he'd been crowned. So my attitude was: you lot enjoy yourselves however you please, and best wishes to all, but I'll sit this one out.

Of course, things are never that simple where Royal occasions are concerned. The TV, radio and newspaper coverage, augmented nowadays by the internet and social media, rolls in inexorably, like a gas attack on the

Somme, and even if you manage to minimise it you're still all too well aware that it's going on. On top of that I had to deal with events going on at the library where I volunteer, one of which was a 'Coronation Street Party'-themed Drop In. (Every Wednesday afternoon we host a Drop In aimed at elderly people living on their own, with home-made cakes, pastries etc). In fact, by the time Saturday came around I felt as though I'd already lived through the Coronation and needed no more of it.

Sunday 30 April 2023

Dropping in mostly to record my weariness and mild irritation with the run-up to the coronation next Saturday. Practically the entire front page of this morning's Times given over to the proposal that every citizen should stand up and pledge allegiance to the Crown, for example. Really? What's the point? Most of us wish the King and Queen good luck and fair winds, so to speak, and even if we're sceptical about the institution of monarchy we're not sufficiently exercised about it as to want to make trouble for the poor sods up at the sharp end. But equally, why go out of our way to self-consciously make a pledge we regard as completely unnecessary? It seems to me that even to articulate such a proposal is to tacitly acknowledge that indifference towards the monarchy is widespread, especially among younger people, and that in the long term it's indifference – seeing no reason to value or continue with the institution, the very opposite of fervent republicanism – that will bring the monarchy down.

Friday, 5 May 2023

... On Wednesday I went to the library for the Drop In. I was only involved with the physical setting up, waiting on table and washing up and clearing away and putting the library back to normal afterwards, but even that meant six solid hours of very hard work. The women who made the food were working for thirty-six hours with only snatched breaks for sleep. In two and a half hours the oldies pretty much levelled the mountains of cakes, cheesecakes, pastries, trifles etc put before them, being serenaded all the while by a nonagenarian neighbour of J's, who turned up with a karaoke machine and carolled his way through the hits of the Forties and Fifties. Then, as no one else was prepared do it, I had to get the forty-odd-strong crowd on their feet and toasting the King in prosecco. It took some doing, as they were too busy forcing down yet more cake and gossiping at the tops of their voices, but eventually I cut through the racket and got them calling out God Save The King! I decided to test the water on one supposedly contentious point, so added in an extra toast for 'Queen Camilla'. Hmm. Quite a few women looked sour-faced at that. Some people.... One of the volunteers has declared her house a Coronation-free zone on Saturday, in memory of

Princess Diana, f'Chrissakes . . . she's been dead twenty-five years, get over it, I felt like saying. Home by five, exhausted and with my feet aching.

6 May 2023

. . . It's far too small a sample to base any observation on, but from speaking to them and also sounding out fellow volunteers over the past fortnight I've formed the impression that people were prepared to go along with the Coronation, and might even enjoy watching some or all of it, but felt no great mystical, emotional connection to the ceremony, or any deeper commitment to the King or to the monarchy generally. If you combined elements of a graduation ceremony, a Senior Prom and a passing-out parade you might end up producing the same mental atmosphere, I think . . .

I found L glued to the TV coverage, which had reached the 'procession out of the Abbey' stage. It all looked very grand, and so well lit it could even have been taken for a feature film recreation: all the figures seemed to stand out incredibly sharply, like sumptuously-dressed waxworks of themselves. **M64, M3190**

I think Charles is being smart. We are in a cost of living crisis. For all he's a bit of a tit, he IS switched on to some things and has SOME common sense. It'll still draw in the crowds who will spend which will boost the economy, and it won't cost the public as much from the privy purse. If I can I'll probably have the coronation on TV in the background if its on a day I'm not at the gaming lounge (which is unlikely as that's a Sunday). It is a historical event after all & the pomp & ceremony is interesting . . .

If the government HADN'T approved the extra bank holiday, I think there might have been riots. Given the state of politics right now it would have been an own goal. So they didn't really have a choice. That being said, longer opening hours at pubs will help the hospitality sector and Charles is known for his charitable initiatives (It's not like he had much else to do in the 60ish years he's been prince of Wales) so again, smart to highlight this. **B7843**

I will not watch any of the coronation because Charles and Camilla are a waste of space and money. If he really wants to 'help out', he could donate the millions he has in inherited wealth to all the people having to go to food banks to survive and to the chronic underfunded NHS.

I like having an extra bank holiday. I shall be avoiding all street parties and see this as a way to distract people from the huge mess Charles and the Tory government have made of the country, the worst living standards in generations and their failure to take meaningful action on climate change. I hope Charles is overthrown as soon as possible and I would be happy to protest to make this happen. I am not going to protest the Coronation in person as I plan to be far away from central London to avoid the crowds of flag waving deluded royalists. Pubs staying open later is just another excuse for binge drinking which shouldn't be encouraged and to distract working class people from their tax money being wasted on the ceremonies. Charles can get lost and I hope he is Charles the Last. **F38, M4780**

I feel largely disinterested in the Royal Family and . . . would have preferred the death of Queen Elizabeth II to have brought an end to monarchy in Britain.

I am writing now with an eye on the Coronation service, having switched on the TV as Charles & Camilla arrived at the Abbey. It's all high camp really! I am enjoying all the costumes and of course the whole thing is so very well organised and executed. The music is lovely. It is apparently scaled down, but I dread to think what it all cost! The tv commentator just said that this procession (from the Abbey to Buckingham Palace) is the largest for 70 years. What happened to the plans to include multiple faiths? It all seems very tightly bound to the Anglican Church.

Two of my colleagues and I have been exchanging comments on WhatsApp as we watch the ceremony, entertaining ourselves. Honestly, so much of it just seems daft. And what utter nonsense are the prayers 'may the king live for ever' and 'may he live as long as the sun and moon endure'! The change to the service from hereditary peers swearing allegiance to the king to an invitation to 'the people' to swear allegiance has grabbed headlines this week and been widely seen as ill-judged. My pro-monarchy friend also thought this ridiculous.

My husband came into the room where I'm watching tv, on his way out to the shops, and I said I felt entirely unmoved by it all. He agreed and commented that while this is the first Coronation during our lifetimes, we have seen a lot of this kind of pomp and circumstance, most recently with the Queen's funeral but previously with various royal weddings. **F57, C6574**

As an ex-soldier I was looking for people I know among the troops, and honouring the much loved Queen Elizabeth who I respected as a person. Throughout the day my attitude to the monarchy shifted. I started as a mild monarchist and moved to being mild → moderate anti-monarchy. Beyond the obscene spending involved whilst many are starving, I was shocked by the ceremony itself. I had not realised that the first and strongest oath sworn by the King was not to the people or country, but to the church. The props used made me realise that the monarchy stems from when a Frenchman invaded our Isles and by force of arms killed or subdued any who disagreed with him, such that all monarchs now receive the crown in his chair. Property belonging to the 'Crown' also stems from then – again, frustrating during the crisis. Mostly, being a Pagan, someone historically killed by the institution he swore to champion and who were not represented during the service (despite being *our traditional faith) I saw an insurmountable gulf open. I was glad to watch 'Tangled' after that.* **NB39, HMP Isle of Wight**

We had our usual kind of morning – breakfast, a leisurely trawl of the market, a check on any interesting books in the charity shops – and headed home. I then switched the TV on and to my own wry amusement, ended up watching the greater part of the Coronation service anyway. So much for my Republican tendencies. I was consulting Twitter at the same time and enjoying some of the more irreverent comments, so I admit it was a bit of a sarcastic viewing process . . . . my husband even wandered through to watch it, and joined in the sceptical commentary. We were especially amused by the witty remarks online about Penny Mordaunt, looking like something out of an Arthurian legend as she carried aloft the gigantic Sword of State throughout the entire lengthy service – someone cleverly spotted that the design on her dress and hat was unfortunately similar to the Poundland logo. **F64, G3423**

I won't be watching the Coronation on Saturday and I really think Charlie could've paid for it himself, or better still we could've used his mum's death as an opportunity to reassess how much a monarchy still serves us in the 21st century. I'll aim to spend the day distracted, either with friends, a long walk or a good book. Admittedly I'll read a load of articles about the event afterwards – these solemn public events are always enjoyably memeable so I think there'll probably be some entertainment to be had from the whole spectacle. I find it truly mind boggling that anyone would watch the whole thing live, as I'm certain it will be crushingly dull . . .

I'm not aware of any events celebrating the day in Leith, or even in Edinburgh as a whole, although there must be some. I literally don't know a single person who is excited or moved or anything but pissed off by the whole thing . . . . My friends are all actively anti-monarchy, and my family still range from ambivalent to hostile. I don't know anyone who is celebrating in any way shape or form. **F30, C7632**

The coronation is this weekend coming and seems to have suddenly appeared very fast! As I'm not a royalist I have little interest in the coronation except perhaps its significance as a rare-ish historical event. I have no plans to watch it, even more so since the news that there will be a 'pledge of allegiance' that people around the world will be asked to make. I think, considering this is not a democratically elected but enforced family this is a strange thing to do. With the exception of a grandparent none of my friends or family are royalists and most have no plans to watch the coronation either . . . .

The main information and things related to the coronation has all been on the news or through advertising and shop marketing. In many ways as there are no planned events it just feels like a materialistic event for clothes, mugs and even (as I spotted on an Asda advert) duvet covers!

Our neighbour did suggest that at some point it might be nice to have a village BBQ as the street parties gave them the idea though they did then say this should 'not be for the coronation' – which I guess sums up the general feeling here! **F29, F7710**

I am planning a buffet and special cake. I have made a cake and will fill it and decorate it nearer the day. I will try the spinach and broad bean quiche today and intend to try the mushrooms in filo pastry recipe in advance. I did the quiche for lunch with various salads and the mushrooms mix later. Local shops are selling bunting, napkins etc. etc., not that I would purchase shop made. . . . At home I have made a fabric flower wreath in red, white and blue. I circulated the instructions to family and friends. Originally it was for the door, but as it might rain, I hung it in a front window on 29th . . . I posted a related picture for the Instagram account of the local embroidery society. **B6659C**

Although I am a fan of King Charles III, I have no plans for the Coronation weekend. I have always been a Royalist, and think King Charles is the greenest Royal we have, which is a great thing much needed in this day and age. I think that part of his nature will have contributed to his scaled down plans for his Coronation, and displays a sensitivity to the wider needs of his people at this time; a huge, grand Coronation during a cost of living crisis for his subjects would have been tone deaf, and I'm pleased therefore he is responding accordingly. I intend to watch the occasion on tv, but will not be partaking of any activities – not least because there won't be any street parties in the city centre! **F35, H6924**

On the day of the coronation itself I'll probably go for a walk on the North Downs if the weather is nice, might be empty of people if everyone is glued to the ceremony on their TVs.

I am by inclination not particularly supportive of a monarchical system and I certainly won't be doing this absurd oath swearing shenanigans that somebody has dreamt up – I am a citizen and not a subject. Having said that, I do not object to Charles personally as the head of state; he seems a hard-working, decent chap, who has championed causes in his life such as organic farming, protecting nature, and helping disadvantaged youth, that are very important and presumably benefit from the public profile his interest accords them. In many ways I feel sorry for him and his family, stuck at the heart of an incessant media swarm, with their personal lives under constant scrutiny. It cannot be much fun to live one's life that way, especially as none of them chose this path but had it thrust upon them.

In short, I'd sum up my attitude to the coronation as conflicted about constitutional monarchy as a system of governance and fundamentally uninterested in all the pomp and mythology surrounding it. **M38, K7050**

I am a very luke-warm monarchist. My feeling is that, like Democracy as a form of government, the Windsors are the least worst option. Why would anyone risk getting a Trump or a Boris instead?! At least the royals don't have political power . . . and the recent 'goings on' of the Sussexes and the Duke of York have been good value on the soap opera/gossip front. I very much enjoyed watching the Coronation Special of 'The Windsors' on TV. It was silly but not cruel and the actors playing the various members of the royal family were having a ball . . . mickey taking but in an almost affectionate way. I not only enjoyed the show but found comfort and satisfaction in the confirmation it gave, that I live in a country where royalty can be lampooned with pantomime panache! Although I am usually happy to join in partying with family, friends and/or neighbours, I had no particular wish to be involved in celebrations for the coronation of King Charles 3. He seems a nice enough, well intentioned, guy and I wish him well but flag waving, cheering and forelock tugging aren't really my thing. I was pleased, therefore, that we planned to be on holiday in Scotland on 6th May 2023, where I expected there to be very little celebrating that we would need to avoid! How wrong I was!

We were surprised when we arrived at the hotel on the shore of Loch Awe, that not only was the place decked out in union flags and red white and blue bunting but there were many permanent pictures on the walls, of recent and current royals. We also noted a poster advertising a community celebration on Coronation Day in a local village hall. All were invited and because we had the time . . . and I'm nosey . . . . I convinced my husband that we should accept the invitation. We did!

We were greeted at the door, as if royalty ourselves and ushered in to the very nice village hall where trestle tables were groaning under the weight of cakes, sandwiches and pots of tea and coffee. Having no picnic for later in the day, I asked if our sandwiches and cakes could be wrapped up as take-aways. This was happily done but then, to my embarrassment I discovered that everything was free and I was told, firmly, that no financial contribution would be accepted! 'We have done this for the community to mark the Coronation. No one pays!' On the stage a huge cinema-sized screen was already showing the ceremony, so we sat down with our cuppas to watch. Around us, children ran about wearing foil crowns and battering each other with red, white and blue balloons. (Not sitting still, watching in rather bewildered silence, as we had done as children, watching the crowning of Queen Elizabeth 2nd, 70+ years before, on a neighbours TV bought especially for the occasion!) As I watched the King and Queen enter the Abbey to shouts of Vivat, I was surprised at how emotional I felt. Commitments for the rest of the day, didn't *allow for us staying longer than half an hour but I was sorry we couldn't watch more of the ceremony I had previously been consciously avoiding . . .*

To conclude: I enjoyed the Coronation much more than I expected to. Like most people, I think, I felt that the pomp and pageantry was a great spectacle . . . and spending less on it wouldn't really have benefitted people struggling with the cost of living. Oh! And a quick word about the Republican protesters: I feel they had every right to make there feelings known (in a safe way) and I am pleased they did. I felt some were unfairly arrested. I would be interested to know, however, how they would chose to celebrate the inauguration of a President and how expensive that might be. Even if it were much cheaper than the coronation of a monarch, it could be even more divisive, because political. I'd certainly be holding my 'Not my Boris/Liz/Rishi' banner! **F76, M7803**

We have a photo in our family of my Grandma, long before she was my Grandma, as a teenage girl, my Dad thinks she would have been 18. She looks fabulous. She's wearing a beautifully made suit and has gloves tucked under her arm, she's carrying a small suitcase. She's pictured near a shop which developed photographs and my Dad says it was probably a street photographer who took her photo on that day, that she'd have picked it up from that shop. She was in London for the Coronation of George VI, so it must have been May 1937. She would always remain a royalist, she had a photograph of the Queen up on her wall.

When Queen Elizabeth II was crowned both my parents gathered around new TVs in their neighbourhoods to watch the spectacle. The Queen was young and beautiful and would remain the Queen for my Mum's whole life.

I used to be a royalist. I liked the ceremony. I liked the long history. But I've come to believe that the monarchy entrenches beliefs in elites, that all our histories are valid, that the institution is damaging to the people, and to the members of the institution.

I would say that the area of Scotland where I stay is not very royalist, although the older people sometimes are. For the Queen's Jubilee some bought bunting and had street parties, and we had colouring in for it in the library. People had respect for her, even if they didn't believe in the institution.

When she died there was a book of condolence in the library and people were glad to see it there. There's a photograph in the library of King George VI visiting somewhere local with various people, including Princess Elizabeth. It's very important to the people of the village. She was very important. People wrote in the book of condolence. People wondered what would happen next.

Nobody printed off any colouring for King Charles. Some people put up bunting but mostly to piss off republican neighbours. I didn't hear of any street parties. We did see a crown display outside an old folks home and one of my kids said 'spot the Tories'. The crochet group who meet in the library had taken the little crowns they'd made for the jubilee home. They did talk about bringing them back, but couldn't really be bothered. 'Nobody really cares' one woman said . . .

On the Saturday, I went to my hairdresser to get my hair done. She was grumbling because she'd wanted to watch the coronation and had assumed it would be on the Bank Holiday. Someone told her she could watch it on catch up, and someone else said that way she could skip the boring bits. I was watching it with my older daughter until it was time for my appointment. She'd be doing a lot of skipping to miss the boring bits. It was still on when I got home. Charles and Camilla stood on the balcony in ermine. I was wondering about the choice to wear ermine. I know it's probably old, but it's still disgusting. My daughter didn't know what an ermine was. She googled it and found the cutest picture. I'm not sure she'll ever forgive them.

My Dad watched it on TV too. He found it boring, and wondered how long the monarchy would last . . . [he] was laughing about the cover of Private Eye, and watching the coronation I wished that it was just a man in a hat sitting on a chair, but it was an immensely privileged man requiring everyone to pay him obeisance while he sat wearing immeasurably expensive things.

The Guardian *did a series on how much the royal family costs, and how wealthy they are. They have their own reasons of course, but it really does not sit well with me that so much money has had to go in to the King's Coronation while people can't afford to feed their families. It's like something out of* Game of Thrones *(although they'd have probably done the crowning a lot quicker). I even heard that councils had had to divert funding away from food banks in order to pay for costs of the coronation. That's truly disgusting. It's bad enough that the country is so badly managed that we need food banks, worse that they're underfunded while we're making sure millionaires don't have to pay for things.*

Having watched some of the coronation and talked about it quite a bit, I became convinced that it's time for the monarchy to go. I'm sure my Grandma would not approve. I also wonder how she would have survived in today's world with her disabled husband and her part time job and her four children. No doubt the Tories she loved would have been suggesting she was a benefits scrounger. . . . No doubt she'd have had to make use of those food banks . . .

I partly watched this Coronation as I think it might be the last in my lifetime. Not because I'll die soon or because Charles will live forever (which was an odd thing to wish for), but because it is so incredibly vulgar. I'm hoping we will soon see the end of monarchy, but if not that then at least an end of vulgar displays like this, which aren't done by other countries which still have royalty. **F49, M4645**

I think it is right that the Coronation is expected to be on a smaller scale in these times of high inflation and difficulties with food and energy prices for many. I'm not sure that was achieved as there are wildly differing estimates *of how much it cost. I always think accountants count things twice. A lot of people would have been there being paid to be doing their job anyway, so did they get counted twice?*

We live in greatly different times to Queen Elizabeth's Coronation. Talking to my 80-year old stepmother, she remarked how it was a bright spot in a grey and dreary post-war world where rationing and the memory of war was still fresh. I can understand that greater sense of togetherness that people would have shared back then. Today, we are so fragmented and diversified I don't think there are many things that captivate the whole nation in the same way as they did in the past, or could do. For example, it was a real struggle to get people interested in the Olympics in 2012 until we saw the brilliant opening ceremony and we started winning medals. Similarly, it's only when the England football team reach the semi-finals of the World Cup do we all sit up, take notice, and become football fans . . .

I think the Big Help Out initiative is great, but I did not see any activity in my area. Things like this are where I can support the Royal Family, otherwise I am quite ambivalent about them. Quite unlike one of my daughters who I was most surprised to see joined the Republic protest in London, pictured on her Instagram with a 'Not My King' placard. I know she has quite strong views about various political matters, but I have not known her go on any demonstrations before. I agree with quite a lot of what she believes. I do think the monarchy are something of an anachronism, a symbol of privilege, entitlement and power that has little place in our society today. However, I don't believe we are going to get rid of the monarchy any time soon – it is not a realistic aim. I think there are far more greater evils in the world to be demonstrating about, or positively getting involved with to make a change. It's too easy to get hot under the collar about something that isn't likely to have an effect and feel you are achieving something than get your hands dirty by making a real difference.

A monarchy is only as good as its incumbent. Queen Elizabeth II was very good at that. I think people have more doubts about Charles III. If the monarchy didn't read the tone of the nation, then I think the public could soon easily turn on them. At the death of Diana, those feelings were made readily apparent, and I think some concessions and changes were made, albeit reluctantly and slowly. On one hand, I agree with my daughter, the monarchy is absurd, too slow to change, and has been shameful in the way it has dealt with Prince Andrew and other issues. However, I have been impressed with things like the Duke of Edinburgh scheme, the Prince's Trust, Diana's involvement with AIDS patients and landmines, and latterly Prince Harry's setting up of the Invictus Games. These have quietly achieved great things for many people over the years and have highlighted issues that need to be brought to our attention in a way that transcends politics. It is here I think the monarchy knows its future role must lead to. I am pleased Charles III places the environment at the forefront of his agenda, although as I have said earlier, it is his son that seems to articulate himself far better.

At times of crisis we do benefit from a voice that can stand outside of our political or industrial leaders. It is the role of the court jester, the prophet, of the church, or maybe even a modern royal family – to hold a precarious position in the trust of the people, to take the temperature of the people, and to speak accordingly to power. Paradoxically, power speaking to power. It is for this reason, despite my ambivalence to the monarchy (I am not interested in the family difficulties and squabbles that we all have), that I believe they have a place and a future for us, if they continue to keep a finger on the pulse of the nation and progress a bit quicker. **M56, D4736**

The royal family has had its day. I could see the point of it when people said that they were an example to us all, showing us the correct way to behave, but who thinks that now? Charles and Camilla had an adulterous affair for many years before they were married. There's a widespread belief that Charles isn't Harry's father. Andrew has recently paid many millions of pounds to a woman he claims never to have met. If all of this is an example then it's fairly disgusting. I would dislike having to live down to the royal family's standards of behaviour.

There was a party in my street yesterday but I didn't go because I thought that would have been hypocritical of me. My wife went. She also watched the proceedings on Saturday via the BBC. I decided to do something more interesting and so I cleaned the house. **M69, M4463**

We watched the funeral on tv and, as I was with my youngest daughter on the day, we all found the whole thing to be extremely moving, even though some of my children had professed to having little or no interest in the Royal Family as such.

As for the Coronation I sense that the mood is entirely different. A sense of indifference appears to pervade and when you mention it to others the usual response is one of shrugging shoulders. It does not appear to be relevant to them. I certainly feel no compulsion to go down to London to witness the event. Yet I am no republican and still support the concept of the Royal Family as opposed to having a President, (the USA is proof of the fact that this is often even worse.) I wonder why this is. Could it be the association of the new King with the awfulness of Diana and her fate? Could it be because of the reaction of their youngest son to his family and the terrible manner by which the media has been used to conduct a slanging match of epic proportions?

There is no joy in this process for me. I accept that money has to be spent and don't kid yourself that it will be any cheaper if we have a republic other than a monarchy. It won't be. It might even be worse. GB has a very proud history, and this is the time to celebrate that. It is bound to be quite different to what happened in 1953. We are a small nation which, in the great scheme of things, isn't that important. But I'm proud of my country (Patriotic, not

Nationalist) and I value the history which exists here. We often get things wrong, but we get an awful lot right as well...

In 1953 there were many accomplishments which sort of made it a golden year for GB – a new, young Queen, scaling Everest, various sporting milestones etc. Will there be any such occasions to mirror that in 2023? The big difference is that this King is not particularly young and having a Queen called Camilla reminds me more of a Disney film than anything else. He seems to carry a little too much baggage with him and there is a degree of suspicion as to whether he is committed to anything other than himself. I do not regard him as inspirational, although I accept that initiatives such as the Princes Trust have helped many younger people to aspire and achieve, so perhaps that is a little unfair...

In 1953 the country had come through a war and was just beginning to rediscover its mojo and feel that it had something to offer the world. I'm not sure that that is so at the moment. However, we have come through Covid and that felt a little like a war, (more for some than for others), so perhaps there are some grounds for celebrating that as an achievement. I still miss the Queen though. **F69, K7522**

What I found missing was the magic: for me the young queen about whom I had read in a book celebrating her accession... was a fairy-tale figure and I drank in the robes, the awesome ceremony and the great crown.

At the age of five most of the ceremonial significance passed me by so this time I found it interesting to be able to follow and understand the various stages of the ritual as it proceeded. What struck me in particular was that, just as the Coronation of 1953 was a reflection of the contemporary Zeitgeist, this was definitely a Coronation for a very different Britain. I have always thought of the early 1950s as a time of optimism: the country had emerged from the war; there was virtually full employment; the Welfare State had been established; and a new generation was being born, of whom I was one, to benefit from healthcare and educational opportunities. As a child my world felt very stable, rooted in pre-war tradition, but I can see now that the seeds which would bring about today's multi-cultural, multi-faith, multi-gender Britain had already been sown and would flourish in my lifetime, coming to fruition in the Coronation of King Charles.

I thought that the balance of tradition and modern culture was successfully managed through the personnel involved in the ceremony – the role of women and representation of different faiths, for example – and the range of music from plainchant to contemporary compositions and gospel. The transition of Camilla from Queen Consort to crowned Queen seemed to me in itself a symbol of the monarchy's increasing adjustment to the mores of contemporary Britain...

I do regret that there were (as far as I know) no official mementoes for the young children. In 1953 we were all given a china mug emblazoned with the Queen's portrait, a specially-minted five-shilling piece, and a colourful cardboard certificate inscribed by hand with our names; it had two wings which opened onto a design including the royal insignia, the symbols of countries making up the United Kingdom and illustrations of St Edward's Crown and the Imperial Crown, with a schematic family tree on the reverse. **F75, T7449**

Comparisons with the last Coronation are almost too obvious to be worth saying: a beautiful young woman with a handsome husband being crowned in the aftermath of World War 2 had a great romantic appeal, compared with a crumpled twice-married elderly couple who are now our king and queen. The rehabilitation of Camilla from being an adulterous marriage-breaking mistress, vilified in the press for years and shunned by the royal family, into being a respected crowned queen, is remarkable, and a sign of the more forgiving times in which we find ourselves. They seem very good as a couple...

A bring-and-share Coronation lunch was planned for our church congregation after the Sunday service; I undertook to provide 2 Coronation quiches, the new recipe involving spinach, broad beans and fresh tarragon. The broad beans had to be out of a tin as they're not in season here; the spinach was frozen (although I could have used fresh); the tarragon was unobtainable so I substituted dried tarragon and fresh parsley. I make a small ginger- and-strawberry trifle for us to eat at home, supposedly a Coronation trifle, but was disappointed with the choice as strawberries aren't yet in season here, and the Scottish ones I did manage to find were not very tasty...

The whole event was a triumph for ceremonial style and tight security. Whether that is what we want to spend £250,000,000 on is a different matter. Other modern European monarchs don't bother with coronations; they just succeed to the throne on the death of the previous one, as of course our present king did. I gather that many people took part in Big Coronation Lunches, as we did ourselves at church, on Sunday; there was also a star-studded live concert at Windsor Castle in the evening, although I didn't watch any of it. The line-up was obviously intended for a younger audience.

This is the moment to redefine our monarchy for the 21st century; we will surely have a new king within 20 years, and I have a feeling that William V's coronation will be very different. **F71, H6675**

This is the second coronation that I have witnessed. I was a teenager when Queen Elizabeth was crowned in Westminster Abbey. My family did not have a television at the time, however the Headmistress of my local secondary school arranged with the manager of our local cinema to allow us to watch the showing of the film made for the coronation... I thought it was a wonderful experience to see what actually happens at a coronation, and the colour of the robes and beautiful dresses of the Queen's maids was I thought magnificent. Yesterday I watched her son's coronation in the comfort of my own home on my colour TV. I wonder if I shall ever see another coronation? ... **F82, H2639**

I plan to watch the Coronation of King Charles on television (probably BBC). I've invited some friends over and will bake a cake and buy some prosecco to make it more of an occasion. I also have some bunting to put up. I am not an ardent royalist but would not want the UK to become a republic. I also like to mark the big occasions and watch the big events like royal weddings. However, I don't feel as fondly towards King Charles as I did the Queen.

I have not considered going into central London. I did go with my mum to the Queen's Platinum Jubilee, hoping to watch the celebrations on one of the big screens, but the parks were closed by the time we arrived. We did get a good view of the flypast, however, but I would not want to get up early to be in place for the Coronation. **F44, D7879**

Before the previous one we were bombarded daily with news items about it – we knew every detail of the various scepters and swords and ampullas and rings and crowns until we were all heartily sick of the whole thing. This time things were very much more restrained and all the better for it. The atmosphere was quite different this time, last time it was almost considered one's civic duty to watch it on TV. This time many people didn't bother. In 1953 we still had the awe of monarchy by now that hardly exists . . .

Of course the whole thing was beautifully managed as these things always are, but you do wonder how relevant the monarchy is in this day and age. On the other hand, the thought of a President Boris doesn't bear thinking about! **F81, P1009**

Personally I have to say that it's been surprising how quickly my attitude has changed towards the Royal Family since the Queens' death. I watched the Queen's funeral with great interest. For Charles' coronation I wasn't even sure if I would watch any of it at. In the end I put the TV on but did other things while it was on. Contrary to my feelings on the Queen's Funeral I thought that the ceremony, even slimmed down, was mostly nonsense. No other nation in Europe does these ceremonies and this was so costly that it felt a little inappropriate, especially when in a cost of living crisis. The only positives were the actual crowning, which I found interesting; the fact that the ceremony included a lot of different faiths and the music which I thought was rather wonderful. Few would deny that Zadok The Priest sounded amazing with the acoustics of Westminster Abbey. Funnily enough I do think that if Charles had totally had his way he'd have slimmed down the service even more. As it was, I turned off the TV well before the end.

The irony of all of this is that the Eurovision Song Contest was held in Liverpool the week after the coronation and the BBC and Liverpool hosted the contest so well that it probably did a much better job of unifying the country and at a much better cost than the coronation did. **M39, O4128**

I definitely won't be participating in the event or watching on tv, although trying to avoid it on tv might be quite a challenge! I think it is good that it is smaller, but not good enough really as I don't believe there should be an occasion at all because I don't agree with the royal family. I certainly hope that this will be the last ever coronation, although I highly doubt it. The coverage will all make it feel very forced, like there is an expectation placed upon us that we should be watching this event even if we don't want to, shown by the extensive build up and coverage which costs the tax payer millions. It is just wasted on a pompous old man who couldn't care about anyone else. In the past, I think the vast majority of people would just go along with events like this and celebrate it for celebrations sake. Nowadays, we think a lot more about what these events entail, the costs and whether they're really worth it or not. We realise the royal family is not something to be proud of and shouldn't be celebrated like in the past when people were blind and ignorant to the facts. **M27, R6956**

I have purchased keepsakes for my three godchildren . . . because it is a significant historical event even if they turn out to be republicans. I still have my father's souvenir book of the Coronation of Queen Elizabeth II and I remember him telling me of making his way to Buckingham Palace to see the Queen. So, I think it will be a nice to give my god children a commemorative gift.

Personally, I am conflicted regarding the continuation of the status of the Royal Family. The idea that one family, via accident of birth are so privileged and hold so much wealth is clearly strange and iniquitous. However, I do believe the core family are used for soft diplomacy and dignitaries from other states enjoy seeing them. I also think many of the events such as weddings, funerals and jubilees are quite unifying. People also seem to enjoy Royal Visits which acknowledge charitable and worthy causes which might otherwise go unmarked. **F55, H7753**

My local railway station has been decked out with multi-colored bunting, which I don't object to. It can be re-used for other events, it doesn't hinder my journey and it adds a bit of gaiety to commuting.

I've mentioned in previous Directives that while I'm not a rabid monarchist, I'm not a republican either. It is possible to be neither. I'd rather the workers (that's us) just paid for one royal spouse and one royal house and demand the rest of the royal family get proper jobs because what they do now is not a proper job, and this causes them and us harm.

On the one hand I have some sympathy for the King. His clearly authentic relationship with his now-wife was undermined in the early 1970s by his family (particularly Mountbatten and the late Queen Mother, who have a lot to answer for), also by palace officials, and the Shand family. If they had not intervened on laughably outdated grounds, Charles could have got on and married Camilla and we'd have been spared the farce that followed (*remember, we have to pay for and put up with them, whether they are well-advised or not*).

But on the other hand, I have concerns, particularly after the Qatari cash-in-bags and Saudi cash-for-knighthoods-and-citizenship scandals. What other naiveties were there? Or is he seriously in league with these crooks? The MP Norman Baker was/is right to question the ethics and conflicts here...

The late Queen had three funeral ceremonies (the Abbey, St George's and the Crypt). She did take her job seriously, but nobody needs three, not even a monarch. Perhaps we cannot expect social awareness from a family that knows nothing but uncomplicated riches (or in the case of Kate Middleton, wealth) but then that's the point – they don't know any different because we haven't taken reform to its logical end: we've stripped them of their old jobs but not given them new ones and they, and us, are caught in a vacuous celebrity-entertainment spiral.

It would be a start if the crowds at such events would stop worshipping the royals as if they were superior beings or believe they are 'relatable' in some way: I'd like to think these hordes are not representative of the population, although the tabloids would have us think otherwise.

It really *is* appalling.

(Please) come, the Revolution... **M53, B4290**

Chapter 2

VISUALIZING CORONATION

Lucy D. Curzon and Jennifer J. Purcell

On 12 May 1937, Humphrey Jennings – while working as a mobile Mass Observer during the Coronation of George VI – took photographs in and around the procession route taken by the new king and queen as they made their way to and from Westminster Abbey. His *Coronation Photomontage* (1937) is one of the more interesting artefacts created as part of MO's attempt to define the experience of Coronation Day. Jennings organized twelve of the images into a grid of three pictures across and four pictures down. In the upper left corner is a photograph of the backside of the Wellington Monument in Hyde Park, beside which is a photograph of a police officer standing in the middle of the Mall, seemingly ankle-deep in paper streamers. The remaining images show the backsides of spectators (four of the twelve photos), rubbish on the streets and in the gutters (three photos), and the backside of a viewing stand. Ironically, these photographs are likely a very truthful representation of what most people who lined the streets actually saw on that day – nothing of the pomp and circumstance, and a great deal of seeing others who were also standing around trying to see over the heads of still more people.[1]

The fact that Jennings's image never actually appeared in *May the Twelfth: Mass-Observation Day-Surveys 1937 by over Two Hundred Observers* may or may not be telling of its effectiveness as a photographic message. On the one hand, it provides the viewer with very little information regarding the wealth of sights and sounds, from around the nation and Empire, heard and seen in London on 12 May 1937. On the other hand, it offers a great deal of insight into the experience of George VI's Coronation for the average person, thus highlighting the frequent banality (even boredom) inherent to ritual and national celebration overall. Indeed, depending on what purpose the reading public wanted *May the Twelfth* to serve (insight into monarchy, a broad understanding of British society, discussion of class strife and industrial action, etc.), Jennings's montage – had it been included – could have completely undermined *or* exponentially heightened (or both) the publication's impact as a record of the event.[2]

Much like text-based documents held in an archive, photographs can be read independently or together. On their own, they provide information about a particular location, person or scene; the impact of light and shade; and the photographer's decisions about framing and angle, among other qualities. When examined in series or succession, however, photographs are no longer singular entities; they interact with one another to create sometimes complex narrative(s). Narrative is constructed from the visual information contained in discrete images, as well as from the meaningful shifts in time and space that occur as the viewer reads across a group of photographs. In many respects, the latter mode of reading is the intention of a photographic montage or essay: putting a cluster of images before the viewer and challenging them to seek meaning in *and* between them. This is, of course, the implication of Stuart Hall's famous argument with regard to *Picture Post*, one of the great British photo-magazines. Founded in 1938, *Picture Post* specialized in publishing photographic essays for popular consumption. Given their nearly simultaneous moments of birth, it is perhaps not surprising that Hall intuitively likens *Picture Post* to Mass Observation:

> There is a sort of passion behind the objectivity of the camera eye here; a passion to present ... to present people to themselves in wholly recognizable terms: terms which acknowledge their commonness, their variety, their individuality, their representativeness. ... The *Picture Post* camera finds them interesting enough, complex enough, expressive enough in the detail of their routine everyday lives.[3]

In the end, for Hall, a photographic essay – because of photography's rich documentary capacity – could serve as both documentation and a form of social democratic intervention.

Given Hall's assessment, it now seems even more strange that Mass Observation did not include photography in *May the Twelfth*. In fact, MO did not use photographic images in *any* of its original phase books or pamphlets.[4] There were many reasons offered for this. First and foremost, during the 1930s and 1940s, Mass Observation did not have enough money to support the high cost of printing photographs in a book or otherwise.[5] There were also concerns that, if published – because the early photographs were most often taken clandestinely – the images would ruin MO's efforts to continue observing unawares.[6] Moreover, for Harrisson in particular, photographs were less biddable than a written report. A photograph could illustrate a particular idea, but it could not be as powerful as a text in conveying meaning. And yet, it was not because photographs were incapable of representing British life at the time that Harrisson was reluctant to use them. Their assumed waywardness, in fact, was the result of producing *too much meaning*.[7]

There is something to be said about the ability of a photograph convey meanings that are unintended or outside the photographer's (or viewer's) control. As Roland Barthes, Annette Kuhn and John Tagg, among many others have suggested, the meaning of a photograph always changes from person to person, place to place and time to time.[8] It only *appears* to be, as Barthes argues, a 'message without a code' – in other words, an assumed analogue to reality.[9] A photograph, in fact, is heavily coded. It handily deceives us into believing that what we see is pure denotation – an instant that will remain fixed in meaning for as long as the photograph survives.

But as Tagg argues, it instead repeatedly slips in and out of our grasp. It regularly becomes, he suggests, 'unframed' – particularly when we, the viewers, '[try] to say what there is to be seen' at any given time.[10] 'The picture is always too little or too large', Tagg suggests, 'obdurately saying less than is wanted and more than is wished'.[11]

In the photographic essay that follows, our intention is encourage viewers to engage the images included in ways that appreciate their profusion of meaning. They are set up, therefore, without the intention of imposing an interpretative framework. Instead, we urge viewers to see each image, per Tagg, as 'large' or as 'little' as the situation allows. The essay's purpose, in the end, is not to foist coherent meaning upon Charles III's Coronation, but rather to visualize and grapple with the plethora of meanings inherent to coronation itself. This is especially the case, for example, with looking at the odd mixture of items included in a high street window display in Lewes (a Jeffrey and Janice mug with the caption, 'People say she acted like she didn't give a f*ck . . . It wasn't an act' juxtaposed with festive tea towels and party decorations), particularly when compared to the orderly presentations of decoration in Chichester's or London's major tourist areas; the appropriation of 'Duchy Organic' as a sign of coronation in Waitrose, or the use of 'coronation spirit' to sell subscriptions to ancestry.com on the Underground; and the many uses of masks and paper mannequins to 'act out' daydreams of a royal encounter or becoming a royal oneself. Indeed, these images reveal the rich fantasy life that underlies popular expression, the celebration of which lies at the heart of Mass Observation itself.

Figure 3 Mixed decorations with mug detail, Lewes, East Sussex ('People say she acted like she didn't give a f*ck ... It wasn't an act').

Figure 4 Shop decoration, Chichester, West Sussex.

Figure 5 Bill's Restaurant, coronation marketing, Soho, London.

Figure 6 'The crowning moments in your family story', London Underground, Central London.

Figure 7 Royal faces, Lewes, East Sussex.

Figure 8 Blank royal faces, Lewes, East Sussex.

Figure 9 Man in hat sits on chair.

Figure 10 Duchy Organic limited edition shortbread.

Figure 11 Coronation cakes, Brentford, West London.

Figure 12 Prince of Wales, no decorations, Brixton, South London.

Figure 13 Throne in Victoria Rail Station, Central London.

Visualizing Coronation

Figure 14 Union Jacks in Piccadilly (looking towards Green Park), Central London.

Figure 15 Piccadilly Circus (looking towards Coventry Street), no decorations, Central London.

Figure 16 Open as usual, Thames Embankment, Central London.

Figure 17 Media preparations, Westminster Abbey, Central London.

Figure 18 Rotary commemorative poster (note: Charles's eyes are scratched out), Chichester Rail Station, West Sussex.

Figure 19 Windrush Statue, Trafalgar Square, Central London.

Figure 20 Commemorative royal sign, London Underground, Central London.

Figure 21 Decorations in Soho, Central London.

Figure 22 British campers on the Mall, Central London.

Figure 23 Campers on the Mall take pictures in the hope of capturing very important people, Central London.

Figure 24 Postbox topper, Salisbury, Wiltshire.

Figure 25 Canadians on the Mall, Central London.

Figure 26 Americans on the Mall, Central London.

Figure 27 Protest posters (opposite 10 Downing Street), Whitehall, Central London.

Figure 28 'The King Is Coming', outside Westminster Abbey, announcing a 'special chapel meeting' at Westminster Baptist Chapel, Central London.

Figure 29 Repent, Houses of Parliament, Whitehall, Central London.

Figure 30 a, b, c Union Jack fashion, Hyde Park, Central London.

Figure 31 a, b Diana Walk on the Mall and outside coronation barricades, Central London.

Figure 32 a, b Boating Lawn (first image at approximately 9.00 am and second image at approximately 10.30 am), Hyde Park, Central London.

Figure 33 Morris dancers, Eccleshall, Staffordshire.

Figure 34 Flag on pavement, Hyde Park, Central London.

Part III

Observations III

It couldn't have been worse really! It rained and it rained and it rained and rained and rained. It was just another day in Shoreham-by-Sea . . . Quite funny, really. The weather being particularly English on this very English occasion.

I think the coronation had to happen really, as pageantry and tradition are about the only things left that we can do really well. Didn't make me feel proud really. Amazed that we can do something really well. Disgusted at all the expertise, planning and resources that can go into an event like this, whereas the very important requirements of everyday living are starved of necessary financial input.

I guess foreigners get a certain amount of pleasure, and show respect for how we nurture tradition and royalty, but I think celebrating a coronation in such a traditional way is probably a bit too much, in present circumstance, for even the most anglo anglophile. Kings and Queens have been absolutely frightful in the past – rather goes with the territory, but after the Queen's long, respectful and dutiful life, [her children] have done their best to make the Royal Family very un-regal.

For me, (and my tribe) the Coronation came under the headship of 'any excuse for a piss-up', and although King Charles's heart might be in the right place, I can't see what advantage he's going to have over his green agendas, by being king rather than prince, but maybe he has a cunning plan for what he intends to do, with his power of position.

I took a photograph of my granddaughter (9) in front of the TV showing the Coronation because I thought maybe by the time SHE had grandchildren no-one will know what a coronation is/was.

In Shoreham-by-Sea there were some street parties planned and barbeques attempted but the weather was too foul for any major outdoor activity, but there wasn't a huge amount of bunting about or general merry-making. My granddaughter wasn't the slightest bit interested. **F76, A1706**

I had been somewhat distracted in the run up to the Coronation due to two things which I will mention here because I feel they are somewhat pertinent in contrast to the royal festivities, a reflection of modern Britain of which, of course, King Charles is now at the helm. Firstly, on the Saturday before the big event, my elderly mother tripped and fell, not only gashing her forehead but also breaking one of her fingers, requiring hours of waiting in a clearly overstretched and underfunded A and E Department at my local hospital, where the hardworking staff nonetheless did their best to help her. I was sat, restlessly beside her, on my second day of what would transpire to be nearly a week of toothache or some kind of infection that had my mouth and the left side of my face burning with searing pain. I had hoped to be able to get access to the NHS dental treatment, which I'm eligible for, and depend upon, on the Monday – but that turned out to be a Bank Holiday. So, after enduring yet another 24 hours of painkillers and squirming in distress, I began calling dental surgeries on Tuesday – and even NHS 111, who told me not to call back if I was unable to find a dentist – but I couldn't find a single place in my city that would treat me unless I paid privately. By Wednesday, the agony was thankfully beginning to subside but I had developed what appeared to be an abscess on the roof of my mouth. Worried, and in desperation, because I know that an abscess can be fatal if left untreated, I booked an emergency appointment to see my GP in the hope he could refer me to a hospital dentist. By the time of my appointment, the swelling in my mouth had gone down which led me to believe the abscess had popped or somehow shrank, and my doctor glanced briefly and disdainfully in my mouth, told me he couldn't refer me to any dentist and sent me away with a prescription for antibiotics – whilst urging me to see a dentist! I walked home in disbelief. This is 21st century Britain! . . .

Anyway, my point is, as I rolled around on my bed at night, clutching my face in agony, I occasionally thought of how King Charles would never have this problem – they would probably bring a dentist to him. So, was I in the mood to cheerfully pledge allegiance to a multimillionaire, one indifferently living a life of luxury and fame, only due to being born in the right bed? Well, I felt more like joining in with a football match chant that I had seen performed by Celtic fans in a YouTube video recently: 'You can shove your Coronation up your a**e. You can shove your Coronation up your a**e. You can shove your Coronation, shove your Coronation, shove your Coronation up your a**e . . . ' I gather that there will be a few street parties in my local area but I won't be celebrating – I'll be too busy looking after my mother. It's more like Charles is showing off anyway rather than including us – we already know that he is king, regardless of whether a crown is ceremoniously plonked on his head for half an hour or not – and would you go to a friend's party if you had to pledge allegiance to them? It has to be said that old Charlie is not much of a mate. What has he done for me or, indeed, any of us lately? I suppose the extra bank holiday – and the pubs staying open later – will not go unappreciated. I do hate to be a killjoy, because if people enjoy themselves during over the Coronation weekend then that's fine by me – all the better, less tax money wasted – but I don't think we should be dazzled by all the royal uniforms covered with unearned medals or the attention showered on these boring descendants of people who murdered their way to the top of society (and just consider subsequent rulers like Henry the VIII's attitude to matrimony . . .) We may as well be saluting the offspring of a mafia dynasty. If the monarchy stuck up for the public by pressuring the British government into giving us all a better quality of life, I'd have more respect for them, but, no, the Royal family carry on in their anachronistic and ineffectual way, smiling and waving, then disappearing back to their lives of self indulgence while leaving the rest of us to get on with it.

The Big Help Out volunteering initiative is a good idea but we know there is some shrewd thinking behind it. 'We've just blown millions of pounds of the proletariat's money – let's all be seen to do a bit of charity work to show unity and give something back. Of course, it'll be the public that do most of the work . . . ' Perhaps I'm just jaded. We've have had over a decade of austerity measures in this country. We're also having a cost of living crisis that we had to ignore to suddenly celebrate the Queen's Platinum Jubilee – which came not long after we were pressured to grieve Prince Philip's passing – then we were obliged to mourn the Queen's death; now we're expected to be happy at having Charlie's Coronation rammed down our throats. Stop telling me what to feel, monarchy! **M45, N5744**

Although I did not, I gather that many people in my local area watched the coronation on the TV but I was not aware of any local events.

As a paid-up 'Life Member' of Republic (www.republic.org.uk), the anti-monarchy campaign organization – and regarding myself as a 'citizen' of the UK and not a 'Subject' of anyone – in no way whatsoever do I approve of or support anything associated with the monarchy, including a grossly expensive and constitutionally unnecessary Coronation (I understand that most countries who still have a monarchy do not indulge in Coronations when a new king or queen is appointed). To me, the monarchy and its on-going maintenance represents much of what is morally corrupt about the UK – England in particular – and its archaic institutions.

The monarchy and the UK government even mislead the public about the costs to the taxpayer and the financial benefits to the UK of the monarchy, the former being enormously more and that latter enormously less than what they claim, which they cannot support with evidence when challenged.

Like a growing number of people, I believe that the monarchy, and all it represents – in terms of obscene material and status inequality, unearned privilege and deference, a clear sense of 'superiority' to 'the commoners', and 'class division' – it is, in my view, a long outdated institution, and should consequently have been consigned to the history books long ago, as it has in many other more enlightened republican countries in the world. That said, I do appreciate that surveys still show that currently, more people support the monarchy than do not, and so I am enough of a realist to know that they will be around for some time to come more's the pity in my opinion. However, interestingly, one survey I heard of did show that the support for the monarchy dwindles to about 25% or so when asked if they would be willing to pay for the monarchy if they had the choice. Either way, my view is that those who do support the monarchy should pay for it out of their personal taxation; not that will ever happen, of course. **M61, B8148**

The Archbishop of Canterbury has invited the public at large to join in the homage to the new King. This will involve pledging your allegiance to the King along with those in Westminster Abbey. I think this is yet another example of the Church of England being completely out of step with both society and the King. The King since the death of his mother, has repeatedly said his reign will be one of service to the people of the UK. It therefore seems somewhat contradictory that a King who has pledged to serve his people would expect those very people to pay homage to him. Also from what I have read about the King over many years, I don't think he would have any wish for the public to pay homage to him. The Coronation will end the previous tradition of Peers paying homage to King, the only person reported as doing so will be William, Prince of Wales. So why is the Archbishop suggesting that the public take up the homage mantle? I am a committed monarchist and anti-republican but even I won't be paying homage to the new King, it seems a somewhat vacuous exercise.

Having said that and although I live in Spain, I will watch the whole of the Coronation live on television with my husband. We won't be decking out our house in Union flags (we wouldn't have done so if we still lived in the UK) but we will settle down on the sofa with an ample supply of wine and snacks and raise a glass or two to toast the new King.

Although I am not aware of any street parties in our region in Spain (Valencia) the national Spanish news broadcast a report saying that Coronation parties were being organised by local branches of the British Legion in Madrid and various towns in Andalucia. These areas have large British immigrant communities whereas where I live we don't. Even if they did have street parties here or in the UK (if I still lived there) neither I nor my husband would go, we are not really lovers of 'community' events!

I do however have two elderly Spanish neighbours who for reasons probably they cant even explain, are great supporters of the British monarchy. They have told me they will be watching the live coverage of the Coronation on Spanish TV where it is being broadcast live.

I think the extra bank holiday and the pubs staying open are great idea and the whole occasion is an opportunity to celebrate something after Covid, and to forget for a few days about the doom and gloom of the cost of living crisis, political shenanigans and wars. I would certainly be taking advantage of it if I were still in the UK! **M58, W5965**

I'm in Spain today (Sat 6th May), so my experience of the Coronation is a little distant. On the other hand, I wouldn't have paid any attention at home either, so maybe things are equal.

The Spanish seem moderately interested – there were a handful of articles in El Pais and one of the TV channels showed it live. There are a couple of points of local interest – one is that the Spanish also have a monarchy and so they got an invite to the ceremony, the other is that one of the crown jewels being used was stolen from the Caliph of Granada and is potentially cursed. I get the feeling the Spanish see the monarchy a bit like a telenovela – in the three weeks I've been here I've read several stories about 'Enrique de Inglaterra', each of which has an over the garden fence 'you'll never believe what he's done now' sort of feel to it. Which, to be fair, feels an entirely appropriate response to him and his travails, the poor little mite . . .

It's now Sunday, so I've got El Pais reviewing the Coronation. They were most interested in Enrique – straight in for the wedding and then straight out – and Andrés – driven in by official car but not invited to wave from the balcony. They were also a little let down by the limits of gestures to modernisation – as far as I can tell, El Pais take an anti-clerical line, so did not feel that substituting olive oil for whale oil was a change sufficient to compensate for swearing to uphold the Church of England. (I have enjoyed the way El Pais translated everyone's names into their Spanish equivalent, which added to the telenovela feel. It took me a while to work out that Catalina, wife of Guilberto, was Kate, though.) **M37, J5734**

I avoided watching any of the Coronation. There is just something about all that privilege on display that was and remains abhorrent to me. I didn't take part in any events, and where I live, there was very little sign that it was happening – Hebden Bridge is not a Royalist kind of place! There were some union jacks in a display in the window of the Yorkshire Soap Company, but they were muted, with sacking-coloured canvas used for the white. On the day, we drove to the coast and I went body boarding . . .

Everyone made a big fuss about Penny Mordant carrying a sword: she did have a very nice outfit, and the sword looked heavy. She said something about how people had a right to protest, but 'most people don't feel like that'. She said 'duty' was a way of expressing love for your country when we don't like to talk about love. It is easy to love your country if it seems to love you back. If you are at the very top of the tree, with all the privilege that entails, the whole thing must feel pretty nice. If your country doesn't do much for you, however, you're probably not going to feel like that. I think a good country would look after people who are injured or ill, and care for people who are disabled or elderly. We will all be those people one day. It should provide education to everyone to help them realise their talents and ambitions, and offer equal opportunities to everyone, including parents. That is a decent way to live, and I'd rather spend money on that than some apparently petulant old man in a cape and a crown. **F47, M5113**

I am happy for King Charles III that he is finally fulfilling his destiny and I think he is/will be a good king. Probably more down to earth than Queen Elizabeth II was, though of course we were all very fond of her.

Sadly, I don't think we will be joining in any celebrations. I am not sure that our village has planned anything. Every year we used to have a picnic in the Abbey ruins just down the road and I would have expected the village hall committee to be organizing something like that, but there has been no word yet and it is getting a bit near for them to be organizing it now.

My husband and I will probably watch the Coronation on the television and enjoy the day off, pottering in the garden and walking our dogs. We'll *probably have a nice meal to mark the occasion. I have never seen a coronation, but he remembers the last one . . .*

People who have said that William should be king instead, although there are less of them now, are wrong, I believe. Charles is giving William the chance to bring up his children, who are still so young and be there for them more. Charles no doubt remembers that his own parents were absent during a lot of his childhood and he is sparing his grandchildren doing through the same loneliness. Given Charles' age, I do wonder how long it will be before we have another coronation though! **F63, A7000**

I'm not sure of any events to make the Coronation in my local town. Certainly our road is not one for street parties. There are events in Truro I think.

Personally I don't mind the Royal Family, and as a nation we do the pageantry really well. That's so important for tourism and behind the scenes diplomacy. However, in Cornwall it's clear that there are a lot of people who are monarchist and view Cornwall as a separate Duchy. For them, Charles is not our King. This has really come to the fore on social media over the last week. When the Coronation Order of Service was released we discovered that whereas Welsh, Irish and Scots-Gaelic were being included in one of the hymns, Cornish is not. There was a lot of debate online as to whether or not letters should be written to the Lord-Lieutenant, Lambeth Palace and Cornwall Council regarding this snub. Then the anti-monarchists weighed in with lots of comments about how Cornwall should be represented in the Coronation at all. This all became fairly vitriolic on certain Facebook groups. (If you want to research this look at 'I Pledge to be More Fluent in Cornish').

I will be watching the Coronation. The main reason for this is that seven of the girl choristers from Truro Cathedral are singing with Westminster Abbey Choir and others (Chapel Royal Choir and some other girls from Belfast?). This will be the first time girl choristers have sung at such an occasion and so is a huge step forward for the importance of girls and women in choral music. I know five of the girls, having taught at the school they attend until a few years ago. I taught three of them and one of them lived with me in the boarding house. I'm delighted for them all, that they get to take part in such an event. I know the upper sixth girls are worried about having to do this just before their A levels. They went up last Friday for a final week of rehearsals. They're all staying in a house owned by the Royal Estate and subject teachers are going up for a few days each to help cover their final exam revision. **F49, B8014**

There has been much talk leading up to the event, of the coronation of 1953, the year of my birth. Society was immensely different then, and I think that reactions to the coronation of 2023, and the shape of it tells us a lot about how attitudes to the monarchy have changed, so the whole thing has fascinated me.

I think that as I get older, I feel increasingly out of touch with popular culture, having previously been a big fan of the latest trends in society, entertainment and media. The royal family has been a constant, and is something I grew up with. I think that they do take criticism on board and are presenting a slimmed down version and have made efforts to reduce spending. If only other private and public bodies could have a go at this and put more effort into putting customers first and not profits!

I was at a barbecue a few days before the coronation, hosted by some very left-leaning friends. The consensus was that it was all a waste of time and that the monarchy was a drain on the public purse. Someone said that we shouldn't be living in a feudal society, kowtowing to the royals. I don't agree with all this. I did say that I had respect for the Queen, and several people agreed.

I think that the Queen commanded a great deal of respect. She was an enigmatic figure, born in a different era. She never gave interviews and presented a wholesome image. We don't really know what she thought about anything, apart from horses and dogs. We are free therefore to construct our own version, untainted by the modern tabloid press and social media. The Queen is a hard act to follow, and 74-year-old Charles with his complicated back story and fuddy duddy image will struggle to win converts, despite having views on ecology that were ahead of their time.

I think that having a monarchy sets us apart from countries that don't. They are a tourist attraction, and organisations such as the Prince's Trust have had a big impact on the lives of many young people over the years. Having just done a search, I see that over one million young people have been helped to date. Astonishing! . . .

I'm all in favour of an extra bank holiday . . . it does set the coronation apart as an occasion. Above all, it is part of our history and unique to us. I feel that we are starting to lose track of all this in the modern age of Instagram, TikTok etc. The royal family is not a trend, but a constant and is all about history and tradition, pomp and ceremony, and I have a reasonable amount of confidence that the younger senior royals will find a way to engage with the modern world which tends to be more about the here and now. **F69, M6897**

I am not a fan of the monarchy, and I would prefer it if this country was a republic. The coronation is a religious ceremony and as an atheist I find it all meaningless. I read that King Charles is going to be anointed with an oil specially prepared in some obscure ceremony and this to me seems to me just a throw back to ancient superstitions.

I usually go on holiday in May . . . I will be leaving for Greece on the morning of the 6th of May, and as I will be away for a fortnight I hope that I will miss most of the Coronation and the subsequent discussion.

I suspect that I will not be able to completely escape the Coronation on the 6th of May. As I have an early morning flight maybe by setting off early enough I will avoid it at the airport, and hopefully it will not get much mention on the flight. I only hope that the hotel I am staying at will not try and cater for the British visitors by having a special coronation event. As it is a relatively small hotel, and as I have booked just bed and breakfast I do not have to dinner there, so maybe I can escape if they attempt something. **M73, M3231**

I am a republican, an anti-monarchist, so I didn't do much in the way of Coronation celebrations, although I did appreciate the extra day off work!

I think the smaller scale to Elizabeth II coronation is just a reflection of the diminishing importance of the royal family, something I expect to continue.

I am writing this after the Coronation and I did see a few minutes of the ceremony on the television. It seemed even more ludicrous and ridiculous than I would have imagined, the orbs, the furs, the 'olde worlde' costumes. Charles looked like a grown man that had been rummaging around a very extensive dressing-up box. The ceremony is so baked in tradition (although much of it not as old as we'd think) that it seems to cease to have any relevance to a modern democracy.

Although I didn't celebrate this, I'm perfectly happy for others to do so and these occasions can help add a bit more social 'glue' to communities. **M51, L7953**

Overall, my view of the RF is that it is outdated, feudal and a propaganda vehicle used by all Governments of whatever colour to distract us from the appalling state of our society and economy in the same way that the Romans used bread and circuses to humour their citizens. I resent also, how this undeserving crowd with all their riches pay no income tax and is willing to take taxpayers' cash to fund their activities. Really the whole RF bandwagon is a waste of space and time and provides little or no benefit to this country.

You will now have gathered from the tirade that I am a Republican and have indeed, signed up to the organisation that promotes this view, Republic. I would add that of the current crop of politicians, except for Caroline Lucas, not one of them would be my president! I would also add that the furore about the lack of invitation to the Duchesses of York and Sussex simply means that they are in good company since I too have not been invited!!

Despite all of this, yes I did watch the Coronation since, like the State Funeral for Queen Elizabeth II, are part of our history and deserve to be watched simply on that basis. Apart from that, I took no part in any celebrations, there was no street party here and only a few residents had hung bunting. I certainly did not. **M76, N6622**

My family and I are strong supporters of the Royal Family. We were all saddened at the passing of Queen Elizabeth II. The sense of being part of history was strong, and the shared sense of mourning was palpable.

I watched the coronation with my son and husband. We felt it was history in the making. My mum was alive for the coronation of Queen Elizabeth II so it felt important to be part of the link to the next monarch. We didn't want to get involved with large-scale activities. We thought that the concert was a slightly embarrassing attempt by the Royal Family PR to seem relevant. The acts were not that impressive so we didn't watch it. I think it's better if they stick to traditional things such as the horses and military that accompanied the king on coronation day. I thought the Big Help Out was a good idea in theory but I'm not sure how much difference it really made. I can understand why many people found the celebrations a bit offensive given the cost of living crisis and that many people are struggling for the basics. However, I still think the monarchy is a valuable institution and that King Charles is doing his best to 'slim it down' and make it more accountable in the 21st century. I think that we have a good balance of power in the UK between a constitutional monarch and elected government. I have always admired Charles, during his time as Prince of Wales, and now, as King. I like his stance on the environment and the fact that he is a quiet, serious man. I think he has done a lot of good through the Prince's Trust and promoting environmental awareness. It's a shame that he's obviously had to scale back on these things now he's King. **F50, G8111**

I keep thinking about all that bunting the residents of Bracondale have hung, so that drivers coming into the city are greeted with the display. It will be hanging there limp and wet, which feels like an appropriate metaphor. It's all so pathetic, this coronation, all the money that's being spent on it. And yet there's something pathetic about my stubborn little boycott. Because isn't there still a part of me that wonders if I am missing out on this great historical moment? But I think that's what they want us to think. . . . The thing that depresses me is that culturally everyone in this country now seems to take sides on everything. It's become all tied up in identity and it doesn't do any of us good.

We go around announcing our opinions, revealing our alliances to each other for validation or brownie points and tribalisation . . .

Anyway, that bunting. There's a long drag of houses with it thrown over front fences, walls and hedges. And on the opposite side, this long section of brick wall (also bejewelled) that beckons. All week I've been imagining what could be written across it in chalk. The cost of the coronation? Upwards of 100 million. A figure so huge I struggle to gauge its weight. The figure Charles has inherited from the Queen, none of which he will pay inheritance tax on after a law change in 1993? 15.2 Billion. Or something simpler and 'calmer'? Coronate the people. Henry said you'll end up in the EDP (Eastern Daily Press) if you do that which put me off. That and the energy required to enact the fantasy. What good would it do? Even the energy that thinking all of this requires makes me feel resentful of them. We're at the centre of such a political shit show – inflation, recession, corrupt politicians, curbing protest rights, trans human rights, Brits living in poverty while oil companies amass huge profits from the cost of living crisis. And then we get given these little bank holidays and encouraged to buy Union Jack bunting and party plates for the Platinum Jubilee, all the stuff around the 10 days of mourning, the coronation. It does feel like proper insanity. And here I am writing about it, which doesn't feel particularly good. **F32**

In the run-up to 6th May, I took it for granted that I would watch the coronation, not only because it was an important historical event, the first of its kind in my lifetime, but also because of my commitment to Mass Observation to report my reactions. Two things began to put me off: the sycophantic attitude of the media, and the duration of the TV coverage I felt I would have to sit through. On the day, BBC1 was showing it from 7.30 to 15.00, as was BBC2 but with signing for deaf viewers. ITV1 was slightly more restrained, not starting until 8.30. The two relevant editions of the Radio Times (29th April to 5th May and 6th to 12th May) were thick with propaganda. Dame Prue Leith ('always a supporter'), giving her recipe for grilled chicken tikka suitable for a street party, said that Charles 'has been right on almost everything: the environment, soulless architecture and the dangers of technology'. . . .

Kay Burley, presenter of a Sky News podcast on the vilification and rehabilitation of Camilla spoke up for its subject. Based on a handful of encounters, she found her 'charming and disarming . . . beautiful'. She also claimed Camilla had been undamaged 'by the publication of Prince Harry's autobiography . . . even though he described her as 'dangerous' and 'the villain' who 'sacrificed me on her personal PR altar'. Children's author Sir Michael Morpurgo eulogized Charles for his early environmental advocacy ('He was brave to do so . . . very much a prophet in his own land') and Camilla ('a power for good in the land') as a 'fantastic ambassador for literature' who 'has worked tirelessly' in bringing attention to the importance of reading, especially for children. I dislike sycophancy, and even if I don't much care for or have no particular opinion on the person doing it, I still feel second-hand embarrassment on their behalf. Fawning over the powerful is craven and undignified, but I suppose once such a person has had a taste of access to royalty, and royalty has seemed to approve of them, they can't help themselves: they get sucked in . . .

My solution to the two issues putting me off were to avoid as much of the toadying as possible, and to only watch the service itself live – so I turned on the television at eleven o'clock just as Charles was entering Westminster Abbey, and caught up with the procession there and back on a highlights programme in the evening. I realized afterwards that this was a mistake, since the interest of such occasions comes from the suspense of experiencing them in real time, of being present in the moment as history unfolds. Fumbles, noisy protests, human behaviour that is a little too human to reflect well on the participants (more likely outside the Abbey) don't make the final cut. The coronation service was the most regimented, least spontaneous element of the day, and consequently hard to sit through. After about half an hour of it, I wondered whether I'd be able to last the course.

At two hours, it was a third shorter than the Queen's coronation but still seemed interminable. For the most part, I found it absurd and rather tedious. I liked some of the music, but overall it felt meaningless, ritual and tradition long divorced from the beliefs that had given rise to them, and incomprehensible to almost all of those watching except theologians and royal historians. I thought the most interesting section – or at least something different to break up the monotony – was when Charles was anointed with holy oil from a special site in Jerusalem. Apparently, it is considered so sacred a process that the Queen was screened from view while it took place. There had been some discussion whether Charles would do the same; I think his decision to maintain the tradition was the correct one. Even so, it was somewhat ludicrous when four decorated screens on poles were trotted into place by guardsmen and held to form a protective rectangle around him – as though he was changing on the beach for a swim, like a modest Victorian maiden. I couldn't help thinking afterwards that more of the service would have benefitted by being screened from public view. Without the element of mystery, it was just random shuffling about and surreal details, some of which felt like they'd been made up in a brainstorming session the week before despite being centuries old.

Another issue I had is that we are used to royalty played in film and television, and described in romance novels as handsome, charismatic, dashing, beautiful and so on, but instead here we had an unprepossessing set of individuals, who if they had ever been considered attractive in their youth – William, Andrew – aged out of that stage rapidly. Any casting director would have turned them down flat. They all looked very silly in their elaborate cloaks and sashes and medals and hats, especially Princess Anne who might have been going on to a fancy dress party later as Napoleon. The lunchtime news on Radio 2 obediently noted that Charles had been 'visibly moved', but if so I couldn't tell. This phrase strikes me as royal reporter speak for not being able to detect any discernible human emotion in a situation where anyone normal would be feeling and showing something. But it isn't really the King's fault: he was brought up a stranger to emotion. The week before the coronation, I came across a video on Twitter of a golden retriever stoically putting up with a toddler heaping him with throws and blankets whilst the parent filmed and laughed. The tweet was captioned, 'What is patience? Basically, patience is waiting with difficulties'. Most of the commentators found it adorable, but some objected that the dog was obviously disengaged and uncomfortable, and that the parent was at fault for not having educated the child to respect the animal rather than treating it as a toy. Thinking about the ceremony later, and remembering Charles swaddled in his embroidered, crimson-lined robes, and it seemed, patiently enduring, waiting for a disagreeable experience to be over, the image of this dog came to mind. The King looked throughout as I imagine prisoners do when a journalist, updating us on a court case, declares that the accused showed no reaction as sentence was pronounced.

I read somewhere, and I can't now remember the context, the opinion of an artist or photographer or art critic who said how difficult it was to create a portrait of Charles that didn't appear a deliberate caricature. I found this really almost revelatory. At this stage of his life, he resembles a Spitting Image puppet. It's as though his face has been made with satiric intent; and the intent is to symbolize the weariness and decline of the monarchy. Afterwards, receiving tribute from the military and waving from the Palace balcony, he and Camilla, in their crowns, looked rather foolish and self-conscious; I was reminded of a pair of commemorative salt and pepper shakers.

My friend N watched only the highlights in the evening ('when you just dip in it seems, I think, all the more ridiculous') . . .

My brother has a more conservative attitude towards the royal family, and usually tries to change the subject if I criticize them. (I find this rather baffling; isn't their unsatisfactoriness apparent to everyone? . . .) He watched the coronation from first thing in the morning, and only switched off before the balcony waving because he had a neighbourhood party to attend. He wouldn't be drawn on how purely enjoyable he had found the ceremony, although we both thought that William's coronation would be shorter still. However, such events can only be trimmed so far before their purpose and meaning evaporates. They almost have to be boring, alien and irrelevant; these qualities, which the television audience would normally reject but here chooses voluntarily to subject themselves to, reinforce the sense of witnessing an important national occasion. History is not entertainment, nor is it assimilable in the moment. One of the best jokes in Channel 4's coronation special of its spoof royal soap opera, The Windsors, was Princess Anne's budget-conscious decision to cancel the service at Westminster Abbey and reserve a function room at the Holiday Lodge Express in Slough instead. Naturally, by the end of the episode, the budget has gone out of the window and the lavish ceremony reinstated . . .

Initially, I was shocked by the implication of so much money being frittered away when it could have gone on essential healthcare; however, on reflection, it actually made the coronation seem something of a bargain. £100 million represents unimaginable wealth to most of the population, but within the context of overall government spending it's barely even a snap of the fingers. I think the difficulty is that if we're going to continue with royalty, then the ceremonies associated with them have to be lavish, otherwise there's a risk people will spot how unimportant and dispensable the royal human beings actually are. But all that spectacle and expenditure brings another risk: that we wake up to how wasteful and foolish it all is, and how hollow everything is at the centre, the centre currently being the humdrum, disappointing, diminished figure of Charles III.

Breakout stars
I. Penny Mordaunt

As Lord President of the Privy Council, Mordaunt played a highly visible role in the coronation. There were times when she just seemed to be standing about rather pointlessly, but her official role involved bearing the Sword of State, and presenting the Jewelled Sword of Offering to the King. She was certainly striking and statuesque in what the Daily Mail described as 'a custom-made teal outfit with a matching cape and headband with gold feather embroidery', which she had commissioned in lieu of the usual (I imagine unflattering) black and gold court dress of the Privy Council, and helped design. She actually looked more regal than most of the members of the royal family; I doubt many casting directors would have turned her down . . .

II. Major Johnny Thompson

From the beginning of May, Radio 2 ran a series of features explaining different aspects of the coronation. Judging from the patronizing, over-friendly tone of the presenter, they were taking a sort of Coronation for Dummies approach. I didn't hear more than a few minutes of any of them, but the trailer, which I heard a lot, included the opinion of an unnamed historian that the crowning of the monarch represented the 'marriage' between them and the nation. If so, then the King's handsome equerry, Major Johnny Thompson, who stuck closely to Charles throughout, and whose role seemed to entail supervising the pages and adjusting the royal train, was chief bridesmaid. Apparently, he has been setting hearts aflutter on social media since the Platinum Jubilee. He was also present at the Queen's funeral, although I don't recall any lustful tweets about him then (I suppose his admirers would have felt it unseemly). This time around was a different matter. @Jebadoo2 tweeted, 'Frankly, and I cannot emphasise this enough, phwoar'. 'He's rocking that kilt', thought @bluecatsarah. 'Fabulous Major Johnny being fabulous as ever. Always providing the eye candy relief, thank goodness', said @wroughtonlass, whilst @jameszebra5 had 'noticed his manly legs when he was sitting down, and wondered if he had gone commando'. And so on. Newspapers, both in Britain (the Daily Mail, the Evening Standard) and abroad, ran stories on his impact (as they did with Penny Mordaunt), for example, the New York Post with the headline, 'King Charles' "hot" equerry Johnny Thompson draws eyes again at coronation'.

III. Sir Karl Jenkins

The appearance of the Welsh composer, a piece of whose music was played during the service, also provided material for social media wags. With his shaggy mop of silver hair, smoky-lensed glasses and drooping moustache, he reminded me of an ageing prog rocker, but others pretended to believe he might actually be a controversial personality who had adopted an elaborate disguise to sneak into the Abbey. Meghan Markle, who had chosen to stay in California whilst her husband attended the ceremony, was the most popular candidate. Jenkins took the jokes in good part, and responded on TikTok that he was 'quite surprised' over the misattribution. 'Someone wrote I was there to steal the crown jewels. I look this way all the time. Oh, and my moustache. . . I've had the moustache since I was 18 years old. It was very trendy then. So that's me. Nothing sinister about it or surprising at all!'

IV. *The Grim Reaper*

I'm not sure whether this mythical figure exactly counts as a breakout star, but the discussion sharp-eyed viewers had about him was one of my favourite aspects of the day. I didn't notice anything whilst watching, but the video posted on Twitter shows a silhouette passing the open door of the Abbey, wearing what looks like a hooded robe and carrying something that might be a scythe. Most people had fun with it and didn't take it remotely seriously. The Mirror quoted (i.e. completely fabricated) the reaction of an unspecified 'royal [who] found the situation quite terrifying as they said: "Not a good sign, is it?"' My understanding of the folklore of the Grim Reaper is that he is not a forerunner or omen of death, but has arrived to do the job of collecting the doomed soul there and then; the royal/Mirror journalist is perhaps confusing him with a fetch, which is supposed to be a signifier of a person's death, except that if this were relevant to Charles, he would have seen the figure for himself and in the form of a doppelgänger. The Reaper was rapidly identified as a Westminster verger, although those with a taste for conspiracies and apocalyptic thinking were unwilling to accept the rational explanation. Amongst the below-the-line comments (all spellings as originally given) to the Mirror's report, athena2 said 'Did u notice that the king s corination was 6months 6weeks and 6days after the queen's funeral 666 the devil's number if there's any other bad omens then he's a dead un'. Charlieboy.1953 felt that 'Maybe it's because the CHURCH IS AGAINST CROWNING DEVORCEE AND ADULTERERS. GOD MOVES IN MYSTERIOUS WAYS' and later followed up with 'Spiratulist have said he would have a short rein'. Even the American author Naomi Wolf made a terrible fool of herself by rubbishing the verger explanation, citing as authority her involvement with two presidential campaigns and opining that 'no one unauthorized can wander across a national stage at a moment such as that. No access'.

Errors of judgement...

II. *Arrests of protestors*

Sometimes the effort to suppress or distract attention from a thing ends up achieving the reverse: those who would never have heard of it in the first place end up doing so via the fallout from those efforts. This is known as 'the Streisand effect' (named, I think, after the attempt by Barbra Streisand to prevent photographers crashing her second marriage by holding the ceremony under a giant cliff-top marquee visible for miles around). An example would be the arrests of anti-monarchy protestors on the morning of the coronation but before it began. According to their statement, the Metropolitan Police had been concerned that 'people were going to disrupt the event, and arrests [were made] to prevent a breach of the peace and conspiracy to cause a public nuisance'. 52 individuals who hadn't committed any offences of any kind were taken into custody. I thought this was completely outrageous, even before I heard the assessment from Human Rights Watch UK, widely quoted on news bulletins throughout the day, that 'The reports of people being arrested for peacefully protesting the coronation are incredibly alarming. This is something you would expect to see in Moscow, not London'. The consequences of the police's political overstepping remained in the news cycle for several days. We heard repeatedly about the length of time the arrestees were held without charge, the threat of legal action from the leader of Republic, the unlucky Australian tourist mistaken for a member of Just Stop Oil, and the Met's self-referral to the Independent Office for Police Conduct so that their behaviour could be formally investigated.

As with Jonathan Dimbleby's attempt to shield Charles, here we had another misfiring effort to protect the monarch from reality. Does Charles have the right, as an unelected head of state, to believe himself universally beloved? Should he be able to look out of the window of his gold coach and see only adoring faces? Or is the right of ordinary people to object more important? The police evidently saw it as their role to erase anything upsetting from Charles's line of sight, but the irony is that the impact of the protesters would have been much smaller had they been left alone to get on with it. The BBC, ITV and Sky were never likely to focus on protestors in the crowd, other than accidentally, and certainly wouldn't have chuntered on about them in tedious detail as they did with every other aspect of the day. It's difficult to imagine Clare Balding cosily remarking to Huw Edwards, 'What a cheerful splash of colour the bright yellow outfits of the Republic protesters make. I can't quite read that lady's sign. Does it say 'Not my King'? 'That's right, Clare, and the one next to it says "Parasite".' As it was, the actions of the police simply increased publicity for the cause of republicanism, and aligned the monarch with repressive tactics associated with authoritarian regimes. This connection was reinforced as developments in the story were tracked by the media, and is presumably set to be revived once the outcome of Republic's threatened legal action and the investigation by the IOPC are known.

III. Camilla as Queen

Was there really any need for Camilla to be crowned Queen? She's far from being the first royal mistress, but she may be the first one to have hung around long enough to win the prize of legitimization and a crown of her own. William and Harry had to watch her usurp their mother's position within the family and then, symbolically, on a national stage. We are supposed to believe that Charles is genuinely puzzled by Harry's anger towards him (and perhaps he is, which doesn't speak well for his emotional intelligence). Strip out the titles and palaces, and it could be fodder for an episode of The Jeremy Kyle Show. Adultery seems to be fairly usual in the royal family: aside from Charles, Camilla and Diana, we had the spectacle of Philip's long-term mistress attending his Covid-restricted funeral, the online rumours of William's extramarital relationship with a friend of his wife's, the fathering of an illegitimate child by Anne's first husband, and I'm sure any number of other examples that have slipped the collective memory or were successfully kept from view. Previously the concept of keeping up appearances was key. How quaint the difficulties of Edward VIII and Princess Margaret with their divorced lovers now appear. I'm sure I heard that one of the revelations in Harry's memoir was that he and his brother had begged Charles not to marry Camilla, but instead to keep her on as – effectively – his unofficial bit on the side. Marrying the mistress is bound to cause resentment within a family, but Charles evidently felt no obligation to consider the feelings of others. That isn't a position I can respect.

I can't say Camilla is making her in-laws look bad: they're quite capable of doing that by themselves. In fact, I was somewhat impressed by her small gestures and facial reactions during the ceremony – the cautious smiling at approaching clerics instead of her husband's dead fish expression, the stealthy rearranging of her hair after Justin Welby squashed it with the crown – which brought a touch of humanity to an oppressive occasion. She's probably a reasonably decent person who was simply operating according to the moral rules at play within her social environment. I am sure that Charles's attitude would be that nothing the King chooses to do could ever be rightfully scrutinized for a lack of taste, but I can't help but feel that it was in rather poor taste for her to be sitting there as Queen. To use a term that's pretty much gone out of fashion: it was tacky. **M56, B3227**

I was a reluctant person going into the 'Carolean Age'.

I stamped my foot and cried, I didn't want change. I liked being an Elizabethan. I wonder how many people thought along those lines?

I did eventually sing the National Anthem for King Charles III. We did have a few months to plan for the coronation. In March I got in touch with the Eden Project, which had changed their format from last year. (Last year I received flags, teabags, etc. This year was frugal.) But I planned the invitation to a street party, approached our library to book a table for display and then the vicar asked if the History Society would put on a small exh[ibition] for the King's Fete afternoon on the Bank Holiday. So my deputy and I were busy plotting, etc. I did nothing on 6th May (my grandmother's birthday) but watched the whole of the coronation and its subsequent load ups and programmes. Thoroughly enjoyed it and felt it was a privilege to be able to see the coronation and go through the drama of the Royal Family with them. I hope they felt the nation's support and love we sent.

Our street party was great. 17 of us met round two tables, suitably covered in red white and blue, we had quizzes, food and tiaras and were home by 5.

God Save the King. **F79, R860**

Chapter 3

'TIMID, BOOKISH, AND UNPRODUCTIVE'?

MASS OBSERVATION, MONARCHY AND ACADEMIA

Lucy D. Curzon

In the spring of 2023, we asked a group of scholars to reflect on Charles III's Coronation – whether on the day itself, in anticipation of the event, or in the wake of it. Inspired by decades of scholarly engagement with MO's study of George VI's Coronation, *May the Twelfth: Mass-Observation Day-Surveys 1937 by over Two Hundred Observers*, participants were given 'free reign' to examine the place of royal ritual – its meaning and significance – in the twenty-first century. We did, however, offer suggestions regarding possible themes, which included discussion of monarchy and its recent history; commentary on *May the Twelfth* and Mass Observation; dialogue about national identity, popular politics, and/or the government; reactions to television, social media, radio, and newspaper coverage (or non-coverage) of the ceremony; reflections on mood and feeling about the Coronation (boredom, excitement, anger and/or disillusionment, to name a few); and the role of memory work in historicizing national events, among many others.

Asking scholars to respond to Charles III's Coronation, at first, may seem antithetical to the project originally established by Mass Observation in 1937. After all, the 'average person' or the 'person in the street' was usually the object of MO's interest, rather than the university-trained researcher (who was, in fact, often denounced in early MO publications). And yet, academics have been involved with Mass Observation since its inception, whether directly or indirectly. Julian Huxley, professor of zoology at King's College, London, wrote the foreword to the organization's initial pamphlet, *Mass-Observation*, in 1937. Harrisson's professional relationship with Bronislaw Malinowski, whose academic career made the London School of Economics an interwar leader in anthropological research, led Malinowski to contribute an essay to *First Year's Work, 1937–1938*. In turn, at least two generations of social historians, particularly those studying the Second World War, have shaped their practices based upon the influence of materials collected by early Mass Observers. And, in Britain, the scholarship of life writing (the study of popular autobiography, in particular) is intrinsically linked to the continued development of collections held in the Mass Observation Archive. As such, it is not an overstatement – as I explore below – to suggest that while academics and MO have often found themselves at fierce loggerheads, they have also found mutually transformative ways to work together.

Similarly tangled, however, is the relationship between academia and the British monarchy, especially in the twentieth and twenty-first centuries. While monarchs have been a subject of investigation for historians of early modern and modern Britain (e.g. assessments of Elizabeth I's statecraft or the expansion of empire under Queen Victoria), the Windsor dynasty has not garnered the same level of professional attention. Often viewed as promoting a culture of celebrity or an irrelevant holdover of hereditary power, the contemporary Royal Family – for many scholars, though certainly not all – is a decidedly unacademic topic. But as Mass Observation has always demonstrated, what makes royalty worthy of study is often what occurs 'around' the monarch, especially the rituals of monarchy in everyday life. Some of the most interesting – indeed revealing – accounts of what happened on 12 May 1937, for instance, had nothing to do with the Coronation. And this information, of course, was pivotal to understanding society at the time.

In this essay, I first highlight significant 'points of contact' between Mass Observation and academia from MO's inception until the present, showing how scholars and Mass Observation have 'encouraged' one another in the study of everyday life for decades. I follow this with a discussion of the ways in which scholars (including those who use Mass Observation materials) have approached the current Royal Family and, in particular, underline why academic engagement with current royalty is both problematic and necessary. And while the first two sections of this essay provide context for understanding scholarly reactions to monarchy, the last section directly engages the reflections of twelve academics who agreed to observe, in the broadest sense, the Coronation of Charles III. Overall, what follows confirms that Mass Observation and its methods not only provide valuable information about monarchy in the past, but also are a lens through which to interrogate contemporary monarchy and its rituals. Not least of all because MO has historically provided a framework for examining phenomena that appear out of place or no longer relevant but, in fact, play a pivotal role in social organization and its experience.

Scholars and Observers

Despite early feelings of frustration regarding 'the "timid, bookish and unproductive" attempts by the... academic disciplines of anthropology and sociology to undertake' the anthropology of ourselves, Mass Observation nonetheless has a long history of directly engaging with academia.[1] But as Dorothy Sheridan, Brian Street and David Bloome argue in *Writing Ourselves: Mass-Observation and Literacy Practices*, this history is anything but smooth. Tom Harrisson's enthusiasm for 'applying the principles of research on so-called "exotic" societies to his own society' led British anthropologists of the interwar period to '[deliver] some powerful criticisms that have remained in the memory of the discipline and still colour its relationship to the project.[2] The methods and scope of Mass Observation, through the late thirties, were ridiculed as the product of 'poor social science'[3] – a letter to *The Spectator* famously declared that MO's early work was, 'scientifically, about as valuable as a chimpanzee's tea party at the zoo'.[4] And yet, the endorsement of MO by anthropologists, especially, was needed for the organization to survive: their validation was necessary for MO to be seen as intellectually relevant. Mass Observation's early leadership thus tried to both 'reject academic anthropology and also to court it', which left, at best, confused excitement about the possibilities presented by the organization and, at worst, palpable disdain.[5]

Through the 1950s, there was some indirect (perhaps ironic) justice for the organization when Charles Madge was appointed first chair of sociology at the University of Birmingham (without himself holding an undergraduate degree). Yet this achievement was likely offset by a publication from leading British social scientist and market researcher, Mark Abrams. His 1951 book – *Social Surveys and Social Action* – offers a scathing assessment of MO's methods (particularly its use of untrained observers) and concludes that, after 'thirteen years of prolific activity[,] they have contributed nothing that can be called a scientific method of content analysis'.[6] But starting in the mid 1960s, a significant shift occurred. Data collected by MO in the 1930s and 1940s started receiving attention from professional historians.[7] As Paul Addison reflects in his obituary for Angus Calder, any historian working on the social history of the Second World War at that time was stymied by the fifty-year seal on wartime government papers.[8] Moreover, the history of topics like Britain's wartime home front was not even considered history per se (Addison's and Calder's PhDs were both classified as 'social studies'), a view reflected in the 'Oxford History Faculty [ruling] . . . that academic history terminated in 1914'.[9] So when Addison (re)discovered the archives of Mass Observation – 'all higgledy-piggledy under layers of dust' in the basement of Mass Observation Limited on London's Cromwell Road – he and Calder were left, by themselves, 'to roam far and wide like prospectors panning for gold'.[10] In 1969, Calder published *The People's War*, which drew heavily upon MO materials and remains in print to this day.[11] That same year, the Mass Observation papers were brought (with help from Calder) to the University of Sussex by then Sussex Vice-Chancellor, historian Asa Briggs (who was 'sufficiently convinced of the papers' value that he was prepared to expend his own resources . . . to accommodate the collection').[12] In 1975, the Mass Observation Archive was officially opened at Sussex and Addison's *The Road to 1945* was published by Jonathan Cape. Other early books that helped legitimize Mass Observation materials as ripe for scholarly engagement include Michael Balfour's 1979 volume, *Propaganda in War 1939–1945: Organizations, Policies, and Public in Britain and Germany*, followed by James Cronin's *Labour and Society in Britain 1918–79* and Penny Summerfield's *Women Workers in the Second World War: Production and Patriarchy in Conflict*, both published in 1984.[13]

The development of what is now called the Mass Observation Project was ultimately another opportunity for academics to engage MO and its materials.[14]

In the summer of 1981, Sussex professor of anthropology, David Pocock (with Dorothy Sheridan), began the process of reviving the programme by soliciting popular responses to inflation from early Mass Observers, as well as those who had responded to Phillip Ziegler's 1977 Jubilee efforts,[15] and newly interested persons recruited through national daily and Sunday papers.[16] They were asked, via mailed directive, to respond to questions about rising costs and the wedding of the Prince of Wales to Lady Diana Spencer. The 'particularly demoralizing' impact of high prices, unemployment, and increasing civil unrest were, in fact, well highlighted against 'the extravagance of the preparations' for what promised to be 'the biggest royal jamboree since the Coronation of Elizabeth II in 1953'.[17] As Sheridan, Street and Bloome assert, the situation 'seemed to demand some kind of documentation which might reflect a different, more nuanced perception of the ways in which people were responding to the event than that which was available in the British media at the time'.[18] Although the MOP 'initiative did not begin life as a formal, funded research project with clearly defined academic objectives and an explicit research methodology',[19] Sheridan (particularly after Pocock's retirement in 1990) came 'to understand the enterprise as part of a broader upsurge of history from below'.[20] And as MOP's reputation grew, Sheridan worked (often collaboratively with Sussex-based and outside researchers) to ask pressing questions about ageing, death and bereavement, hobbies and pleasurable activities, infidelity and the role of the Royal Family in contemporary British society, among other subjects. The development of oral history, which recognized the value of 'memory and ... personal life stories ... [,] helped to place such material at the forefront of innovation in the writing of social history'.[21] The burgeoning history of emotions, as well as histories of gender and sexuality similarly made MOP a rich source of data for late twentieth and early twenty-first-century scholars.

Not surprisingly, by 2007, Susan D. Pennybacker felt that arguments over the scholarly relevance of Mass Observation materials could be dismissed once and for all. She argued, instead, that 'the debate should continue over *how* ... to use' Mass Observation as an academic source.[22] Subsequent discussions have thus revolved around, for example, the issue of MO's representativeness. A prominent claim, in this context, is that Mass Observation does not reflect, statistically, the totality of the British population. In the early days of Mass Observation, as Penny Summerfield suggests, the organization's membership was marked by a 'preponderance of middle-class volunteers located in South-East England whose politics leaned to the left', while the newer MOP 'recruited a majority of middle-aged women'.[23] Recently, Khaleda Brophy-Harmer has argued, 'Across both periods of MO, the vast majority of respondents have been assumed generally to be racially categorized as "white"'.[24] Despite clearly problematic sample sizes and demographics, scholars have nonetheless worked productively within these limits to emphasize the value of studying, for example, individual lives – that is, 'luminosity of [the] single [case]'[25] rather than the representative sample.[26] As James Hinton argues, 'for the historian, close study of individual life stories can often alert us to experiences overlooked or marginalized by existing accounts of the larger history, forcing us to revise or re-think'.[27] Indeed, one of the early projects of Dorothy Sheridan, as an archivist, was to encourage scholars to see that the 'subjectivity of Mass-Observation was an asset, it was a resource, that people telling their own stories was a resource'.[28]

Beyond emphasizing the value of individual cases, scholars have found other innovative ways to work with Mass Observation. As Rose Lindsey argues, because panellists can reply to MO Directives year after year, MO offers rich possibilities for longitudinal study, a central tenet of sociological research.[29] Liz Moor and Emma Uprichard, in turn, demonstrate how the 'unwieldy materiality' of Mass Observation materials, while presenting a challenge for social scientists, also offers an opportunity for developing sensory-based research models.[30] Reflecting on data collected by early Mass Observers, Rachel Hurdley argues that, in its effort to upset the status quo (academically and socially), the organization's eclectic vision presents 'a compelling future for sociology as a politicized, public endeavour of active citizens and engaged academics'.[31] All of these examples suggest that – in the twenty-first century, at least – academics are well aware of the pivotal role that Mass Observation data can play in assessing the complexities of British society in the past, present and future.

The monarchy and the academics

Academic engagement with the British monarchy has similarly been dogged by doubts about its validity as a scholarly subject, particularly regarding the House of Windsor. As such, while MO has collected opinions about the Royal Family since 1937, scholars have had a tendency to engage with this body of materials obliquely. Charles Madge and Humphrey Jennings's *May the Twelfth: Mass-Observation Day-Surveys 1937 by over Two Hundred Observers* is a case in point. Technically, this volume records reactions to and events around George VI's Coronation. But it has been used by scholars to examine, first and foremost, Mass Observation's history as a movement/organization and its methodology. Indeed, the text has proved to be of pivotal importance to scholars of British surrealism, the Documentary Film Movement (and Humphrey Jennings's career), the study of everyday life, interwar British literature and a host of other topics.[32] Scholars have also used MO's royalty materials to contextualize significant events in British history, including the Second World War, as well as broader issues or themes including: class identity; kinship; emotions; myth and religion; national identity; and the impact of film, television, radio and other communication media.[33] As the conceptual variety evident in this list suggests, Mass Observation has certainly demonstrated to scholars that 'the way people write about the Royal Family tells us much more about other things than the Royal Family'.[34]

Relatively few scholars have used Mass Observation materials to discuss the monarchy for its own sake.[35] In fact, while the landscape has changed somewhat, Ross McKibbin's claim – made nearly thirty years ago as he reflected upon MO and the death of Diana, Princess of Wales – that 'historians and sociologists of the 20th century have approached the subject of royalty and its audience gingerly, and few have done so at all' still has an air of truth to it.[36] McKibbin explains that 'the dominant intellectual categories of the 20th century are secular and rational' and thus scholars have been, essentially, 'taught not to be able to understand such "irrational" phenomena' like the heightened public reaction to Diana's death.[37] Obviously, in the time since McKibbin wrote this response, the consolidation of emotion as a category of analysis for historians, sociologists and anthropologists alike, among others, has given scholars the opportunity to better understand how 'feeling' provides insight into major historical events. Regardless, McKibbin's claims remain relevant – there is still significant reticence towards studying the Windsors in a scholarly way. Laura Clancy implies that this may be the result of professional discouragement. 'Academic anthropological accounts', she suggests, 'often position royalty as superficial, and nothing more than symbolic', thus scholars who study royalty may not be considered 'serious' social scientists.[38] Matthew Glencross, Judith Rowbotham and Michael D. Kandiah argue that 'the emergence of post-monarchical systems in Europe after 1918' has proved more interesting to political historians, thus 'books . . . on both monarchy as a modern form of government and on individual monarchs as political and diplomatic agents have been few and far between in the last half-century of substantial historical writing'.[39] And while many competent biographies have been written about the Windsors, 'biography has [nonetheless] remained an area of academic historical writing that continues to be under-appreciated in terms of the contributions that it can make to the understanding of the past'.[40]

Part of the issue of studying the Royal Family is its idiosyncrasy (even in relation to other European monarchies). King Charles III is Head of State for one of the more powerful countries in the western world, and yet – because of a centuries-old understanding – he does not exercise this power and plays what often appears to be a ceremonial role in the government of the United Kingdom and the Commonwealth. As Andrzej Olechnowicz contends, academic study of the monarchy has historically existed at the margins because, 'the modern monarchy is an institution which reigns but does not rule'.[41] In many respects, then, as Jennifer J. Purcell argues earlier in this volume, the power of the Royal Family has more to do with – among other things – branding and celebrity (and the money and attention that comes with them) than it does with traditionally understood political power.[42] The theatricality or overt performance of monarchy put on by British royalty (made evident in the significance, largely attributed by the press, of golden coaches, massive real estate holdings and crown jewels, among other assets) and the fact that it is as popular in the United States (which spectacularly divorced the monarchy in 1776 but now bears at least two HRHs with dual American-British citizenship) as it is in Britain suggests that this is true. Certainly, no matter how many (or how few) Britons, Americans or even Commonwealth citizens may love, hate or feel indifference towards the Royal Family, it is nonetheless stalwart in its contemporary presence. It permeates the activities of everyday life including the monarch's presence on currency (in the UK, Canada, Australia, New Zealand and other nations); monarchy's dramatization, on a global scale, via television shows (i.e. *The Crown*); its representation on passports and postage stamps; and even – during the May 2023 Coronation weekend – the King and Queen Consort advising Transport for London patrons to 'Mind the Gap' while entering and exiting London Underground trains.

Precisely because of its staying power, monarchy needs to remain a subject of genuine academic investigation. The apparent sacredness and intangibility of monarchy do not make it any less viable as a subject of study – as Edward Shils and Michael Young argue in their 1953 assessment of public reaction to Elizabeth II's Coronation.[43] Olechnowicz similarly questions, albeit implicitly, scholarly reserve. He asserts: 'monarchism should be considered both as a pervasive cultural fact, which often goes unremarked, and as a distinctive ideology articulated in print and other media, which needs close historical investigation'.[44] More directly, Laura Clancy suggests, ignoring the monarchy (and the aristocracy generally) demonstrates, arguably, a significant oversight or even a willingness to neglect how power operates in British society.[45] 'The aristocracy's invisibility in contemporary Britain is incredibly powerful' and has allowed the monarchy to act 'as a façade, through which the mechanisms of inequality are disguised and naturalised'.[46]

Monarchy, furthermore, is pivotal to understanding British national identity. As Purcell argues, national identity and monarchy – as concepts – are firmly tied to one another. Indeed, the 'linking of monarchy and nation . . . enacts a sense of timelessness which binds the two together such that one cannot exist without the other'.[47] As such, major events in the lives of monarchs have served as outlets for expressing what it means to be British (or, more specifically, to be English). For example, on the occasion of Queen Elizabeth II's Silver Jubilee in 1977, a 40-year-old woman revealed to Mass Observation: 'I'd feel very insecure without a monarchy, so I think the Jubilee is a good idea because it is an excuse to do something traditional'.[48] Upon the one-hundredth birthday of Queen Elizabeth, the Queen Mother, an Observer noted the joyous state of the crowd around her at Buckingham Palace: 'Everybody seemed very happy and friendly. If only we could always have this feeling around us, wouldn't it be great. I did feel proud to be English again, something I have found lacking for years'.[49] An Observer of Charles III's Coronation, in turn, asserted: 'I thought William and Kate and the children performed very well. It made me feel very proud and very British'.[50] Analysis of this discourse suggests these sentiments may revolve around how powerful the idea of 'family' (a point also discussed by Purcell)[51] is in the social construction and legitimation of the Royal Family as a symbol of nationhood. Becoming more 'familiar' in appearance and outlook – via the *The Royal Family* (1969) documentary, the crowning of the Princess of Wales as the 'People's Princess', young Royals discussing mental health issues or the 'progressive change' ostensibly marked by Meghan Markle's marriage into the Royal Family – has made the Windsors more identifiable or 'knowable' in general.[52] And as Michael Billig argues, 'family' tends to neutralize or make invisible the social and economic distance between the monarchy and 'ordinary people', such that monarchy can appear to play a quite comfortable role in everyday life – that is, the Royal Family can be framed as just another family in the 'national family' to whom we can all, in theory, relate.[53]

In many instances, though, public reaction to monarchy is also a barometer of how foundational myths and other aspects of national identity have stood the test of time. As Ed Owens suggests, 'the monarchy exists as a kind of screen on to which the UK public has been encouraged to project ideas of perpetual national greatness that simply don't bear the weight of scrutiny'.[54] This is particularly the case when thinking about how non-English populations connect (or do not connect) with the monarchy. The House of Windsor receives mixed reactions (at best) in Scotland, Northern Ireland and Wales, as well as in historically recognized Celtic nations like Cornwall and the Isle of Man. This is unsurprising given that the monarch is the head of the Church of England (not the Church of Scotland, for instance), the monarch's main residence is in England (as is the seat of the UK government), the monarch's primary titles are those recognized by the English, and the English benefit most from the Royal Family's investments (e.g. the Duchy of Cornwall and the Duchy of Lancaster). More pointedly, that the House of Windsor is directly descended from the Norman conquerors, who colonized, by force, the British Isles and continued to tamp insurrection through a long line of monarchs thereafter, is rationale enough for huge swathes of the UK to deny any unifying 'national' narrative, full stop, let alone one based upon a so-called 'shared' sovereign. As one woman from the Isle of Skye declared about Charles III's Coronation, 'I couldnae care less. It'll just be another day for me'.[55] Indeed, despite Walter Bagehot's suggestion that the British monarchy was a '"dignified" symbol around which the nation could gather', this is hardly the case.[56] In the end, different relationships to the monarchy have produced quite different national identities (often based upon the cultivation of dissent rather than country-wide unity and agreement), and – perhaps more than ever before – it is these identities that are integral to understanding Britain historically and today.[57]

Responses to the Coronation of Charles III

The short essays that follow this introduction are written by twelve scholars who reflect upon various aspects of Charles III's Coronation. All of them consider, directly or indirectly, the ways in which Mass Observation has documented and cultivated meaning around the monarchy from 1937 to the present day. For instance, they engage the subject by using one or more of MO's established forms of data collection, including the Day Diary (e.g. what they or others were doing at the time) and direct observation (about the weather, fashion, dreams, sounds, objects, feelings). Others consider the relationships (similarities and differences, for example) between George VI's Coronation, Elizabeth II's Coronation, and Charles III's Coronation, and the role that Mass Observation played or plays in exposing the complicated place of the monarchy in national life. Still others focus on themes or contexts historically dear to Mass Observation, including how superstition and rumour operate in tandem with mass public events.

What is central to many of these responses, however, is a notion of the 'personal'. More than half of these scholars contextualize Charles III's Coronation via their own experiences as emotional beings, as historians, as cultural critics, and as citizens and non-citizens (or even anti-citizens), to name but a few categories. Much as the Mass Observers themselves do, these writers tell us what coronation looks like to *them*. Focus on singular lives is hardly surprising given the role that 'the historical study of the individual' – first evident in scholarly 'preoccupation[s] with "great men"', which have now been productively challenged by micro-history, oral history, revisionist ethnography, popular writing and so forth – has played in the development of history, literature, cultural studies and related fields.[58] Study of the self has also been fostered via the application of specific theoretical frameworks, including 'post-structuralism, post-colonialism, feminism, and psychoanalysis', which illuminate how individuals interact with one another, as well as institutions, in the context of power and/or precarity.[59] More recently, the efforts of scholars to 'situate' themselves inside of their scholarship demonstrate how critical the personal (as a category) is to research agendas.[60] Indeed, in the last ten years (and especially in the wake of the global Black Lives Matter movement), scholars have actively denied assumptions of objectivity and instead have identified themselves – by race, in particular, but also gender, age, ability, training and nationality – in order to make clear the subjective nature of their work and, moreover, engage in critical self-reflection as a form of anti-racist and anti-colonialist practice. Revealing the often-unstated hegemony of whiteness in the academy is a central objective of this type of engagement.[61]

The self, in other words, while it has always been a subject of study, is now even more present in contemporary scholarly practices. Of course, Mass Observation has recognized the value of selfhood as a subject of study since its inception. MO has always been, as James Hinton suggests, an 'available cultural resource' that everyday people have used 'to weave meaningful narratives of their personal identities'.[62] Put differently, MO is 'a reflexive space in which [respondents] . . . pause to take a look at contemporary life and their part within it'.[63] And yet, as Anne-Marie Kramer indicates, the methods of Mass Observation are also useful for the ways in which they promote self-reflexivity *generally*. MO is a body of knowledge constituted by a series of 'negotiated' relationships, Kramer argues, ones that actively demonstrate how individual selves are consciously formed in relation to others. In their responses to contemporary Mass Observation Directives, for example, panellists engage in direct discussion with other 'subjects or agents' including 'the University of Sussex . . . the Director and Trustees [of the Mass Observation Archive], individual staff members . . . those who use the archive, both those who commission Directives . . . [and those] who use the archived Directive responses for research'.[64] As such, they are well aware of presenting a constructed 'self' to other equally constructed 'selves', whether in their own time or to those who read/use the documents in the future.[65]

Given the awareness of panellists to these negotiations, it is hardly surprising that the archivists, researchers and other entities who engage with the panellists, through time, also experience consciousness (and conscious construction) of self. Rachel Hurdley, for example, reveals that her engagement with the Mass Observation Archive has regularly humbled her as a scholar:

My first visit as a very serious doctoral student disturbed my orderly thesis, upset its textbook methodology and transformed both its aesthetic and the monograph that followed. Subsequent visits over twenty years have led to annoyance, captivation, confusion and delightful excursions into other lives, times and places. . . . To hold it at arm's length as a collection of datasets for analysis would be both misguided and reductive.[66]

Even different platforms or approaches (e.g. the ease of searching a digitized archive versus the spadework involved in searching an analogue archive) used to engage Mass Observation materials make scholars more conscious of their limitations *as scholars* (and thus more aware of the power of panellists to influence the outcome of a project).[67] Hurdley's experiences, in the end, exemplify Lucy Robinson's claim that 'MOP [and MO] respondents remind us that as archivists, commissioners, respondents, the observed and the secondary researcher, we are all in it together'.[68]

Beyond self-reflexiveness being endemic to the scholarly study of Mass Observation, there are also arguments to be made about its relevance to investigations of monarchy. Upon approaching scholars to write about Charles III's Coronation, for example, it became clear to me – in many instances – that communicating through anything other than the first person would be inappropriate. The first person is often used to signal the urgency of particular claims, ones that are routinely silenced by mainstream media and publishing. For instance, due to the current cost of living crisis across the UK – the weight of which is particularly oppressive to immigrant, minority and working-class communities – there is good reason for social historians and sociologists (many of whom have been trained in Marxist analysis and its successor paradigms) to aggressively highlight the amount of wealth and hereditary/unelected power behind the throne. The same level of insistence is evident in discussions about the monarchy's entanglement with white supremacy and misogyny. Meghan Markle's and, more recently, Adjoa Andoh's treatment by the press and public (often using the trope of the 'Angry Black Woman') suggest that Black women in particular are more susceptible to racist violence in the context of monarchy.[69] In these and other instances, the immediacy or directness of a first-person address actively courts readership for the sake of amplifying an issue that might otherwise be dismissed. Certainly, whether in response to racism, classism or sexism, among other oppressive discourses, scholars have historically used 'I' or 'we' to stress the exigency of identifying and denouncing society's power imbalances.[70]

Whatever the motivations are behind those who have written for this volume, what is clear in these short essays is that using Mass Observation – its methods, its history, its formats – as a lens through which to assess or reflect upon coronation is a productive way to highlight why monarchy (and Mass Observation, for that matter) is continually relevant to historians, sociologists, anthropologists and others. As Mass Observation has always shown, however eclectic, energized, wistful, angry, sceptical or mundane the response to an event may appear, this response nonetheless tells us something valuable about the construction of selfhood; how the self, in turn, interacts (or chooses not to interact) with other selves; and how these interactions (or non-interactions) are foundational to ideas of community, historically and in the present. Indeed, whether someone treats coronation as extraordinary and magical or they experienced 6 May 2023 (or 12 May 1937 or 2 June 1953) as just another day is, in many ways, irrelevant. Mass Observation records and affirms the value of both (and all those in between).

These scholars' voices are but a handful among the welter of opinions shaping the archive of coronation. And each engages – directly or indirectly – with the relevance of questioning monarchy as a cultural, political and social phenomenon. Paul Deslandes' thoughts on the body of Charles III and historical notions of male beauty and masculinity; Martin Francis's imagined versus real experience of Elizabeth II's death and the waning place of mysticism in coronation ritual; Nick Hubble's reflections upon Welsh identity; and Catherine Ellis's sonic and visual notes from the Azores all suggest that, however annoyingly spectacular or pleasantly ordinary the Royal Family is, there is intellectual value in assessing its impact nationally and globally. This type of thoughtful evaluation is continued through the rest of the essays. Janet Wolff's reflection, along with my own, ponders the indirect presence of coronation in the study of family and memory. Khaleda Brophy-Harmer, in turn, questions the emotional performances of coronation, tying them to race and the (re)production of whiteness. Claire Langhamer and Lucy Noakes's discussion of weather and crowds, feelings of division, and the oath of allegiance works in tandem with Kimberly Mair's analysis of rumour to present coronation as a particularly British social ritual that expands and contracts over time. Finally, Christina Baade and Trevor Nelson assess the Coronation Concert, particularly its choral performances, as disappointingly blind to – among other things – the legacies of colonial oppression. Each of these essays, in the end, points to new questions or reconsiders old ones that highlight *why* observing coronation is quintessential to our understanding of contemporary life.

Part IV

Part IV

Chapter 4

MAJESTY, MAGIC AND MASS-OBSERVATION

Martin Francis

1972 saw the publication of a slim volume, *Dreams About Her Majesty The Queen*, in which the author Brian Masters sought to use the monarch as a means to better understand the inner lives of her subjects. Masters had been struck by how frequently the Queen appeared to ordinary Britons in their sleep, suggesting she had a subliminal effect on millions of people who had never met her in person. Many of these dreams were clearly exercises in displaced anxiety, involving scenarios in which people were required to negotiate the abrupt and unanticipated appearance of the monarch on their doorstep or in their local pub.

I never myself dreamt of the Queen, but, in the last decade of her reign, I found my mind frequently wandered to thoughts about her demise. Such reveries were clearly no exercise in clairvoyance, given the Queen's advanced age, and they all too clearly betrayed the empirical fastidiousness of the academic historian. Indeed, these visualized thoughts and imagined situations were both thickly textured and highly particularized. A visibly ailing monarch would spend her last Christmas at Sandringham, in the last days of a year which had witnessed the celebrations that marked her hundredth birthday. On Christmas Day, the Royal Family's attendance at the service at St. Mary Magdalene Church would be led by a clearly preoccupied and sombre-faced Prince of Wales, constantly fussing with his cufflinks and the strap on his wristwatch. The Queen, for the first time in living memory, would be absent. The opening weeks of the New Year would entail a trickle of imprecise and platitudinous bulletins on the monarch's failing health. Then, at the very beginning of February, on one of those quintessential Norfolk winter mornings, in which meteorological logic seems to have been totally confounded by a combination of brittle frost and lugubrious fog, Elizabeth II's long reign would finally come to a close.

In my musings, I knew exactly when and where I would be when I was to hear the sepulchral intonations of the official radio announcement: at home, about to leave for work, at some point in that period of relative serenity that immediately follows the chaos of the school run and the office rush hour. For two days, the Queen's coffin would sit in the nave of Sandringham's parish church, as workers from the Royal Estate paid their respects. Then, the arrival of the coffin, draped in the Royal Standard, at an eerily deserted King's Cross station. Next, the snaking line of mourners in thick overcoats and mittens filing past the catafalque in the austere grandeur of Westminster Hall. Finally, the Queen's body carried into the Abbey while flurries of snow danced around Dean's Yard.

Providing a classic illustration of why the historian's aptitude for scrutinizing the past is likely to be an unreliable indicator of their capacity for anticipating the future, very little of the projected scenario which featured in my daydreams actually came to pass. The Queen died, not in her centenary year, but in the year of her Platinum Jubilee. Her death was announced, not shortly after breakfast but just before dinner. She died, not in the harsh midwinter but during a glorious Indian summer. She died, not at her winter home in Norfolk but in her summer home in Scotland, her body returning to London, not by rail but by plane and motor hearse. It undoubtedly came as a relief to realize I did not possess the gift of supernatural divination, but I remained intrigued by my apparent personal investment in what had proved to be an ultimately flawed version of a death foretold. From what material and psychic sources had I assembled an ostensibly authoritative and well-defined – but ultimately erroneous – narrative of the death of a sovereign?

Was it merely a product of local pride, a residual emotional attachment that required relocating the Queen's death to the county of my birth and upbringing? Or was it a testimony to my overfamiliarity with the narratives of the deaths of the Queen's father (George VI) and grandfather (George V), who had both died at Sandringham in midwinter (in February 1952 and January 1936, respectively)? Did repeated reacquaintance with these previous royal deaths through the Pathé newsreels I regularly shared with my students indicate that even the most dispassionate historian is far from immune to the prerogatives of a densely mediatized mythologization of Britain's hereditary monarchy?

In the periods both between the Queen's death and state funeral in September 2022 and the Coronation of Charles III in May 2023, Mass-Observation served as a beneficial template for how to engage with a historical event as it was happening in real time. On the day after the Queen's death, I joined the crowds flowing out of Green Park tube station on their way to place tributes at the gates of Buckingham Palace, and a week later took my place in the legendary 'Queue' of ordinary Britons shuffling along the South Bank in a ten-hour epic march to view the Lying-in-State in Westminster Hall. Prior to the Coronation, I talked to officials setting up outdoor viewing screens in Grosvenor Square. These were clearly all opportunities to assume the mantle of the MO investigator, to record behaviour or attitudes, to even seek to establish the 'state of the nation' at the close of the first quarter of the twenty-first century. There were certainly arresting parallels between what I overheard in 2023 and what respondents to an MO survey immediately prior to Elizabeth II's 1953 Coronation had averred. Some statements were virtually identical: 'It will be good for tourism'; 'The Americans can't do anything like this'; 'It seems like a lot of money to spend when many people are so hard up'; 'It's really a London event, with not much for anyone else to get excited about'. While public enthusiasm for the 2023 Coronation lacked the hyperbole that accompanied the onset of a 'New Elizabethan Age' in 1953, there was a similar sense that the ceremony marked a renewed optimism after three years dominated by the Covid pandemic.

Here, one was reminded of the value of MO as an anthropological or sociological exercise, providing evidence of group behaviour and social attitudes that could be measured and even statistically analysed. However, this seemed less pertinent to me than MO's no less significant appreciation of the indiscriminate, the eclectic and the esoteric, its willingness to acknowledge aspects of personal subjectivity which refused any unifying interpretative coherence. As long as a queen regularly appears in the dreams (or, in my own case, daydreams) of her subjects, understanding the survival of a hereditary monarchy in a democratic age clearly requires engagement with what has been termed the 'poetics' of MO, the aspect of the organization that asked its panellists (including notables such as Nella Last and Naomi Mitchison) to record their dreams or what they deemed uncanny coincidences.[1] Among the trinity of MO's original founders, maybe we need a little less of Tom Harrisson and a little more of Humphrey Jennings and Charles Madge.

The rewards of acknowledging the continued power of enchantment in the modern age might seem to be borne out by the ritual of coronation, where temporal power is assumed only after spiritual obligation is affirmed. Coronations are clearly moments of consecration, much of the ceremony embedded in what is effectively an extended Communion service. In 1953, the sincerity of Elizabeth's commitment to the principles of Christian witness was only too apparent, and we might want to remind ourselves that in 1956 thirty-four per cent of respondents in an opinion survey believed that the Queen was somebody specially chosen by God. In 2023, the imperatives of post-1960s secularization and multiculturalism created a starkly different context. Nevertheless, the presence in the ceremony of the leaders of other faith groups, there at the express invitation of a new monarch of decidedly ecumenical sensibilities, suggested that matters spiritual and sacred had not lost their significance. Despite the fact that only 15 per cent of the British population were now professed Anglicans, Archbishop of Canterbury Justin Welby discharged his duties in the Abbey in a manner that seemed no less serenely (and, at times, even smugly) complacent than Geoffrey Fisher seventy years earlier.

However, any element of the mystical in Charles' Coronation was kept securely confined to the domain of officially-sanctioned civil religion. Both unsanctioned magic and a decidedly vernacular conception of the supernatural, which had played such an important role in the long history of the British monarchy, were notable by their absence. This not merely made Charles' Coronation distant from those of his medieval and early modern predecessors. Less obviously, it also marked a distinction from the crowning of his own mother, at least in terms of how it was conveyed in certain critical contemporary texts. There is a moment in the colour film recording of the 1953 Coronation, *A Queen Is Crowned*, in which the narrator, Laurence Olivier, in an (inevitably) theatrically hushed timbre, informed cinema audiences that the Queen, taking her seat in the venerable King Edward's Chair under a canopy of cloth-of-gold, was about to receive the royal unction. The ceremony has reached 'the moment of the anointing – the hallowing – a moment so old that history scarcely goes deep enough to contain it'. Such preposterously inflated rhetoric might seem jarring to us, especially when we remember that this ceremony had effectively been reinvented for the Coronation of Edward VII in

1902. However, the film captures both the magic and myth of monarchy at this weighty moment, its profundity reinforced by the way the camera then cuts away, only to return once the anointing is completed.

By contrast, the anointing of Charles III took place behind a rather more prosaic three-cornered screen, but with the camera still rolling. Many a Briton watching the ceremony on television might have been forgiven for querying at this point what exactly was going on behind the awning. For those who were not totally perplexed by the arcane ritual, the bizarre disappearance of monarch and prelate behind the screen for several minutes came with definite intimations of the furtive, the fumbling and the farcical. There was undoubtedly abundant mystification, but insufficient mystery. There may well have been majesty, but there certainly wasn't magic. Nor, for that matter, any poetry. The Coronation of Charles III may well mark the final and definitive, if long anticipated, eclipse of what Ross McKibbin termed the 'quasi-magical' monarchy.[2] In light of the banality of his coronation, whether Charles will feature in the dreams of his subjects to the extent his late mother did is seriously open to question.

Chapter 5

CHARLES III'S ROYAL BODY

SOME REFLECTIONS

Paul R. Deslandes

Royal rituals have at their core royal bodies. Royal weddings showcase the gendered attributes of bodies, heterosexual pairings and romantic fantasies, as well as the perpetuation of dynastic lines. Funerals sanctify and lay to rest the royal body, frequently commemorating its earthly appearance in effigies carved in stone. Somewhat more morbidly, these events also remind us of the ephemerality of the human physical form and the organic processes of decomposition. Coronations, as spectacles that have historically celebrated the secular and spiritual authority of kings and queens, centre on both the adornment and marking (through the ritual anointing) of the royal body. Each of these themes crossed my mind as I observed, from my living room across the Atlantic, the Coronation of Charles III on May the sixth 2023. While clearly a moment marked by celebration and pomp (but also one in which viewers were reminded of the legacies of the British Empire and the violence perpetrated in its name), it was also an occasion for me, as a historian of both male beauty and masculinity, to reflect on Charles's place in these long histories. In my ruminations, many images flashed before my eyes: Charles shirtless at the beach or playing polo as an eligible, young bachelor; Charles and Diana at the announcement of their engagement and again at their wedding; Charles as Highgrove House gardener and environmental advocate; Charles as father; Charles as mourning ex-husband; and, finally, Charles as king. Each of these moments has been associated with different modes of bodily presentation that tell us something about the place of the monarch (and, by extension, the monarchy as an institution) in the larger histories of gender and sexuality in Great Britain.

Separating Charles's Coronation from his longer life history is difficult, particularly when reflecting on his physical self and bodily presence. As he processed through the streets of London on the auspicious day of May the sixth, Charles bore all the hallmarks of the modern celebrity monarch for whom appearance has generally mattered greatly. The figure most closely associated with this new vision of the monarchy was Queen Victoria, whose nineteenth-century reign roughly coincided with the emergence and rising popularity of photography. Victoria was very savvy when it came to the cultivation of her royal image, using portraiture (in painted and photographed form) to emphasize both her authority as a female monarch and her status as a paragon of domestic and national motherhood. The imperial queen's great-great-granddaughter and Charles's mother – Elizabeth II – also carefully employed photography and, more significantly, television in reinforcing her own status as monarch. Her image, captured countless times over the course of her long life, conveyed a variety of distinctive feminine roles, alternating between wartime worker, skilled horsewoman, warrior queen and doting (but also sometimes admonishing) mother, grandmother and great-grandmother. Like his female predecessors, Charles's public image, as presented in photographs and televised broadcasts, communicated to viewers a range of narratives about his place in the gender hierarchy, his (sometimes dubious) commitment to family and nation and his engagement with a celebrity culture that he simultaneously relied upon and seemingly, at times, reviled.

As Charles came of age in the 1960s and 1970s and increasingly into the public's eye, his cultivation of the media, and his own bodily presentation for it, drew on tropes that were present in popular culture at the time. Most notable was a growing sexualization of the male body in the popular press, in tabloids and in magazines geared towards teenagers and young women. It was in this period that his body tended to be most prominently on display as an example of youthful muscularity and athleticism. In a single 1970 image, he was captured by one photographer at the age of twenty-two in swimming shorts and with an exposed torso, an image that would not have been out of place in publications such as *Honey*, a glossy mag that featured television and film stars and was directed at a young female audience. Charles's muscularity was usually made evident and was most typically on display on or around the polo field. One 1974 photograph, taken at Windsor Great Park, shows Charles's taut, smooth and subtly ripped torso partially revealed as he pulls on a light blue polo shirt. Another image from a year later reveals his muscled body under a tight shirt following a match. Polo was not the only sporting activity in which Charles's body was readily on display or subjected to the photographer's gaze. He was regularly captured, throughout youth and middle age, on the cricket pitch, on ski slopes, fishing or on horseback, bodily poses that marked both his considerable leisure pursuits and his embrace of athletic masculinity as a particular marker of status within the hierarchy of gender attributes.

While Charles's body continued to be showcased on the polo field throughout his engagement and during different points in his marriage to Lady Diana Spencer, his physical form was particularly on display throughout the 1980s and 1990s as a kind of clothed spectacle. The Royal Wedding of 1981 saw Diana dressed in an ivory gown that resembled, in some ways, an elaborate meringue. Charles, on the other hand, was resplendent in his Royal Navy commander's dress uniform, a nod to both his military service from 1971 to 1976 and the long-standing valorization of martial masculinity in British culture. Other components of Charles's identity were displayed through his clothed body on many occasions during his marriage to Diana, which ended in divorce in 1996. Most notable, perhaps, were those occasions when Charles donned specific forms of dress that highlighted his family's strong connections to Scotland. Both in terms of bloodline (his grandmother – Queen Elizabeth, the Queen Mother – was, according to the official website of the

Royal household, 'descended from the Royal House of Scotland') and in terms of emotional attachment, these links were often directly expressed through clothing the lower half of Charles's body in a tartan kilt. Two well-known images, both taken in the countryside (a favoured spot for Charles), come to mind. The first of these captured the prince during his honeymoon with Diana when he and his young wife walked casually on the grounds of Balmoral and the second, taken on the River Dee, showed Charles wearing a pleated, knee-length garment while standing next to his younger son Harry.

As a somewhat closeted royal watcher who could not resist the televised ceremony on May the sixth, all these images, and many more, flashed before my eyes as I watched the events of that day unfold. Bedecked and bejewelled, the new monarch's body functioned as a beautifully attired and robed spectacle that drew both on medieval precedents and ecclesiastical traditions associated with certain forms of male power and privilege. The Tunic, Supertunica and the Robe Royal – all garments donned at different ritual moments in the Coronation – are also articles of clothing that are curiously body-obscuring and androgynous, especially when compared with the many other garments that Charles has worn throughout his life, most notably his trademark double-breasted suits. Whereas Charles's body during his long tenure as Prince of Wales often reflected traditional masculine poses and identities (usually in keeping with, but sometimes departing from, prevailing British ideals), at the Coronation these physical manifestations of gender were subsumed by the golden trappings of Church and State. The King's body was, during the ceremony, adorned with symbolic representations of the constituent nations of the United Kingdom, emblems of royal power and authority and reminders of the monarch's spiritual responsibilities, all of which had not been gendered specifically as male since Mary Tudor's accession to the throne in 1553 (when women were allowed to reign in their own right for the first time). In sum, my own viewing of Charles III's Coronation was not only an opportunity to reflect on the meaning of this illustrious ceremony but also an occasion to contemplate the new king's humanity, his relationship to gendered roles and gender ideals, and, ultimately, the way in which he might be situated in the larger histories of male beauty and the male body that have consumed me, of late, in my own scholarship.

Chapter 6

OBSERVING THE CORONATION FROM WALES

Nick Hubble

The tradition of awarding the title of Prince of Wales to the heir to the English throne dates back to 1301, when Edward I invested his eldest son with that title following the conquest of Wales and the death in battle of the last Welsh prince. Charles III is the first Prince of Wales to become king since Edward VIII in 1936, but Edward was never crowned, abdicating after less than a year on the throne. Therefore, the last time a Prince of Wales was crowned king (George V) was over a century ago in 1911. However, Edward VII, whose Coronation took place in 1902, is probably a better comparator for the current monarch. Like Charles, Edward had been Prince of Wales and Heir to the Throne for many decades in the shadow of his powerful mother. One of the ways he sought to assert his authority on becoming monarch was by appeal to tradition and the reintroduction of ceremonies that had been allowed to lapse in the nineteenth century, such as the State Opening of Parliament – a ceremony which Charles conducted for the first time on 7 November 2023. By participating with full pomp and regalia in the processes surrounding the delivery of 'the King's Speech', Charles confirmed, what had already been made clear by his Coronation, that he seeks public legitimacy through the performance of tradition. Thus, the opportunity to introduce a modern, slimmed-down version of the monarchy fit for the twenty-first century has been missed, and Charles is now committed to reenacting the same and similar ceremonies for the rest of his reign.

That Charles would take the traditional route became obvious to those of us living in Wales when his first act following accession to the throne on his mother's death was to announce that his son, William, was the new Prince of Wales. The fact that this proclamation was made on the day after the Queen's death and before the funeral suggests that it was deliberately timed to take advantage of a period when it was impossible to organize political protests. In contrast, Charles himself was only made the Prince of Wales on 26 July 1958, six years after Elizabeth had become the Queen, and the official investiture took place at Caernarfon Castle on 1 July 1969. While the monarchy was generally popular in Wales as a whole at that time, this feeling was not so widely shared in Welsh-speaking Wales. During the 1960s, following the flooding of the Afon Tryweryn valley and the village of Capel Celyn to create a reservoir providing water for Liverpool, there was a shift in consciousness which fuelled the political rise of Plaid Cymru (The Party of Wales).

Furthermore, although it is often ignored by unionist accounts of British history, Northern Ireland is not the only country within the UK to have seen paramilitary activity. The aftermath of the drowning of Tryweryn also saw the foundation of Mudiad Amddiffyn Cymru (Movement to Defend Wales), which primarily targeted infrastructure carrying water to Liverpool. In the late 1960s, MAC ran a bombing campaign targeting government installations (as opposed to people) in the run-up to the investiture. Two of its members died when a bomb exploded prematurely on the evening before the investiture, and later a ten-year-old boy was seriously injured when he discovered a device that hadn't yet exploded.

While such bombing campaigns are thankfully a thing of the past, the contexts have not been forgotten. The most famous piece of graffiti in Wales is the message 'Cofiwch Dryweryn' (Remember Tryweryn) first painted on a wall a few miles south of Aberystwyth in the 1960s, which now has the status of a national monument and has become an icon for the independence movement. Since the foundation of the campaigning group Yes Cymru in 2014, inspired by the campaign surrounding the independence referendum that took place in Scotland that year, support for independence has grown to around 30 per cent of the population. Independence is one of the options presented by the independent Constitutional Commission set up by the Welsh Government, which produced its final report in January 2024. Under these circumstances, many had hoped that the title Prince of Wales would be retired once Charles had become king. As soon as it was made emphatically clear that this would not be the case, it became obvious that Charles would be embracing tradition.

Indeed, not only did Charles's Coronation embrace the pageant of the past but it also attempted to introduce a new tradition in the form of a 'homage of the people', an unprecedented public vow of allegiance from the millions of UK citizens watching on television. As it happened, criticism beforehand caused the framing of the pledge to be altered so that the Archbishop of Canterbury, Justin Welby, 'invited' a show of support from the congregation and watchers rather than 'calling' upon them to take the oath. This was indicative of the mixed messages sent out by the event, which looked embarrassingly at times to be a low-budget state coronation. While UK viewing figures peaked at twenty million for the actual crowning of the King, a similar figure to the number who had watched the Queen's Coronation in 1953, this was still nearly ten million less than the viewing figures for her funeral last autumn. The continual switching of camera angles made the event feel more like a televised sporting occasion than a historical event. There was one part of the ceremony where the camera kept tilting up and right to the upper tiers and the eaves of the Abbey, which made me think of the famous scene in *Citizen Kane* when we see a stagehand in the gantry far above Kane's second wife singing in an opera, holding his nose to indicate that she 'stinks'. This colour footage will never achieve the iconic black-and-white newsreel quality of the previous coronation.

Watching the Coronation from my living room in Aberystwyth, the town where Charles attended university in order to learn Welsh in the run-up to his 1969 investiture, was a curiously flat experience. There were no flags in the town. As the local newspaper had reported some weeks previously, there had been no applications at all for road closures to hold street parties in the county. In short, there was little interest in what was an empty spectacle taking place in another country. During the twentieth-century heyday of the late Queen's reign, it often seemed as though the end of the monarchy in the UK would be a revolutionary event, but in practice it's fading from significance not with a bang but with a whimper.

Chapter 7

ANOTHER CORONATION

Janet Wolff

I still have my souvenir coronation mug from June 1953. I was ten years old that year. I don't really know why I still have it. In the intervening seventy years I have moved house more than twenty times, moved city eight times and moved country twice. Many things have disappeared in that time. And the mug is not exactly a treasure among my possessions. Strangely, I can't actually remember whether I watched Elizabeth II's Coronation. I thought I had – we have all seen that television footage, though the fact that I 'remember' the original black-and-white and the later-colourized version suggests it's a false memory, not a real one. Others of my generation remember getting their first television specially for the occasion (acknowledged as the first mass television broadcast) or going to neighbours' houses to watch. I have no memory of doing either. I do have a very clear recollection of the day the King died the previous year (6th February 1952), when I was eight. Miss Harrison, the headmistress at my primary school – King's Road County Primary, in North Manchester – came into the classroom and told us we all had to stand up because she had something important to say. She told us the King had died. I can't remember what else she said, but I remember that my friend Linda had the hiccups, and we were trying very hard not to giggle, knowing that we were supposed to understand that this was a momentous event.

There were plenty of other things going on in 1953, in retrospect perhaps competing in memory space with the Coronation. A car ferry sank in the Irish Sea in January, killing 133 people, including three Northern Irish politicians. A North Sea flood killed 307 later that month. Rationing of sweets ended in February, followed by rationing of sugar in September. Convicted murderer John Christie was hanged in July. Much-loved contralto Kathleen Ferrier died tragically young. On 29th May, a British expedition became the first to climb Everest. The first 'Panorama' aired on the BBC in November (still running today). In the same month, the House of Lords voted in favour of proposals for commercial television. The first James Bond novel, *Casino Royale*, was published, as was L. P. Hartley's *The Go-Between*. The term 'Teddy Boy' was coined by the *Daily Express* on 23rd September, naming the first youth subculture in London. And the first Italian espresso coffee bar in England opened in Frith Street, Soho.

* * *

Figure 35 1953 postcard, courtesy of Janet Wolff.

This postcard, dated 21st July 1953, perhaps explains the relative insignificance of the Coronation, a month earlier, in my emotional world at the time, and hence my unstable recollection of those months. It was written from Metz in Lorraine to M. Jules Schwarz in Wissembourg, Alsace, and signed by several people, including my mother, my father, my sister Veronica (aged seven) and me. We were visiting family members, those who, like my father himself, had managed to leave Germany in the 1930s. At the bottom, my father tells his uncle Jules (my grandmother's brother Julius, who had left south-west Germany and survived the Nazi period in France) to expect us on 10th August; he asks him not to go to any trouble. These two photos show us, that summer, in the two places.

I've written about them before (in my book *Austerity Baby*) but I only acquired the linking postcard in July 2022 from my French cousin Catherine, daughter of Claude (the tall young man at the back of the second photo, taken in Wissembourg). I had 'rediscovered' Claude in 2016, sixty-three years after our meeting in 1953, and spent two days with him in Paris that year. He died in April 2020 at the age of eighty-nine. In the first photo, we are with our Metz family (my

Figure 36 1953 family photographs, courtesy of Janet Wolff.

paternal grandfather's side). One signatory of the postcard is cousin Edgar (far right of that photo). I have only recently discovered that the Thérèse who also signs, standing behind the smallest girl (a French cousin), was the widow of my grandfather's brother, Leopold Wolff, murdered in Auschwitz on 30th May 1944. To the left of Thérèse (and standing behind me) is my father's cousin Julie. Her son, Marcel Siesel, was in the French Resistance and was executed on 2nd June 1944 in Villefranche-de-Rouergue in the south of France.

I don't remember the visits any more than I remember the 1953 Coronation. And I'm sure that at the age of ten, I knew nothing about that recent history or about who these strange foreign people were. But by now, I know enough about the subtleties of transmission of trauma through generations to understand that in those ten years, and living with my German grandmother who had lost many family members, the importance of this visit must have been something I felt. In Manchester, arrangements were being made, emotional reunions anticipated, while in London, coronation ceremonies and pageants were performed and broadcast. It's far too long ago to know, but it seems likely that my own young inner world, responding to the intense affect of the grown-ups around me, had little room for investment in the crowning of a new monarch.

Chapter 8

RAIN, REVELS AND REBELLION

THE PEOPLE'S CORONATION 1937 AND 2023

Claire Langhamer and Lucy Noakes

In the end, of course, it rained. Any casual observer of history, not to mention the British weather, would not have been surprised. It had rained for the Coronation of George VI in 1937, and for Elizabeth II in 1953. Mass Observation had been present in the London crowds for both occasions and recorded the 1937 view of the *Daily Telegraph* that 'the enthusiasm of the Coronation crowds in the West End remained undamped by the almost continuous rain in the morning and afternoon'.[1] The material collected by Mass Observation supported this claim. Charles Madge noted in his description of his early morning journey from Blackheath to central London that although the day had started with 'a thick ground fog or river mist, but clear deep blue sky above', by late morning it was overcast and by the time of the return procession from Westminster Abbey to Buckingham Palace in the early afternoon it had started to rain. By 3.00 pm, it was getting wetter and colder and half an hour later an Observer recorded 'people throwing balls of wet newspaper at each other' near Marble Arch.[2] In 2023, *The Guardian* focused on the Royal procession rather than the crowds, describing the Royal couple going 'forth into the drizzly day'.[3]

It was not just the inclement weather that 1937, 1953 and 2023 had in common. We are often told that the coronation of a monarch sits at the heart of British tradition, linking the people of today with those of the past in an observance of ritual and deference. It is one of the mechanisms whose function is to tie the British people together, linking them in an unbroken chain not only to the past but to one another today; a performance of nationhood and national identity.[4] *The Times* put this well in its leader column on 12 May 1937, where it emphasized the unifying nature of the ceremony and its power to enchant:

> This coronation day breaks upon the world like some sublime chord that is the climax of a long crescendo. It has been expected, awaited, counted upon; yet when it comes it stirs the blood like a sudden revelation. . . . The grocer's paper bag has been gay with flags, and portraits of their majesties; the schoolchild's buttonhole has borne a red, white and blue ribbon, the houses and flats of the

workmen are all aflutter with 'baby bunting'; but at the other end of the social and financial scale the enthusiasm has been just as hot.⁵

As *The Times* acknowledged, and as Mass Observation shows us, it is what happens outside of Westminster Abbey, and indeed beyond London that really matters. In a democracy, there can be no coronation, no monarch, without the consent of the people. Within the context of coronation, 'the people' are subjects; Mass Observation shows us their lives as citizens, as active or reluctant participants, or sometimes vociferous critics, of the pageant and pantomime of privilege.

In their book *May the Twelfth*, first published by Faber & Faber in 1937, Mass Observation provided a bricolage of Britain on one day, combining detailed observations of the crowds in London, newspaper coverage of the Coronation, responses to questionnaires and day diaries sent in by their National Panel of reflective respondents from around the country. In this short piece, we reflect on what the 1937 material tells us about Britain *then*, in order that we may better understand Britain *today*.

In the interregnum between the death of Queen Elizabeth II in September 2022 and the Coronation of her son Prince, now King, Charles in May 2023, some wondered whether the 'decline in deference', observed since the 1960s, and the more recent appetite for grassroots power and for political populism seen to such effect in the Brexit referendum of 2016, would mean that Britain was now more inclined towards republicanism, and less inclined to assent to a hereditary Head of State. Did acceptance of such a Head of State in the twenty-first century depend upon the kind of personal affection for the monarch that had been on display after the death of Elizabeth II? Such a dramatic representation of birthright appeared, to many commentators, to be out of step with a post-Brexit Britain where 'the people' had shown their power in the controversial referendum of 2016 on leaving the European Union, and which was not only deeply divided but was also experiencing a cost of living crisis.⁶ These anxieties were not new. In 1930s Britain, itself still suffering the effects of the Great Depression and heading towards a second global conflict, voices critiquing George VI's Coronation and all that it represented could be heard. Mass Observation recorded that a series of pamphlets produced by the British Communist Party, called *The Plain Man's Guide to the Coronation*, received a mixed response from Cambridge passers-by, with an elderly woman crying out 'up the Reds' and an undergraduate shouting 'when's the next war going to start'.⁷ Meanwhile in Birmingham, a veteran of the First World War vocally expressed his feelings about the social stratification of both his home city and of the nation as a whole. The Observer who recorded this wrote:

> He . . . shouted 'We're as good as Broad Street, we're as good as Hagley Road (These streets belong to the West End of Birmingham, and all the buses stopping here were going in that direction) . . . Then [he] said to me 'I fought in 1914'. He tore open his overcoat and continued. 'I ain't got any decorations up but I fought for England.' He put his hand on A's head and A grinned up at him. 'This little girl' he said 'is as good as the woman who was crowned Queen today. Ain't she?

... she's as good as royalty, the little duck. I fought for England, for the *people* of England. Not royalty.'[8]

In Scotland, a letter to the *Edinburgh Evening News* saw a vivid illustration of the decade's social and economic divisions in the financial costs of the Coronation:

> We are going to burn £200 in a bonfire on Leith Links. In a few moments it goes up in flame and smoke. Do we expect the disabled and unemployed ex-Servicemen of Leith and Edinburgh to gather round with their wives and children and throw up their caps in jubilation at the beginning of a new reign when the debts of the last have not yet been paid?[9]

The London Vegetarian Society sent letters opposing planned ox roasts, and the principal of the Royal Manchester College of Music complained that northern musicians had been overlooked by the Coronation authorities in favour of those based in London.[10] In 1937, as in 2023, a diverse range of voices, views and experiences of coronation coexisted side by side.

Yet the majority of people acquiesced in or embraced the festivities. In 2023 the country enjoyed an extra Coronation Bank Holiday; in 1937 many workers were given an extra day's holiday, but not always with pay, as the *Daily Express* noted:

> Two thousand workmen of the Ocean Colliery have decided that as the coal owners were not prepared to give a day's holiday with pay on coronation day, they would go to work as usual.[11]

In both cases, any extra holiday was not necessarily spent reverently listening to the Coronation on the wireless, or watching it on a screen, but in a multitude of other ways. In 2023, *The Guardian* described Charles III's Coronation as a 'mix of serious and absurd', a description which could apply just as easily to many of the people and events recorded for Mass Observation in 1937.[12] An Observer in a suburb of Birmingham described a scene worthy of inclusion in Humphrey Jennings's famously surreal depiction of working-class leisure, *Spare Time*:

> The bus passes through meaner streets past a council school playground full of middle aged men and women dressed in all types of costumes, hats and false noses, apparently playing some kind of game (Nuts and May?), a poor looking girl of about 18 is watching them unsmilingly through the gate. A fantastically dressed couple of about 45 walk past wearing false noses and looking round to catch the approval of passers by.[13]

In south London, a woman called Maggie described to an Observer how she had 'gone on a spree':

> I went up to the pub first and had some drinks, then all my relatives and myself went to a neighbour's house and we spent the rest of the day singing and drinking until midnight.
>
> [Observer]: What did you drink?
>
> Guinness of course she said, and slapped me on the back.[14]

The prospect of spending leisure time with friends and family, a chance to dress up and play, and the opportunity for 'a spree' meant that the King's Coronation was as much an occasion for people to break out of their daily routine as it was a display of national and imperial unity.

In 1937, as in 2023, media coverage of Britain on Coronation Day focused on the crowds that gathered in London and elsewhere to watch the ceremony itself. Viewed from this perspective, we see a largely united nation, participating in a collective act of ritual designed to symbolize continuity and stability in an often unstable world. In contrast, Mass Observation's survey of the nation shows us a Britain that was often less reverent than such accounts suggest. It offers up a 'people's coronation' that might only tangentially relate to the ceremony itself.

If 12th May 1937 delivered a people's coronation rooted in everyday life, then 6th May 2023 was designed in more self-consciously inclusive terms from the outset. The guest list for the ceremony included 850 so-called 'ordinary people', as the *Daily Mirror* enthusiastically explained:

> The King is axing centuries of royal tradition to invite 850 local heroes to his People's Coronation. From fundraisers to firefighters and carers to community workers. Britain's local heroes are to play a key part in the event.... The event at Westminster Abbey on Saturday, May 6, is being hailed a 'People's Coronation' to honour those who work tirelessly to help others.[15]

More controversially, a proposed 'oath of allegiance' would have called on 'the people' to pay homage to the King during the ceremony, placing the relationship between crown and subject at centre stage. It was not widely welcomed – in part because it drew attention to the tensions between subjecthood and citizenship that the event needed to sidestep. A 'Homage of the People' that was widely derided as out of step with the times, thus became an invitation to 'a moment of private reflection', followed by an opportunity to say 'God save King Charles'.[16]

If those organizing the 2023 event attempted – with degrees of success – to find an explicit place for 'the people' within the pomp and circumstance, Mass Observation material from 1937 demonstrates that they have long played an active part in the shared traditions and rituals of British life. From its very inception, Mass Observation was fascinated by the place of 'ordinary people' in the national story, mobilizing its diverse methodologies to forensically unpick the relationship between the monarchy and the people, in 1937, in 1953 and in 2023. Here, as elsewhere, the material that it draws together provides an archival alternative to the homogenizing accounts offered by the media. Fundamentally, Mass Observation shows us that the inherent tension between the sanctification of an unelected head of state and the democracy within which it exists – and on which it has to depend for its continued existence – can best be observed through a record of the feelings and the actions, of the people themselves.

Chapter 9

ROYAL FAMILIES

Lucy D. Curzon

In *Family Secrets: Acts of Memory and Imagination*, Annette Kuhn discusses a photograph of herself – at seven years of age – on Coronation Day in 1953.[1] Kuhn uses the image, taken by her father, to recount her memories of that day (particularly being dressed in 'a special frock' for the occasion). Yet it is also a context for reflection upon the strained relationship she had with her mother, expectations of femininity, the impact of mass communication, cultures of gift-giving, conventions of portrait photography and postcolonial identity. The fact that Kuhn, through a personal artefact, can not only address a lifetime of family tension but also navigate something so vast as the end of the British Empire (among a host of other topics) has always struck me as simultaneously ordinary *and* extraordinary. On the one hand, the indexical quality of a family photograph (and, indeed, any photograph) suggests that Kuhn's progression from personal to national context is as pragmatic as it is insightful. On the other hand, it is astonishing that one image can be the site of so much intertwined meaning.

What I have always appreciated about Kuhn's analysis is her genuine effort to prioritize popular memory over 'official' history. 'Formally speaking', she argues, 'Popular memory typically involves the remberer, the subject, placing herself – what she did or where she was at the time of the big event – at the centre of the scene; as it were grounding the remembered event in her everyday world, domesticating it'.[2] These memories, Kuhn reveals, are more often shaped *not* by the moments that an outside observer might assume to be the most important or pivotal. Kuhn, in fact, recalls 'the setting and the circumstances in which . . . [she] watched the Coronation on television far more vividly than what . . . [she actually] saw on the screen'.[3] The dress she wore, her mother's anger over a young neighbour sitting on the floor with 'her hand in her knickers', and the new Sobell television set that had 'a flap that pull[ed] down to cover the screen when it . . . [was] switched off', seem – to Kuhn – far more central to the meaning of that day than the anointing of a new queen.[4]

Mass Observation's approach to analysing the 1937 Coronation of George VI is, of course, sympathetic to Kuhn's assessment of Elizabeth II's. Rather than document what might be considered official facts, the Mass Observers instead recorded what everyday people said and did on 12 May of that year. From those who lined the procession route with mirrors and cardboard periscopes to those who went to work as if it was any other Tuesday, Mass Observation sketched an image of the nation at a particular moment in time. Striking, of course, are the varieties of meaning that the events of Coronation Day in 1937 generated. One London Observer, while watching 'mounted escorts from distant parts of the world', felt overwhelmed 'to think that England's influence reached so far'.[5] Another 'suffered tortures of the damned listening to the wireless from 10 a.m. till 11:30 p.m' in order to mollify an 'old housekeeper who was unable to go out and join in the fun'.[6] A third, in Lancashire, noted both the dissatisfaction of a bus conductor because he was not receiving 'double pay' for the day ('which, he considered, was a day of rest') and that his grandfather had 'taken no notice of the Coronation' and thus his day passed 'no different to any other'.[7]

While Kuhn's approach is more systematic than the eclectic vision of Mass Observation, both are nonetheless attempts to frame coronation as a site of meaning that extends far beyond an actual coronation ceremony. My own experience of coronation, like that of Kuhn and the interwar Mass Observers, crisscrosses private and public, personal and political. As an art historian trained in the social history of art, Marxist critique of the power structures that underlie systems of hereditary privilege is a cornerstone of my professional life. And yet, fond recollections of my father's collection of commemorative mugs (marking royal births, weddings, coronations and deaths), which was proudly displayed in my childhood home, and my mother's carefully curated collection of royal yearbooks and souvenir programmes marking official visits to Canada, suggest that monarchy is also a personal touchstone for me.

My experience of coronation began, not surprisingly, in the late afternoon of 8 September 2022. I was walking back to my hotel in Hammersmith. Auspiciously, I had flown to London from Aberdeen that morning. I saw through a window, on a television mounted in the lobby of an office tower, a scrolling BBC news ticker stating that Elizabeth II had died. I became, almost immediately, profoundly sad. But who was the Queen to me (a white middle-aged Canadian woman) that I should hold back tears on a busy London road? Or that my young son – in that moment – felt the need to pet me gently on the arm? Andrew Marr, the *New Statesman*'s political commentator, similarly teared up on that day as he announced the Queen's death on LBC Radio. He later revealed that his reaction was caused by remembering his father's death two years prior.[8] Marr's revelation, or the wealth of commentary[9] on the Queen's status as a 'beloved grandmother' figure whose loss was necessarily personal, suggests to me that I was not – in fact – upset that Elizabeth Windsor, the person, was dead. I was sad because I had experienced – very clearly – the impact of time's passing. I was now old and so was everyone else. My kids were growing. My mother was no longer a girl, nor was I a child in her care. And my father, soon to enter the end stages of a wasting disease, would not be alive to experience the reign of Charles III. In short, Elizabeth II's death and the accession of Charles III were made meaningful to me in so far as they were triggers to my own memory work.

In an effort to understand this moment, I turned to thinking about family as a 'useful category of historical analysis'.[10] In her discussion of the hit BBC series

Who Do You Think You Are? Anne-Marie Kramer examines the role that the show's celebrity participants, whose personal genealogies are linked to major historical events (including the Holocaust or enslavement), play in fostering what Alison Landsberg has identified as prosthetic remembering.[11] The popularity of this show, Kramer suggests, is based in not only the allure of exposing 'the real person' behind the star, but also the average viewer 'experiencing some of . . . [the] emotion' *themselves* as 'celebrities experience the shock and surprise of unexpected findings'.[12] In other words, 'in identifying emotionally with the historical experience through the emotional journey of the celebrity participant', viewers can 'similarly . . . experience the uncanny, engaging with ghosts of the past'.[13] As Kramer concludes, the success of *Who Do You Think You Are?* can be explained, in large part, 'because a celebrity "family history can stand in for so many others"'.[14]

While Kramer's argument focuses on how family genealogy can personalize or otherwise challenge 'official' historical narratives, and thus shape new identities for celebrities and viewers alike, it also explains why so many people – myself, Marr, Kuhn and the Mass Observers included – felt or feel a range of emotions around the phenomena of accession and coronation. Family is an accessible idiom through which we can all, potentially, operate. This is particularly true when bridging the distance between celebrity families, like the Windsors and the rest of us. As Michael Billig and Laura Clancy suggest, we can identify with the Royal Family because we understand the notion of family and family dynamics.[15] Through the mediatization of Elizabeth II's death and Charles III's Accession and Coronation, viewers were offered the opportunity to experience – alongside the Royal Family – a highly relatable event (i.e. the death of a family member and, in turn, adjusting to life after that death). As such, otherwise remote royal observances provided opportunities for individuals not only to reflect upon their own familial histories but also for highly localized family stories to become, in essence, a part of national history.

While Kramer reveals that many present-day Mass Observers, who responded to a 2008 Directive that included questions about media coverage of genealogy, felt duped by what they believed were the emotionally excessive responses of celebrities on *Who Do You Think You Are?*, others were genuinely 'very touched' and even inspired.[16] In the end, though, the type of response people had to this show, I think, is irrelevant. Their engagement with (whether positively or negatively) the concept of family is, to me, more meaningful. Indeed, the tone and range of answers provided by Directive respondents in 2008 reflect the tone and range of responses provided by Mass Observers more than a decade later (as this volume demonstrates) on the topic of royal deaths, accessions, and coronations. Regardless of whether people felt an overpowering closeness to the celebrity/ monarchy, a pronounced and angry distance or sustained indifference, what is significant is that these reactions are all ones that reflect sentiments commonly felt in the context of family.

Chapter 10

CARLOS III E CAMILA

NOTES FROM A VERY SMALL ISLAND

Catherine Ellis

Before

Early morning, 6 May 2023. Outside it's mild, grey and misty. British weather, but I'm on a different island in the Atlantic – São Miguel, the largest of the small islands that make up the Azores, an Autonomous Region of Portugal. I'm here with four friends on a much-anticipated, pandemic-postponed adventure.

This is supposed to be a holiday, but I should know better: historians of modern Britain are never on holiday when the Royal Family is in the news. Having ducked Canadian media inquiries on the grounds that I will be away, I'm pulled back into the fray when I and the two other Canadians in our party walk through the airport terminal in Ponta Delgada, fresh – more or less – off an overnight flight from Toronto. We see multiple large television screens tuned to an 'Edição Especial' looping live street scenes from London, where crowds have been waiting overnight for the arrival of 'Carlos III e Camila'. I'm a bit surprised but give it little thought.

Our taxi driver only wants to talk about the Azorean diaspora in Canada, but as we pull our suitcases into the hotel lobby, I realize there's no escape: a flat-screen TV is showing the Coronation 'direto' from 'Londres' on Portugal's cable news channel, SIC Notícias. I snap a couple of photos to send to my coronation-mad cousin back home. It's shortly after 9.00 am local time and dignitaries are arriving at Westminster Abbey while onlookers and busbied guards shelter under umbrellas. The three of us check in and head to the breakfast room to meet a fourth friend who had arrived from Switzerland the night before. Breakfast is much appreciated and I'm grateful there's no screen in the restaurant. The reprieve is short-lived, however. Once ensconced in our shared suite, it turns out my friends are very keen to tune in again.

During

The popular appeal of the monarchy is well documented and much studied, but on a personal level, it remains a mystery. As Edward Shils and Michael Young famously observed at the time of Queen Elizabeth II's Coronation, '[t]he heart has its reasons which the mind does not suspect'.[1] Mid-century explanations for the monarch's popularity focused on ordinary people's reverence or their susceptibility to 'quasi-magical thinking' but those claims have not held up, and indeed there is a longer history of working-class people's views of the monarchy distinctly lacking in reverence.[2] On Edward VII's Coronation Day in August 1902, for example, American author Jack London contrasted the indifference and drunkenness of impoverished East Enders with the enthusiasm of well-heeled crowds in London's West End. Never, London thought, had he witnessed 'anything so hopeless and so tragic' – a people who, like the elders who asked the Prophet Samuel to make them a king, would only recognize too late the punishment they had brought upon themselves.[3]

As my friends tune into SIC Notícias on the TV in our room, I speculate on the appeal of this Coronation's coverage for Azoreans. Perhaps there's a simple explanation, like a dearth of Saturday morning programming on local television? Or maybe royal ceremonial is exotic and exciting in a country where the last king was dethroned in 1910? King Manuel II lived in exile in Twickenham and was an acquaintance of George V, so there is a tenuous connection. The sceptical historian in me suspects, though, that interest in Charles III's Coronation is a barometer of Britain's significance in the European sphere – evidence of the nation's reduction to impressive symbol and ceremonial.

For those of us from Commonwealth countries, the relationship with the monarchy presents other complications. As the ceremony gets under way and my interest is slightly piqued, I wonder if I'm witnessing evidence of Stephen Turner and Edward Kissi's claims for the 'continuing emotional power' of the monarchy post-decolonization, 'especially among intellectuals' – 'something to reject and embrace simultaneously'?[4] Perhaps on some level we really are suckers for the 'theory of the Coronation' advanced in *May the Twelfth* that 'all members of the British Empire . . . belong to one big family'.[5]

Only one member of the group has any facility in Portuguese, so we decide to supplement the live television with BBC coverage on my laptop. iPlayer is blocked in Canada, but I'm bemused to find that it works seamlessly in this European territory. The dual-screen approach proves to be a sensory challenge, however, not only because the stations' producers chose different camera angles but also because streaming BBC via wifi is about forty-five seconds behind the hotel's satellite feed. The impression is that BBC 'live' can't keep up with SIC Notícias 'directo'.

Our musical interests lead to the discovery of a separate official programme posted online with details of all the music selected and commissioned for the Coronation – so the viewing party becomes a three-screen event. For the remainder of the ceremony, we follow the musical elements closely and debate their merits and significance, fuelled by Swiss chocolate bars imported directly from the source.

The juxtaposition of old and new, with highlights including Bryn Terfel's Welsh 'Coronation Kyrie' and Pretty Yende's stunning performance of 'Sacred Fire', reminds me of the role of music in other recent royal landmarks. In 1977, the Sex Pistols' 'God Save the Queen' became *the* musical story of the Silver Jubilee. Subsequent jubilees channelled such energy into surprisingly successful 'Parties at the Palace'. Charles III's Coronation music seems like a similar attempt to present the monarchy as both traditional and contemporary. The inclusivity of both the pieces and the performers feels forced, but it's the most interesting part of the event for me.

After

Coronations and jubilees reinforce the somewhat enigmatic – some would say irrational – ties observed between the 'common people' and the monarch, a symbiotic relationship in which each side seems to demonstrate a genuine fondness for the other. Based on relative knowledge of British politics vs. the monarchy both now and in the last century, I'm inclined to think undergraduates would more readily grasp modern British history if my courses were framed by royal landmarks rather than the more conventional election- and war-based divisions.[6]

As the Coronation coverage is wrapping up, the fifth and final member of our party arrives from Germany. She presents everyone with matching commemorative tea towels selected on a recent visit to England. The tea towel features a large painted portrait bust of King Charles in full scarlet military regalia, hands folded. It's framed in royal purple with a delicate gold filigree of crowns and leaves. The King's brow is slightly furrowed and his expression looks more petulant than regal. To avoid any confusion, 'C III R' and the Coronation date are stamped just above the King's left ear. It's cringy, as the kids would say. My Welsh husband refuses to allow it into the domestic tea towel rotation. A company in Broadstairs, Kent, claims credit for this striking piece of memorabilia. The label reads 'Designed in the United Kingdom'. I infer that it was manufactured elsewhere, although the label is silent on that point.

A few weeks later, I see the same tea towel for sale in a 'British Shop' in a small town in southern Ontario. Global Britain.

Chapter 11

RUMOUR AND THE CORONATION RITUAL

Kimberly Mair

The Coronation will not happen. An actor will be crowned instead of Charles, as the King is secretly already dead. Princess Diana, however, was never actually dead and will emerge from hiding in her current service to the US military to be crowned instead of Charles.[1]

As the Coronation of King Charles III and Queen Camilla approached, these were among the several rumours and predictions that circulated in the attention economy of the commodified digital public square of Web 2.0. Dire warnings came from astrologers and psychics concerning the event occurring on Mercury's retrograde and an eclipse, citing a short or troubled rule for the King.[2] A mother-son team of royal-watching psychics reported having visions of a falling crown and an orange carriage. The colour orange, it was speculated, might suggest trouble from Just Stop Oil.[3] The arrival and passing of the Coronation did not put an end to the rumours. Among them: a conspiracy theorist tried to show that imposters donning masks were crowned in place of Charles and Camilla;[4] Sir Karl Jenkins, the Welsh composer of a song performed at the ceremony, was rumoured online to be either a jewel thief or Meghan in disguise;[5] and a robed verger seen on the ceremony's broadcast was rumoured to be the Grim Reaper, Meghan, Diana and the ghost of Father Benedictus, a monk who haunts Westminster Abbey. Joining other online lifestyle influencers who claimed the Coronation never happened, an astrologist referring to it as the 'uncoronation', insisted that what seemed like a coronation was instead a *real* wedding for Charles and Camilla.[6]

Rumours about the Coronation of King George VI in 1937 in Mass Observation's *May the Twelfth* share striking similarities with those of 2023. In 1937, it was widely speculated that George VI's Coronation would not take place. Most vividly, there were two separate reports of a fortune teller giving a double warning to people that they would see a death in their car 'before night' and that the ceremony would not happen. Other rumours – often described as a 'feeling' – that George VI's Coronation would not take place report that this would be due to the King's ill health; his anxiety; his assassination; his choking death; or because he was not the rightful or desired king. There was also a claim that the King was only being kept alive artificially. Edward VIII, who travelled to see Wallis Simpson upon news of the finalization of her divorce one week prior to the Coronation, was said to be scheming to steal attention from the event, yet was also reportedly spotted watching the procession in a disguise.[7]

With such striking patterns of similarity shared by rumours concerning events separated by eighty-six years and circulated in vastly different media environments, how can we make sense of these speculations? Although rumour is often assumed to be disruptive to the social order, it provides ways for people to communicate about subjects for which they have strongly felt emotions and unsettled interpretations. A coronation is not merely a singular and bound event but rather a heterogeneous social object that, as MO had observed, can be put to a 'variety of uses . . . to advertise hair oil, or a political party, or the beauty of the English countryside . . . all producing their own special shift of emphasis'.[8] As a complex social object, a coronation is made from multiple and conflicting meanings for members of different social groups, and, as *May the Twelfth* illustrated well, the meanings it held then were conflicted for groups and even within individuals. One Observer noted their own strain and tension – from thrill to political opposition simultaneously – and that the carnival spirit is a 'dangerous weapon' for those in power.[9]

Two considerations that inform the function of coronation rumours are historical context and the sacred character of coronation ritual. Both the 1937 and 2023 Coronations occurred during periods perceived to be marked by crisis. In 1937, the intertwined threats of fascism and war grew, and MO had begun its work with a focus on public opinion concerning King Edward VIII's abdication, noting that rapid change had produced a 'sense of continuous crisis' against which people had built up defences.[10] In 2023, the global public consciousness of the urgent need to decolonize institutions and practices ran up against the conception of royalty as an essential part of national culture, perhaps as central to the nation as family itself. Significant events, such as the Sussexes' exit from their official roles and the Queen's passing after a sustained reign, produced breaks in the perception of continuity that monarchy had historically provided. Additionally, strain had been acutely felt from the financial consequences of Brexit, political instability (signalled by three prime ministers in the calendar year of 2022), and a cost of living crisis. At the same time, social movements of particular interest to law enforcement, such as Just Stop Oil, Republic and Animal Rising, provide insight into some of the critical texture of social concerns that stood at odds with the event or the resources expended upon it and appeared to be key targets of the controversial Public Order Bill and the zero tolerance security policy that were publicized in the days prior.

A coronation consists of several constituent rituals that are undertaken in the passage to a new status for the one who is crowned, yet the crowning also has transformative implications for all whose roles correspond with the one being entered by the subject of the ritual. In this sense, the ritual prepares everyone for the 'incorporation' of the new monarch.[11] While there are many rituals of status passage observed in the life course of modern individuals, crowning rituals are unique in the reach of their sacred character that, although socially constructed, presents the apprehension of legitimized meaning, stability and continuity.[12] Symbolically, the sacred power that rituals attempt to draw upon in this process has historically been seen as dangerous. In a practical sense, transitions are disruptive to the fabric that supports a sense of continuity and rituals aim to suture meaning.

MO's study of the intricacies of everyday life revealed that there is considerable planning that precedes any normal day, but a day like that of a coronation unfolds from preparations that are 'infinitely greater and more protracted'.[13] Despite meticulous organization, the potential for inadequate preparation and the unexpected hangs over imminent events taken to be significant, expensive and expressive of multiple meanings. Yet, it ought not to be forgotten that we not only prepare ritual ceremonies; their very function is to prepare all for the transformations they bring into being. In 2023, Charles III's Coronation was tied to struggles over definitions of what the continuation of the monarchy means. Would it offer a sense of stability and social cohesion at a time when the political scene felt increasingly transitory and chaotic? Would it suggest the intractability of the violence and global inequities forged in Empire? It seemed to do both simultaneously. Rumour and speculation about a sacred ritual imbued with accumulated historical meanings and functions of legitimation that, for many, are disjointed from the concerns of the present time may be a critical part of the planning process that people undertake to incorporate the event, its contradictory meanings, and the emotions that it evokes in everyday life.

Chapter 12

'CORONATION ORGIES' AND A 'TERRIBLY WHITE BALCONY'
EMOTION AND RACE IN THE CORONATION OF KING CHARLES III

Khaleda Brophy-Harmer

On the day of 6th May 2023, 'a bejewelled couple' rolled through the streets of London in a two-tonne golden coach. Throughout the day of King Charles III's Coronation, news bulletins reported on the details of proceedings, while we are told, at its peak, over twenty million people tuned in to watch the live event.[1] In the week preceding, schools had assemblies, 'enrichment' lessons, made flags and had parties to make it clear: *we* are excited, and *we* are proud.[2] In step with this, news outlets, newspapers and daytime TV shows claimed to both represent the feelings of the nation, while looking to garner anticipation and excitement.[3] They declared emotional responses, while simultaneously asking others to share in them. Following the Coronation spectacle itself, the day was unpacked and recreated in news articles and on screens. These processes required and encouraged active engagement from their audiences: reading, discussions, imagining and re-imagining. Indeed, both pre- and post-Coronation events, in sharing emotional performances and looking (wittingly or unwittingly) to construct one, might be understood to have formed part of a coronation performance 'complex' or 'web'.[4]

But were 'we' excited, who was the 'we'? As one of ITV's *This Morning* viewers wrote: 'Jesus wept. How much time can they devote to the coronation. I am switching off for the rest of the week. Soul destroying listening to it. #noteveryoneisobsessedwiththeroyals #ThisMorning'.[5] I imagine my own young, impressionable children were far more confused by the end of the Coronation week than they were at the start, caught between two very stark emotional responses: that of school and that of home. They were no doubt a little frustrated and slightly bemused that I could not, in this instance, heartedly agree that dressing up, waving flags and eating cake at school were preferable to doing maths. Throughout Charles III's Coronation performance, I could not help but recall the phrasing of Irish revolutionary James Connolly and his depiction of the 'Coronation orgies' of King George V in 1910.[6] 'Orgies' does seem rather fitting if defined as excess and overindulgence (mixed in with a little hysteria).[7] In his pamphlet, Connolly had implored Irish workers to 'unanimously refuse to countenance this visit, or to recognise it by [their] presence at its attendant processions or demonstrations'.[8] Indeed, to refuse to partake in a ritual and to deviate from a prescribed emotional performance en masse, for Connolly, seemingly contained powerful and even revolutionary potential.

This Coronation and its surrounding performance web, though grand in scale, was woven into and around familiar feelings and discourses of Britishness.[9] Drawing on emotional and discursive frameworks such as prestige, pride, nostalgia, benevolence and tolerance, as a mobilizing spectacle it was cushioned in a 'cocoon' of national and, as argued here, 'racial comfort';[10] feelings and discourses that have also been understood as synonymous with the visible and 'invisible empire' and liberal 'whiteness'.[11] As Georgie Wemyss outlines, such 'discursive formations' cannot be dissected from the racialized social structures they support, nor the 'bundle of silences' that make up their core.[12] Indeed 'white supremacy and white identity', Robin DiAngelo argues, rest upon a 'foundation of (superficial) racial tolerance and acceptance'.[13] A 'tolerance and acceptance' arguably very present in the diverse coronation ceremony itself.[14] Yet, as Wendy Brown, Ghassan Hage and Wemyss all remind us, 'tolerance' is a value based upon a dynamic of power; it is by nature always within reach of the 'tolerator' to withdraw it from the 'tolerated'.[15]

During ITV's coverage of the Coronation, Black actress Adjoa Andoh commented: 'Looking at all those young people, there is a bit of me that has gone from the rich diversity of [Westminster] Abbey to the terribly white balcony.... I'm very struck by that.'[16] Following the comment, Ofcom received 8,371 complaints and media outlets were keen to jump on the 'story'.[17] Andoh, albeit far from critical of the monarchy, was quickly targeted for speaking *out of turn*, and seemingly *out of place*; perceived as giving an unfavourable nod to the absence of Meghan Markle, and prevalent debates over racism in the Royal Family.[18] Following the further amplification of her comments, on BBC's Radio 4, Andoh felt the need to clarify what she had meant:

> I think I may have upset a few people yesterday.... I was talking about the day and how marvellous it was and then looking at the balcony at the end and suddenly going: 'Oh it's so white!' because the day had been so mixed, and I didn't mean to upset anybody.[19]

Keen to emphasize her adherence to the prescribed emotional performance, in an additional statement she added: 'I continue to celebrate the king.... It's an exciting moment in our history'.[20]

As DiAngelo writes, 'white fragility' can be understood as a 'powerful means of white control and the protection of white advantage'.[21] Protected and encased by emotional uproar, white privilege does not like to be exposed, nor its 'systems of feeling' disrupted.[22] While talk show pundits contemplated whether Andoh had apologized (and been chastised) enough, the discursive violence of race in the everyday was laid bare. On the 6th of May, as King Charles stood ceremoniously displaying his inherited inordinate wealth, born of systems of racialized inequality and adorned with the spoils of empire,[23] a woman of colour received a barrage of complaints for acknowledging that he, and his fellow adorned, were all white. The ensuing media debate fixated on what was, or was 'not racism', with declarations of whiteness being under attack.[24] In so doing, any critical discussion on the persisting structures of race that uphold and privilege whiteness (arguably embodied in royalty itself) remained muzzled and untouched.[25] Andoh was publicly brought into emotional order (if she had ever really left).

It could be argued that the kinds of performances of racialized outrage that Andoh endured at the receiving end of this discourse have become a mainstay of our society. News channels, social media platforms, phone-in radio shows, and political influencers stake claims to the performance of outrage, with many making careers out of it. In keeping, they present themselves as rigid characters, fixed and unwavering. But, in reality, identity is none of these things, and nor is race; in fact, it has been argued to be quite the opposite. As Black Marxist Cedric Robinson wrote: 'Race presents all the appearance of stability. History, however, compromises this fixity. Race is mercurial – deadly and slick'.[26] Pointing to the fragmentation and discord of race – its 'matrices of identity' and 'lived multiplicities' – Robinson notes how critical to understanding race is the chaos of its production, in which 'racial regimes' can be best understood as 'unstable truth systems'.[27] As Stuart Hall reminds us, race as a 'floating signifier' must be given meaning to exist.[28] In a 'constant process of redefinition and appropriation', race must be reforged and reinvented; it is a process that is not only fluid but also messy.[29]

The Coronation performance web looked to present a fixed national emotionally performing body. However, much like my children caught between family principles and their school parties, we all constantly negotiate the emotional avenues and communities that we inhabit, and the systems of power that we straddle and work within.[30] It is argued here that there is a great deal to be learnt in the negotiation of such performances of emotion and identity – from the royal state spectacle to the banal and everyday. The nuance, contradictions, 'stickiness' and subversions of racialized identities and emotional performances have much to tell us about the replenishing and maintaining of social structures.[31] These interests align with much of the initial ambitions of Mass-Observation, which in its early work viewed the royal spectacle as the starting point from which to unearth and lay bare the fragments of everyday national 'social consciousness', and placed an onus on the feelings that make up the 'ordinary' social world.[32]

In view of the unsettling social and cultural symmetry between the beginnings of M-O in 1937 and the societies we inhabit today (in line with M-O founders Tom Harrisson, Charles Madge and Humphrey Jennings) it might be argued that observation and reflection on the 'everyday' can be powerful.[33] Critically considering the emotional responses of ourselves and others around us has the potential to offer not only insights into the intimacies of systems of power but also a glimpse into a means of their disruption. In short, it encourages us to consider: who requests an emotional performance from us, what are these performances doing and who do they benefit?

Chapter 13

'LIGHTING UP THE NATION'?

SOUNDING MULTICULTURAL BRITAIN AND THE COMMONWEALTH AT THE CORONATION CONCERT

Trevor R. Nelson and Christina Baade

On 7 May 2023, the Coronation Concert aired on the BBC for a domestic audience averaging 10.1 million and in over 100 countries.[1] In contrast to the Coronation's seriousness, the Coronation Concert represented the planning team's pursuit of pop culture relevance, although few critics agreed they had succeeded, calling it a 'bizarre musical confection', 'a cobbled-together bunch of B-listers', 'a cheesy display' and 'a Sorry Sales Pitch for a Brand New King'.[2] Perhaps more than any other event marking Charles III's Coronation, the Coronation Concert embodied the contradictions inherent in the contemporary British monarchy amid the cost-of-living crisis, Brexit, Megxit and a fraying Commonwealth.

An examination of the programme – particularly the two large, amateur choirs – demonstrates the challenges of musically representing and speaking to the people of Great Britain and the Commonwealth. *The Times* situated the concert's appeal in the uncool, normative, English middle: it was an 'extravaganza for Middle England . . . brimming with good cheer and undemanding, populist appeal'.[3] Its repertory hewed to the family-friendly, Anglo-American mainstream of pop anthems, Broadway and Disney show tunes, and light classical selections. Populist appeal often embraces spectacle, which the Coronation Concert delivered with a huge, purpose-built, Union Jack-shaped stage on the Windsor Castle grounds. It accommodated a seventy-piece orchestra, hundreds of performers, video projections and drone light displays.[4]

In contrast to the serious music dedications that marked Elizabeth II's crowning,[5] the Coronation Concert recalled the eclectic tradition of Royal Variety Performances with acts ranging from DJ Pete Tong playing the party-oriented Ibiza classic 'Feel the Love', to the Royal Collaboration, an act uniting the Royal Academies around Shakespeare's *Romeo and Juliet* – an accessible dose of distinctly British high culture (although the music selected, 'Somewhere' from Bernstein's *West Side Story*, infused an American twist). Eclectic programming is a time-honoured way to recognize a diversity of tastes, and it also recalled the tradition in which British coronations since 1900 have 'served as a magnificent showcase for the glories not only of Britain's musical present but also of its great heritage'.[6] Charles III's Coronation service featured dramatic shifts in musical style from Georg Friderik Handel to Andrew Lloyd Webber, but the Coronation Concert went farther. Admittedly, some of its eclecticism was rooted in the challenges of recruiting performers. Before the concert, media coverage was dominated more by who had declined to attend (Adele, Elton John, and Harry Styles) than by who had agreed – Lionel Ritchie, Katy Perry and Take That.[7] With two of the headliners hailing from the United States and the generally 'undazzling star wattage',[8] the concert did not offer a 'magnificent showcase' of British popular music.

Of course, communicating the values of inclusion, multiculturalism and belonging does not necessitate glamour, and both the audience and the Coronation Choir expressed the concert's democratic thrust. Free tickets were given to the audience of 20,000, which was composed of volunteers from the King's and Queen Consort's charities and winners of a national ballot.[9] Embodying the night's community spirit was the over-300-member Coronation Choir, which brought together Britain's eighteen 'most enthusiastic' community choirs, including 'refugee choirs, NHS choirs, LGBTQ+ singing groups and deaf signed choirs'.[10] The ensemble gave an uplifting rendition of Black Scottish singer-songwriter Emeli Sandé's 'Brighter Days', while their presence offered a diverse vision of the nation: a mosaic of NHS scrubs and Royal National Lifeboat Institution uniforms, shalwar kameez and dashikis, neckties and hoodies. In the BBC telecast, the Coronation Choir's performance, together with intercut shots of audiences around the UK, underlined the concert's theme: 'Lighting Up the Nation'.

The theme rendered the Commonwealth an afterthought – although the indifference probably cut both ways. Media coverage suggested that appearing in Charles III's Coronation Concert was a risky proposition for Commonwealth artists; Kylie Minogue, for example, reportedly withdrew due to republican sentiments in Australia.[11] Indeed, several Commonwealth member-states, especially Jamaica and Belize, were exploring independence and calling for apologies and reparations for the transatlantic slave trade, a dynamic highlighted in William and Catherine's 2022 Caribbean tour.[12] Ultimately, the Coronation Concert's only solo Commonwealth performer was the Nigerian Afrobeats star, Tiwa Savage. While many Nigerians celebrated her representational work, others decried her participation, noting the devastating legacies of British colonialism.[13]

Amid this fraught terrain, the Virtual Commonwealth Choir became the concert's primary vehicle for Commonwealth representation. Early press coverage framed the Virtual Choir as the Coronation Choir's supplement: '[The Coronation Choir] will be accompanied by a Virtual Choir featuring singers from across the Commonwealth as the King signals his commitment to the international "family" of 56 nations.'[14] As the concert approached, the number of participating nations fell to forty and the description of the Virtual Choir constricted from 'choirs' to 'voices'.[15] There was also the matter of keeping the choir virtual. On one hand, eschewing international air travel underlined the concert's ecological themes. On the other hand, they lacked the Coronation Choir's physical presence and were represented in a video montage that showed them in iconic outdoor settings, often dancing or wearing ethnic dress – a decorative, colourful mosaic of global diversity.

Musically, the voices of the Virtual Commonwealth Choir were blended into the mix that accompanied Steve Winwood singing 'Higher Love'. Winwood's song had first hit the charts with his 1986 solo album, followed in 1990 by Whitney Houston's well-known cover, and in the 2019 remix of Houston's record by the Norwegian DJ Kygo. In the Coronation Concert, Winwood became the performance's auditory and visual focal point, with the Virtual Commonwealth Choir in the background, more seen than heard. The performance recalled rock tropes in which English, white male artists are cast as the protagonists, supported by the authenticating presence of Black women backup singers.[16] In the mini-documentary preceding the concert, Winwood linked Commonwealth representation in the 'Higher Love' performance to world music: 'It's wonderful that the Commonwealth are included because they are a very important part of what Britain is . . . . I've always loved world music and in fact this song does contain many of those elements, so hopefully it will be the perfect vehicle for the Commonwealth Choir to sing on'.[17] Recalling the colonial 'west and the rest' framing that dominated the marketing of world music in the 1990s, Winwood's comments suggested a conception of diverse global musics as seasoning for Western rock – and the Commonwealth as an ingredient in British identity.[18]

The treatment of the Virtual Commonwealth Choir in 'Higher Love' recalls the ways, since the Second World War, UK representations of the Commonwealth have been sculpted around British values and culture, recalling earlier habits of Empire. For example, when producing a radio variety series celebrating Elizabeth II's Coronation, BBC executives believed that light classical and show tunes performed by Commonwealth musicians were more representative of the Commonwealth than musical styles indigenous to Commonwealth nations.[19] For those in Britain to hear the Commonwealth as something to be shaped to their priorities and tastes helps explain the resentment felt by Commonwealth citizens seeking republican reforms and, in some cases, to leave the Commonwealth altogether. The inaudible Virtual Commonwealth Choir backing Winwood in his preferred style at the Coronation Concert recalled a long representational tradition within the UK of treating the Commonwealth as a source of exotic colour while failing to explore the potential of meaningful collaboration.

Winwood's performance with the Virtual Commonwealth Choir was, obviously, a symbolic event. But, given the importance of symbolism to the Commonwealth's stability, as well as the sovereign's role as its head, it also represented a missed opportunity at the start of Charles III's reign. Unlike the stately Coronation, the Coronation Concert provided Charles III and his supporters a chance to highlight how the monarchy might adapt to reflect a post-Brexit nation and the Commonwealth as a truly 'equal partnership of nations' as Queen Elizabeth II optimistically described it in 1953.[20] Unfortunately for the House of Windsor, that chance seems to have been missed because of multiple musical and political factors. Perhaps that made the Coronation Concert representative in its own way, not of Commonwealth aspirations, but of contemporary British sentiment. As the apogee of British music at his mother's Coronation signalled the dawn of the New Elizabethan Era, the meagre hodge-podge of musical acts welcoming King Charles III did little to assuage the misgivings of many about the new-Carolean age.

Observations IV

Although I recognise that the royal family brings tourists and money into the country, by and large I have Republican leanings and am appalled at the amount of money spent on the Coronation Jamboree, during a time of financial desperation for so many. I have to acknowledge though that it was for many a chance to celebrate an historical event with all the 'glamour' of pomp, circumstance and celebrity spectacle, needed at a time of wall-to-wall depressing news. These rituals have been around for a thousand years, and many find them uplifting...

In the event, and although I hadn't intended to, I did actually watch the coronation on TV as it was a historical event, but I was glad it was shortened...

On the Big Help Out volunteering initiative, I visited a venue which was hosting various charities, hoping to find another charity to join. On leaving the hall, I noticed quite a small child with a mini litter picker, who was being encouraged by her parents to grab scraps of litter and deposit them in a nearby bin. That was great community action to witness and a positive end to the subject. **F75, K7595**

As an antimonarchist I tried to avoid anything coronation related – not easy! I believe the monarchy should have been ended in 1918 – after WW1. I actually had a hospital appointment on the morning of the coronation for pain management... so I can honestly write I preferred having needles stuck in me than watching King Charles in an although historically interesting ceremony, now seems outdated and archaic. I've not heard many people say they were looking forward to it. There's been a few houses with bunting up. The main road... was closed for a few hours for a 'village celebration' – small fairground rides, stalls, shops open I believe. A few people I know watched the ceremony, out of interest; it was the main topic of conversation... where I work, but the general feel was its costing too much money when people in this country are really struggling.

It might have brought well needed money into the hospitality sector in London but it still was of an horrendous cost to the taxpayer, for an over privileged man who has an obscene amount of money which he hasn't worked for.

I saw a photo of the royal family in the robes and garters and the King and Queen with the crowns on and it just looks wrong, feudal, archaic, out of place. I love history and reading about previous monarchs but I don't feel the argument about the current royal family bringing in money stands. It costs more to keep them and their many homes, palaces. I think people would still visit and tourism still be good for the economy without them. **F52, G3187**

Most of my friends watched the Coronation on television. It was different for my children and grandchildren. My daughter and family went out to avoid it – they are completely disinterested in the monarchy. My son and family watched a little, but their young daughters soon got bored after seeing the royal coach, so they didn't see any more.

I believe that this divide was fairly typical round here. I have one friend (ex-Catholic from N. Ireland) who is vehemently opposed to royalty, but I think most of my contemporaries, like me, had mild curiosity.

I watched most of the footage. It was a wet day and I cleaned the sitting room at the same time. I found a great deal of it boring and out of keeping with our times. The best bit was the marching and music in the ceremony.

I thought that the clothing Charles and Camila, and William and Kate had to wear was rather ridiculous. Charles looked particularly silly when partially clothed in what looked like a dressing gown, and I was reminded of Masonic ceremonies. I am aware of the historic significance of all the accessories like the sceptre, orb etc. etc., but again I found them not to be relevant to the present.

I disliked the religious overtones of the coronation and was uncomfortable about the oaths. The Church of England should be dis-established from the state. As for the Archbishop of Canterbury's idea that we should all swear an oath of loyalty to the king – that was just stupid.

I have no wish to get rid of the monarchy. I am sure Charles is sincere, and believe him to be a good man who wants to be a conscientious king. However, things need to change. I am amazed when I see how many people come to London to stand for hours in the streets to watch events like royal funerals, weddings and coronations. I think we are a sentimental people who have need to worship celebrities.

In the locality where I live there were no parties or celebrations, not even flags or bunting. Only a couple of miles away there were street parties. My friend who lives in a residential establishment in Bristol experienced plenty of coronation related events. Another friend who lives in a Yorkshire village was involved in special teas, dances, and royalty related activities throughout the long weekend. She had a great time. I did not feel I missed out as I did not feel much enthusiasm for the Coronation, nevertheless I am glad I watched the ceremony so know what it was all about. **F72, D826**

I am not a Royalist but am enough of a snob to appreciate the pomp and circumstance of the Royal Family and we took part in the platinum jubilee as well as attending the proclamation for King Charles. Personally I am not motivated by the republican argument although I agree with much of their argument. So I suppose it could be summarized thus: I am happy enough with the way things are but would be deeply unhappy if there was still a King or Queen with the same role and position in society in the next 30 years.

My late mother would have liked watching the coronation as I remember her recording such events on video but as Diana became the patron saint of wronged women, I am sure she would have been triggered by the joint coronation with Queen Camilla. So I thought about my mum and the feelings of 'wronged' women all over the world when I saw Queen Camilla. That's a bit reductive but I am sure that's how a lot of people felt. **P7688**

On Monday 8th May, our neighbours had planned a barbeque, to be held outside our house and others. However, the weather was dreadful. Our immediate neighbours sent a message round, that everyone was invited to their house, so an impromptu party was held and we had a happy afternoon.

That day was supposed to be the 'Big Help Out', but nothing specific had been planned in the village – a lot of voluntary work goes on in the normal way – and the rain would have probably prevented it anyway . . .

My husband and I are of an age with King Charles. Throughout our lives, we have seen him waiting to take up his designated role, while we got on with our lives. Now we have retired and are ready to do less, but he is having to do more. So far, we think he is doing well. We wish him well. **F74, I6609**

Charles 3rd was born the same year as me, 1948, that simple fact has made me compare my life with his, as we age. I often ask myself would I care to swop lives with him the answer is a resounding NO. As I understand it, he has from a child been groomed as a future king. To play the game of Monarch, all the rules that have been generated and followed through centuries, who to suck up to and who to snub.

Elizabeth 2nd was 'my' queen and monarch, she died as we all must and I miss her as I would a relative. Yet Charles, the new kid on the block at 75 years old calls us 'his people'. Well in my view he has not earned the right to spout such piffle. I would not wish to begin a new career at 75, and yet Charles has proudly accepted the task with no thought of the pressures that will arrive on his doorstep. I do not believe he will gel with the population, and will reign as a tolerated monarch, but unloved. An old boy out of touch with the people of this land, mainly because of his insulation from us, but secondly because of his age. I feel out of touch with the younger generation, and I have not been coddled with the finest that money can buy.

Perhaps you can detect an air of anti royalty in what I write, maybe so, but I think his son William is the person best suited to the task for this generation and for the country. In the light of my comments therefore I cannot celibrate Charles 3rd accession to the throne. I did not watch the ceremony, I did not attend a party, nor have I a union flag flying, neither did I read in the press about the events. Unable to avoid comments via my laptop, I under stood the whole affair to have cost the taxpayer a cool £20 million, or more if *the truth is known, when folk are struggling to pay energy bills to cook and to keep warm, and to avoid starvation, I believe its all a bit insensitive to say the least.*

Good luck to those people that tell me to give him a chance, and that the £20 million was well spent, the world leaders were well impressed with the show.

What is the 'Big help out initiative' Have I not heard this from a recent prime minister, from a priviledged background who ran away when the going got tough; 'we are all in it together' phrase rings in my ears. Commoners we may be, but do not treat us as peasants.

Lastly thanks for nothing, bank holidays do not apply to pensioners, perhaps double the pension on special days, we are excluded. **M75, T3155**

The problem is . . . what has become of our royalty? What of their standing within this nation? And what of the nation itself? A generation ago it would have been fair to say that the Royals were held in a degree of esteem. They were on the whole respected. Her Majesty the Queen was our constant. Unflappable, dignified and smiling, she grew to be our Nan, the nations Grandma. Sure Prince Phillip could be a bit of a berk sometimes, talking of 'slitty-eyed' foreigners and the like, but that was just him trying to be a bloke and so he was soon forgiven. But what now in this era of instant communication without censorship? A time where everything is filmed on a hand held device called a mobile phone and then broadcast on social media in all its ugliness. A time when everyone's opinion can be shared without a filter.

What of Charles himself? His doomed relationship with Saint Diana, the beautiful Princess that held the hand of a man dying of AIDS, kissed him on the forehead indeed, pick up and held a starving child in Ethiopia or Sudan, or was it Somewhere Dreadful? Walked with soldiers into a minefield to remind us all that people can, and still do, lose their limbs to these terrible devices of war long after any such war is won or lost. Charles had this woman for his wife, and he lost her in a loveless marriage. It was driven home to us all after her tragic death just how wonderful she could have been as our Queen.

Then there are the other members of the family, the less well thought of. Andrew, younger brother of the King, the royal nonce, sex pest, philanderer, banished from public life and good riddance. The embarrassing uncle we don't want on the photographs. And Harry, the Kings second born son, currently estranged from the family, along with his beautiful but American non-white wife. For she is truly damned if she does, and damned if she doesn't, by this nations scandal sheets that pass for the printed press. She'll simply never be able to do right for doing wrong in the eyes of this dying and antiquated form of news media. This 'Fourth Estate', itself fast becoming an irrelevance to the rest of us, happy to condemn and vilify the woman for things beyond my reckoning.

No, enough is enough in my eyes. I'm not a monarchist by any stretch of the imagination but nor am I a committed republican. I simply don't care anymore. And from what I can fathom from my observations of the general public here in Barrow-in-Furness there doesn't seem to be a great deal of enthusiasm for this upcoming coronation from them either. No street parties, no publicised plan to deck the streets with bunting, no brass bandsmen marching to and from the Town Hall to any church, nothing of that nature at all. Compare this with how it was in times past. I have a couple of drinking buddies of whom I'm fond, and only a week or two back we were talking of the fuss made back in the 70s when it was the Queens Silver Jubilee. Back then there were street parties, newly-minted commemorative coins, flags and bunting by the furlong stretched across the streets, and it was all done to a soundtrack provided by the Sex Pistols, wonderful stuff.

My father met Her Majesty Queen Elizabeth at Buckingham Palace some years ago when she presented him with an OBE, it was a proud moment for Dad, and the rest of the family too for that matter. Dad now has Alzheimer's and is in a care home within the town that specialises in the care of people with dementia. And just two days past I visited him in the home and took him out for a drive over to Walney Island, where we took in the views of the town and the sea, and ate an ice cream each whilst sat on a draughty bench looking out towards the shrouded and invisible Isle of Man. But what struck me most of my visit to the home was that the staff have gone to the effort of decking the place in all manner of red, white and blue, in an effort to stimulate some distant memories of simpler times for the residents. A time when Elizabeth was crowned their Queen, whilst they were still young and vibrant within their own families. Alas I fear their efforts will fall upon stony ground, Dad has no recollection as to who I am or the part he played in my upbringing, we're all lost to him, even though we still hold him dear to our hearts. He knows to trust us, myself and my siblings, but he no longer knows who we are. And it's heartbreaking. **M62, P6988**

I will not be watching the coronation. I have no respect for Charles and Camilla. When Charles divorced Diana, on the BBC news the reporter said that when the Queen dies the Archbishop of Canterbury will have a program because he said that the rules were that no monarch can be divorced or have committed adultery. Well they have both done that. Also I can't forget how they both treated Diana and when Charles said if he died he would like to come back as Camilla's Tampax.

So I didn't watch the coronation and I dislike both of them immensely. I'm so glad Prince Harry went to live in America. He must have hated having to pretend in public that it was ok to have her as a stepmum. **F78, C2579**

I am organising a Coronation Big Lunch on Monday 8 May for our street. I have organised the road closure (I must do a 20-mile round trip to get the Road Closed signs . . .) and a backup venue in case it rains. I issued the invitations with a deadline to 32 houses. I have had five responses and my colleagues in our village committee are helping me and attending. So, in all, there will probably be a maximum of 20 people including children. This is quite disappointing, but since Covid trying to organise events has proved unsuccessful, it seems people just do not want to do this anymore. I am hoping that on the day more people will come out and join us. **F72, L7499**

Due to being wrongly convicted and contained I spent most of my time trying to unwind . . . However, I managed to watch the coronation and the King's procession. It was also good to see the diversity of Britain and see different cultures and backgrounds come together for this extravaganza. I.e., I saw the St Vincent and Grenadines Flag which made me feel a little bit inclusive . . . the Coronation Concert I thoroughly enjoyed because their was lots of diverse acts. Yet, the Act I resonated the most was with Lionel Ritchie; Katie Perry. Such as 'Roar!' This song helps me feel insurmountable because even though I am in this jungle I will succeed. Also 'All Night Long' song relates to being jubilant. No matter what adversity we face there will always be a tomorrow. Peace and Love. **M34, HMP Ashfield**

WASN'T THERE, DON'T HAVE A TELLY, SO NOT MUCH INTERESTED.

Coronation? I'm not a Royalist, or any longer a Londoner, except by birth so it doesn't mean an awful lot to me. Besides the coronation was a bit off. It should have been Diana being crowned. I mean no disrespect to Camilla. I'm sure she's a perfectly charming lady, and I've heard that she cares about battered women which puts her high in my estimation, but, it should have been Diana . . .

As far as I'm concerned the main thing about the coronation is that it has once again opened up the whole discussion about what really happened to Diana. (That's something that I do find interesting.) Whatever her faults, and let's face it she wasn't without them, 'the firm' did the dirty on Diana. I have never been entirely satisfied with the news about her death . . .

Shortly after that first announcement the news bulletins changed and she was supposedly seriously injured. Was she really? Personally I hope they buried an empty coffin and that she's living an alternative life somewhere in an obscure part of the globe under a new identity. This is a topic J and I have discussed many times but the bit that stumps us is – would Diana do that to William and Harry? But perhaps they do know that she's secretly alive and this is another one of the firm's well kept secrets. It's great fun having a conspiracy theory or two to gossip about now and again and sometimes it is hard to remember that they are real people with varying emotions, thoughts, preferences and ailments just like the rest of us.

Anyway, back to the coronation. (I'll be marked down to C – for that digression.) Yes, the coronation is a fabulous piece of theatre and possibly means a great deal for a few thousand commoners who stood in the Mall cheered but what about the rest of the country? What about the homeless who get swept off the streets so as not to offend visiting dignitaries? Perhaps it is time to stick to just the legal formalities, ditch the jewels and ermine even though their maintenance does, of course, provide employment for many craftsmen and women. There is a cost of living crisis in the country, people are going without food, going without heating, going without medical treatment because important, though minor things, such as eye tests, ear syringing, tooth filling and so on are no longer available on the NHS. Schools and hospitals are in desperate need of repair, so can we afford to spend such lavish amounts of tax payer's money on such a spectacle as the coronation? Is it all paid for with tax payer's money or is there always a sum government money ring fenced for such occasions? Who gets paid what for all the overtime work that surely goes into it? . . .

Sure it probably is excellent for tourism but tell that to a junior doctor who has worked a seventy hour shift on an understaffed ward somewhere in the midlands. Tell that to a teacher who spends coronation day catching up with marking. Tell that to Mrs So and So's elderly relative who cannot come home from hospital because there are no care services in place where she lives. Also, I cannot help but think that it's a perfect distraction for 'the public' from the messes and mucks the current government is engaged in. What is the government up to behind closed doors whilst 'the public' are waving union flags, eating picnics and downing pints in the local? Echoes of bread and circuses perhaps? It's no good saying 'it was ever thus' I still come back to the question of cost.

Is not the King super rich? It feels indecent that the tax payer should even have to foot the bill for the coronation. I don't wish Charles ill, I would not like his lifestyle although I wouldn't mind his clothing and bed linen allowance. Imagine never having to worry about money. Personally I do not mind if he expresses opinions on issues such as architecture but I'm furious to learn that 'the throne' is allowed to interfere secretly with government policy. Interfere all you like Sir but do it out in the open where us commoners can see you. We need to know what is being done in our country by whom, as some of it will surely affect our lives. Well done to a certain left wing broadsheet for bringing that story to light . . .

I really do admire some of the initiatives the King put in place as the prince of Wales like the Prince's Trust. However when many of us who are actually 'running the country' such as nurses, teachers, bin men, supermarket staff, school dinner ladies and public loo attendants' have to go to food banks just to survive and don't have the money to heat our homes a theatrical style coronation that most of us cannot get to seems utterly immoral. If we really are such a poor country that we cannot fund education, health, transport, and defence properly then perhaps we cannot afford to have a lavishly theatrical pageant such as the coronation either? Give us the chance to rebel and dethrone you Sir as they did in centuries past. **F67, B8133**

I watched the coronation on tv, pretty much all day on May 6th. At first I was at home alone and then later I watched with my sister and her family including her grandsons aged 2 and 11 and her mother-in-law aged 91. We didn't attend any external events and I wasn't aware of any in my immediate neighbourhood but I wasn't interested in that.

I was very moved by the day's events, particularly by the ceremony in Westminster Abbey. Although I have no religious beliefs nowadays, I was brought up in the Church of England and consider it part of my heritage if not of my spiritual life. The familiar hymns and prayers and the fact that as a member of a choral society I have often sung or listened to the traditional pieces moved me deeply and at times I felt tearful. I was born in 1955 so I have never known any monarch other than Elizabeth II. Her death was a profound experience for me and many of my friends. In her later years I often wondered if it would be better if Charles just sidestepped the Crown in favour of William but I don't think that now. I have always admired Charles and I think that he is a good man and will be a good monarch and I wish him well. This is partly because of what I know of his life but also because of the great thoughtfulness and generosity that I think he contributed to the coronation ceremony.

Extended pub opening hours didn't affect me. They seem to be open all the time nowadays anyway. The Big Help Out seemed like a patronizing piece of Tory propaganda. I expect that those who participated were mostly people who already help out in all sorts of ways. **F67, B7763**

The coronation has been and gone. I did watch most of it, although I was doing other things while it was on TV, and I got quite bored after a while. I actually found it far less interesting than the Queen's funeral last year, which really felt like quite an historic occasion. The bit that was the most interesting was watching Charles get oiled up and undressed on his special throne behind a screen. It all felt very Game of Thrones. In fact the whole coronation felt very Game of Thrones, which to me sums up royalty; like a medieval fantasy TV show.

The whole idea of a monarchy is quite ridiculous, and the idea that they have a God given right to rule is equally ridiculous. The richness and opulence that was on display was a bit obscene, especially these days when so many people are struggling to afford food. And the origins of the wealth and jewels made me feel quite uncomfortable. It was an unsavoury reminder of our colonial past. I watched the coverage as a historical document really and haven't given the new King much thought since. I do object to how much money was spent on the event and think that the royal family should have paid for it themselves. The Coronation concert which was on the Sunday evening was a bit embarrassing. They seemed to have struggled to find any decent acts for it and it all seemed a rather forced celebration. Again, the Queen's Jubilee concert was more enjoyable. Just as I think the Queen will always be more popular than the King.

There were no street parties or celebrations anyway near our neighbourhood but the supermarkets made attempts at Coronation celebration cakes etc. and one of the supermarkets, Sainsburys, was selling Charles and Camilla face masks which I thought was quite funny. Commercial interests trying to whip up interest in the Coronation for profit.

I have an elderly family member who really doesn't like Camilla, which seems to be based purely on her looks; he loved Diana and we have had some spirited conversations about the Royal family and how it is unfair to judge people on their looks! . . .

I'm not a Republican, but I think that the royal family need to change and become a bit more down to earth, do more real work and pay for their own lifestyles more. I hope that when William becomes King, things will change a bit more. **54, T8072**

It's almost three months since the Coronation now, and at this distance it almost feels like a dream – did it really happen? It was so out of this world really. Beforehand, I wasn't particularly interested in it – and this was a common feeling among my friends and family (especially younger generations). We had all been captivated by the Queen's funeral, for the sheer brilliance of the organisation, and the sense that some people, somewhere, could get things done well – unlike our government leaders.

However, the funeral felt like a rite of passage into a new era. The Coronation less so. The talk of a pared-down ceremony seemed appropriate, both for a modern age and for the fact that so many people are struggling in their daily lives. The idea of street parties seemed out of step with the mood – as if we were children being told everything was alright. And, in the event, the ceremony didn't seem in any way pared down.

I am not a royalist, though at the same time, like many, I accept the role of the royal family, however anachronistic and mad it seems. The place of ritual and ceremony in national life does have some emotional validity, I feel. Personally, I like the theatre of it. And the eccentricity is also consoling in some way. But during the Coronation, half of my brain was shouting 'ridiculous!'. Was it necessary to have hundreds of soldiers in red and gold military regalia riding around on horseback to accompany a Cinderella coach through the streets of London? Why were there so many members of the armed forces present? Did they need to have so many guests or 'celebrity' faces? Did the barons of the Cinque Ports really need to be there? . . . When Charles was disrobed and dressed in the simple tunic he looked rather like an invalid being helped into nightwear, rather than appearing as a 'humble man', if that was the intention behind it.

But Penny Mordaunt holding her Excalibur sword was tremendous. She was genuinely admirable in her steadfastness and unifying in her appeal – everyone was Whats-Apping, 'Penny!' 'The sword!' and she was a hit on Twitter.

As for the new King Charles himself, he did look moved, and sad, most of the time. And quite tired. Lots of people were looking after him, including William. Like many, I wondered whether it wouldn't have been better just to skip Charles and make William king and introduce a whole new era of simple ceremony and vastly reduced public display. The music, though, was superb. **G7926**

Appendix

SPRING 2023 MO DIRECTIVE

Part 1: Cost of living and support

In recent months, we've all experienced rising costs for energy and food, along with increases in mortgages, rents and loans (including student loans). At the same time, real wages have declined, and pension funds have been exposed to greater risks. We welcome your thoughts and experiences about how you have been coping under these circumstances. What has the rising cost of living and increasing uncertainty meant for your everyday life, as well as your future? We hear a lot about individuals struggling with the cost of living and are particularly interested in how this has affected the kind of support that exists between generations. Such support can be material, practical and emotional assistance which you provide or receive from family, friends, neighbours or people in your community, both from the younger and older generations.

The everyday

Can you start by sharing a list of any everyday habits or activities you've changed recently because of the increasing cost of living? For instance, the way you cook or heat your house, reducing your travel or how often you socialise.

Family, neighbours and friends

Please tell us if any activities you do with younger or older relatives have changed. For instance, do you spend more time together in one heated room; do you visit each other less or more; have you changed the way in which you celebrate special occasions; do you talk to your family more about managing expenses?

What about places where you interact with different generations of friends, acquaintances or colleagues, such as leisure activities, volunteering or work? Has the cost of living impacted this?

Do you think that family and relatives are increasingly supporting each other through gifting or lending money and material items, or is it more difficult to do so with the recent cost of living rises? Does this also apply to friends and neighbours?

Do you have any experience in receiving or giving any kind of material support from family, friends or neighbours? Were they living with you, nearby or far away? Has any support you were usually giving or receiving declined in recent times? Why was this?

Have you helped any relatives or friends with daily tasks? For example, assisting with childcare for a relative who has recently started to work longer hours, or doing the shopping at a discount supermarket for an older person who could not afford groceries at the smaller local shops?

How do you think people are coping emotionally nowadays? Have you or any of your relatives, friends or neighbours become in need of emotional support? If so, please share your thoughts on this and what has made a difference.

Living arrangements

Have you, or anyone you know, made changes to their living situation, such as moving areas, selling their home, or living with relatives or friends? Do you know anyone who has started to rent out a room or their home? Have you considered this? If so, please share your thoughts.

There has been talk of some Britons taking a 'winter work-cation', going abroad in the winter months to save money. What do you think about this?

Community

What changes do you see happening in your community? Do you volunteer for a charity, food bank, church group or similar, or do you use services provided by such organizations? If so, do these experiences bring you into contact with people of different generations to yours? Please share any experiences of this. How do you think different generations have been affected in your area?

General

Are there any other changes you can think of that people have made over the past few months to cope with the rising cost of living? How do you think these changes may have affected the support between the generations? What do you think will be the longer-term impact of these rising costs? Please share any other comments you may have on this subject.

Part 2: Everyday ritual, materials and magic

The elaborate and precise ritual of Queen Elizabeth's recent funeral reminds us of the elaborate mourning rituals of past generations and the following of traditions such as grandparents keeping their curtains drawn on the morning of a neighbour's funeral.

In Part 2 of this Directive, we are interested to hear your thoughts and experiences, not on formal ceremonies and religious customs and norms, but instead focusing upon ordinary, everyday rituals and the use of objects. We would like to know about those things that you do, without really knowing why, as well as those that have particular significance for you.

This may also reflect changes in daily rituals over time, such as any familiar routines your older relatives or friends would do compared to what you or younger generations do now.

Before you start, please share the area in which you live and if this is different to where you grew up. We are interested in regional differences for this subject.

Ritual

Please share any experiences of and feelings about rituals, in as much detail as you can. For example, do you use different plates for Sunday roasts or reserve clothes for certain events? What forms of 'ordinary' ritual/repetition do you have in your life? For example, do you have the same meal on a Friday, or, when driving to work, do you take the usual route or park your car in the same space? Is there a distinction between what is a ritual and what is a 'usual' task (e.g. using special glasses for celebrations vs. putting out the rubbish bins)?

Autopilot

Are such routines so habitual that they are done on autopilot, such as washing up or making the bed? Have you ever reflected on why you do this? What does it feel like to do taken-for-granted things without noticing them?

Superstitions

Please list superstitions that you know and mark the ones you engage in. Do you classify rituals or superstitious beliefs as different to habitual routines? For example, saluting a magpie as opposed to leaving for work at the same time every day. Are there superstitious customs which are common, you think, to your locality and region of the country?

Objects

Are there any out-of-the-ordinary events (e.g. a driving test, sporting event or exam) that make you turn to objects which you think 'magical' in such circumstances? We are interested in stories about lucky objects from your past and your life now.

Are there 'lucky' objects you always have with you or take when travelling? Do you have objects that you think contain traces or connections to people, animals, nature or the past? Do you think of these objects as having feelings or as being able to sense your mood? Do these objects change your mood/feelings?

Special objects

When we think of things as 'special' sometimes, we might attend to them in special ways. Do you have any objects that you treat specially? If yes, please share details of what you typically do and how you attend to special objects.

Please share any other reflections on ideas of ritual, 'magic', 'luck' or even 'hauntedness' as particular kinds of 'specialness' in objects and in everyday activities.

Part 3: Coronation

Since its founding in 1937, Mass Observation has recorded royal events. The Coronation of King George VI on 12th May 1937 was one of its first activities, and in 1953 people were called upon again to document their thoughts, feelings and observations on the Coronation of Queen Elizabeth II. The resulting collections provide a 'snapshot' of Britain during these occasions. There are reports of those actively following events and taking part in street parties and writing by those busy at work or purposefully avoiding the celebrations. It provides a picture beyond what the press recorded. In the final part of the Directive, we would like to hear your thoughts and any planned events for the Coronation of King Charles III on the weekend of 6–8 May. The Coronation is expected to be smaller in scale than that of Queen Elizabeth II. What do you think of this? Do you intend to watch the occasion? Will you be helping to organise and/or take part in Coronation-related activities, or will you be steering clear of the event altogether? What are your thoughts about the extra bank holiday, pubs staying open later (Friday 5th and Saturday 6th) and the Big Help Out volunteering initiative? Please share any observations of what is happening (or not happening) in your local area.

NOTES

Introduction

1. See ed. Jennifer J. Purcell, *Mass-Observation: Text, Context and Analysis of the Pioneering Pamphlet and Movement* (London: Bloomsbury Academic, 2023).
2. Humphrey Jennings and Charles Madge, eds., *May the Twelfth: Mass Observation Day-Surveys 1937 by Over Two Hundred Observers* (1937; reprint, London: Faber and Faber, 2009), iv.
3. Jennings and Madge, *May the Twelfth*, v.
4. Jennings and Madge, *May the Twelfth*, 348–9. See also James Hinton, *The Mass Observers: A History, 1937–1949* (Oxford: Oxford University Press, 2013), 71–3.
5. Hinton, *The Mass Observers*, 73.
6. Directive December 1947, SxMOA1/3/106, Papers of the Mass Observation Archive (SxMOA), University of Sussex, Brighton, UK; Directive November 1955, SxMOA1/3/133, Papers of the Mass Observation Archive (SxMOA), University of Sussex, Brighton, UK; File Report 2221, 'Duke of Windsor', March 1945, SxMOA1/1/10/3/4 (SxMOA), University of Sussex, Brighton, UK; File Report 2290, 'Duke of Windsor', October 1945, SxMOA1/1/10/10/1, University of Sussex, Brighton, UK.
7. Tom Harrisson, *Britain Revisited* (London: Victor Gollancz, 1961), 233.
8. A curated collection of MO material on royalty going back to 1937 can be found in Jennifer Purcell and Fiona Courage, eds., *Reflections on British Royalty: Mass Observation and the Monarchy, 1937–2022* (London: Bloomsbury Academic, 2024).
9. 'Coronation 1953 Memories: Cold, Wet, Tired and Happy', *www.bbc.com*, 5 May 2023, https://www.bbc.com/news/uk-england-hampshire-65485348.
10. P3209, 'Coronation', Spring 2023, SxMOA2/1/127/3, Papers of the Mass Observation Project (SxMOA2), University of Sussex, Brighton, UK.
11. See, for instance, Clifton Daniel, '"It Better Be Good," says Iowa Couple. Poultry Packer and Wife Face 9-Hour Wait to See Queen After Rising at 4:30 am', *New York Times*, 2 June 1953.
12. C. L. Sulzberger, "Birth of a New Era Is Britain's Hope: War-Ridden Public Is Yearning for Prosperity that Reigned with the First Elizabeth," *New York Times*, 1 June 1953.
13. For Observers' reflections on the 1953 Coronation, see Purcell and Courage, *Reflections on Royalty*, Chapter 4.
14. Harrisson, *Britain Revisited*, 230.
15. See Purcell and Courage, *Reflections on British Royalty*, Chapters 7 and 8.
16. B8133, 'Coronation', Spring 2023, SxMOA2/1/127/3, Papers of the Mass Observation Project (SxMOA2), University of Sussex, Brighton, UK.
17. R1025, 'Coronation', Spring 2023, SxMOA2/1/127/3, Papers of the Mass Observation Project (SxMOA2), University of Sussex, Brighton, UK.
18. Cele C. Otnes and Pauline Maclaren, *Royal Fever: The British Monarchy in Consumer Culture* (Berkeley: University of California Press, 2015), 295.

19. Lucy D. Curzon, '"Timid, Bookish, and Unproductive": Mass Observation, Monarchy, and Academia', in *Mass Observing the Coronation of Charles III: Monarchy, Spectacle and Experience*, ed. Jennifer J. Purcell and Lucy Curzon with Fiona Courage (London: Bloomsbury Academic, 2025), 126.
20. Roger Mortimore, 'Measuring British Public Opinion on the Monarchy and the Royal Family', in *The Windsor Dynasty: 1910 to the Present, 'Long to Reign Over Us?'*, ed. Matthew Glencross, Judith Rowbotham and Michael D. Kandiah (London: Palgrave Macmillan, 2016), 139.
21. Hinton, *The Mass Observers*, 68.
22. Lucy D. Curzon and Benjamin Jones, 'Historical Contexts or Contemporary Uses? Mass Observation and the Politics of Continuity', in *The Historical Contexts and Contemporary Uses of Mass Observation: 1930s to the Present*, ed. Lucy D. Curzon and Benjamin Jones (London: Bloomsbury Academic, 2025), 1.
23. Dorothy Sheridan, 'Writing for....Questions of Representation/Representativeness, Authorship, and Audience', in *Ordinary People Writing: The Lancaster and Sussex Writing Research Projects*, by David Barton, David Bloome, Dorothy Sheridan, and Brian Street (Lancaster: the Lancaster and Sussex Writing Centre for Language in Social Life Working Paper Series, 1993), 17–23.
24. Early MOP directives, as Ben Highmore notes, explicitly asked panelists to write for future historians and other researchers who would want 'to understand the lives of ordinary people'. Dorothy Sheridan, Annebella Pollen, Joan Haran, and Kate O'Riordan have done the same. See Lucy Robinson, 'Perforating Event and Narrative, Experience and Analysis: Beyond the Retro Eighties', in *The Historical Contexts and Contemporary Uses of Mass Observation: 1930s to the Present*, ed. Lucy D. Curzon and Benjamin Jones (London: Bloomsbury Academic, 2025), 203.
25. Robinson, 'Perforating Event and Narrative', 203.
26. Robinson, 'Perforating Event and narrative', 185.
27. The entire Directive is reproduced in Appendix I.

Chapter 1

1. 'The Guardian View on Coronation Day: A Mix of Serious and Absurd', *The Guardian*, 7 May 2023, https://www.theguardian.com/commentisfree/2023/may/07/the-guardian-view-on-coronation-day-a-mix-of-serious-and-absurd.
2. Roy Strong, *Coronation: From the 8th to the 21st Century* (London: Harper Perennial, 2005), 172–3.
3. Lucy Williamson and Sam Ormiston, 'Fights Break Out in King's Coronation Crowds over Umbrellas as Miserable Royal Fans Get Soaked', *MyLondon*, 6 May 2023, https://www.mylondon.news/news/uk-world-news/fights-break-out-kings-coronation-26858028.
4. Samuel Pepys, 'The Diary of Samuel Pepys: Diary Entries from the 17th Century Diary', 22 April 1661, https://www.pepysdiary.com/diary/1661/04/23/.
5. See, for instance, Jennifer Purcell and Fiona Courage, eds., *Reflections on British Royalty: Mass Observation and the Monarchy, 1937–2022* (London: Bloomsbury Academic, 2024), 20–1.
6. Strong, *Coronation*, 386.
7. Anna Keay, *The Magnificent Monarch: Charles II and the Ceremonies of Power* (London: Continuum, 2008), 4.

8   'Coronation Amusements', *The Times*, 20 July 1821.
9   Strong, *Coronations*, 415.
10 Tracy Borman, 'William the Conqueror', in *Crown and Sceptre: A New History of the British Monarchy from William the Conqueror to Elizabeth II* (New York: Atlantic Monthly Press, 2021), np, Kindle.
11 Lindsey German and John Rees, *A People's History of London* (London: Verso, 2012), 21.
12 Ibid., 104–5.
13 Tom Nairn, *The Enchanted Glass: Britain and Its Monarchy*, 3rd ed. (London: Verso, 2011), 70.
14 Emily Mayne, 'Shows of Joy and Malice: Performance, the Star Chamber, and the Celebration of James I's Coronation in Norwich in 1603', *Early Theatre* 23, no. 20 (2020): 169–82.
15 David Cressy, *Bonfires and Bells: National Memory and the Protestant Calendar in Elizabethan and Stuart England* (Berkeley, CA: University of California Press, 1989), 50.
16 Ibid.
17 See, for instance, activities mentioned across the country for William IV's Coronation from Arundel and Bolton to Winchester and York. Bolton advertised a hot air balloon with the likenesses of the King and Queen to be launched from the marketplace. 'The Coronation', *The Times*, 7 September 1831.
18 'London, Friday, June 29, 1838', *The Times*, 29 June 1838.
19 'Coronation to Be Observed Here with Services and Fetes: City to Celebrate Coronation Today', *New York Times*, 12 May 1937.
20 See Purcell and Courage, *Reflections on British Royalty*, Chapters 1 and 4.
21 'London, Friday, June 29, 1838', *The Times*, 29 June 1838.
22 See Ibid. Also, see Lucy D. Curzon and Jennifer J. Purcell, 'Visualizing Coronation' in *Mass Observing the Coronation of Charles III: Monarchy, Spectacle and Experience*, ed. Jennifer J. Purcell and Lucy D. Curzon with Fiona Courage (London: Bloomsbury Academic, 2025), 80, 83 and 85–6.
23 Quoted in Purcell and Courage, *Reflections on British Royalty*, 90.
24 A2C, 'Coronation', Spring 2023, SxMOA2/1/127/3, Papers of the Mass Observation Project (SxMOA2), University of Sussex, Brighton, UK.
25 See Curzon and Purcell, 'Visualizing Coronation', 80, 83 and 85–6.
26 Judy Bates, 'King's Lynn Proclaims Charles as New King Outside Town Hall', *Lynn News*, 12 September 2022, https://www.lynnnews.co.uk/news/town-proclaims-charles-as-new-king-with-three-cheers-9273523/.
27 'Charles Officially Proclaimed King at Saturday Accession Ceremony', *Daily Gleaner*, New Brunswick, 12 September 2022.
28 Andrzej Olechnowicz, 'Introduction', in *The Monarchy and the British Nation: 1780 to the Present*, ed. Andrzej Olechnowicz (Cambridge: Cambridge University Press, 2007), 33.
29 Billig's inspiration for banal nationalism was the ubiquity of American flags he noticed while in the United States.
30 See Curzon and Purcell, 'Visualizing Coronation', 92.
31 Strand on the Green Association, 'Strand on the Green Association Chair's Report (2022)', accessed 8 March 2024, https://www.strandonthegreen.org.uk/news.
32 Ealing Council (@EalingCouncil), 'After Attending a Civic Service Earlier Today', *X.com* (formerly Twitter), 7 May 2023, https://x.com/EalingCouncil/status/1655212202998083587.

33 Benedict Anderson, *Imagined Communities: Reflections on the Origins and Spread of Nationalism* (London: Verso, 1983), 36.
34 David Morgan, 'The Crown and the Crowd: Sublimations of Monarchy in Georgian Satirical Prints', *European Comic Art* 9, no. 1 (Spring 2016): 63.
35 John Plunkett, *Queen Victoria: First Media Monarch* (Oxford: Oxford University Press, 2003), 14.
36 Edward Owens, *The Family Firm: Monarchy, Mass Media and the British Public, 1932–1953* (London: University of London Press, 2019), 373.
37 Plunkett, *Queen Victoria*, 170. For a discussion of this phenomenon, see 166–77.
38 Owens, *The Family Firm*, 93; and Philip Williamson, 'The Monarchy and Public Values, 1910–1953', in *The Monarchy and the British Nation: 1780 to the Present*, ed. Andrzej Olechnowicz (Cambridge: Cambridge University Press, 2007), 245.
39 Jennifer J. Purcell, *Mother of the BBC: Mabel Constanduros and the Development of Popular Entertainment on the BBC, 1925–1957* (New York: Bloomsbury, 2020), 36–40.
40 Richard Cawston quoted in John Pearson, *The Ultimate Family: The Making of the Royal House of Windsor* (London: Bloomsbury Readers, 2016), retrieved from https://www.google.com/books/edition/The_Ultimate_Family/EuacWNk3oTwC?hl=en&gbpv=1.
41 Owens, *The Family Firm*, 383.
42 Rowan Atkinson (as Blackadder) in opening speech of programme at 2:10. 'It's a Royal Knockout', 3 August 2020, *YouTube*, video, 1:19:46, https://youtu.be/kwkv0-QlbZY?feature=shared.
43 Daniel Boorstin, *The Image: A Guide to Pseudo-Events in America* (New York: Vintage, 2012), 57.
44 Malcolm Muggeridge, 'The Royal Soap Opera', *New Statesman*, 1955; reprint 30 May 2012, https://www.newstatesman.com/politics/2012/05/royal-soap-opera.
45 Michael Billig, *Talking of the Royal Family* (London: Taylor and Francis, 1991), 221.
46 Ibid., 33.
47 T3155, 'Coronation', Spring 2023, SxMOA2/1/127/3, Papers of the Mass Observation Project (SxMOA2), University of Sussex, Brighton, UK.
48 See Purcell and Courage, *Reflections on British Royalty*, 259–66.
49 David Giles quoted by Laura Mayall in 'The Prince of Wales versus Clark Gable: Anglophone Celebrity and Citizenship Between the Wars', *Cultural and Social History* 4, no. 4 (2007): 531.
50 Nairn, *The Enchanted Glass*, 34 and 36.
51 Ibid., 43.
52 Will Lloyd, 'The Kate Conspiracy', *The New Statesman*, 12 March 2024, https://www.newstatesman.com/politics/uk-politics/2024/03/princess-kate-middleton-conspiracy.
53 Sharon Carpenter, quoted in Natalie Finn, 'How the Kate Middleton Story Flew So Spectacularly Off the Rails', *E! Online*, 24 March 2024, https://www.eonline.com/news/1397809/how-the-kate-middleton-story-flew-so-spectacularly-off-the-rails.
54 Walter Bagehot, *The English Constitution*, 2nd ed. (1872; reprint, Kitchener, ON: Batoche Books, 1999), 67. Looking at the state of the American Republic in the twenty-first century, especially the irrational emotional support for a convicted felon's run for presidential office, one wonders about the validity of Bagehot's assessment.
55 Nairn, *The Enchanted Glass*, 53.

56 Robert Segal, *Myth: A Very Short Introduction* (Oxford: Oxford University Press, 2004), 4. Segal states that, at base, myth is simply story.
57 Rollo May, *The Cry for Myth* (New York: Delta, 1991).
58 Ibid., 30.
59 Ibid., 45.
60 Ibid.
61 Laurence Coupe, 'Myth without Mystery: The Project of Robert Segal', *Religious Studies Review* 29, no. 1 (2003): 5. Using myth in this manner draws on sociologist Bronislaw Malinowski's theories of myth. See Bronislaw Malinowski, *Myth in Primitive Psychology* (New York: WW Norton, 1926), especially 34–5.
62 Billig, *Talking of the Royal Family*, 30.
63 L7536, 'Current Events in 2022', Autumn 2022, SxMOA2/1/126/3, Papers of the Mass Observation Project (SxMOA2), University of Sussex, Brighton, UK.
64 Nairn, *The Enchanted Glass*, 326.
65 HIS MAJESTY'S DECLARATION OF ABDICATION BILL, HC Deb, 12 December 1936, vol 318, cc2199-221, 2213–14.
66 Thomas Mann, *Joseph and His Brothers*, trans. H.T. Lowe-Porter (New York: Alfred Knopf, 1963), 33.
67 Strong, *Coronation*, 8.
68 Nairn, *The Enchanted Glass*, 73.
69 Cited in John Buchan, *The People's King, George V: A Narrative of Twenty-Five Years* (Boston: Houghton Mifflin, 1935).
70 David Cannadine, 'The Context, Performance and Meaning of Ritual: The British Monarchy and the "Invention of Tradition"', c. 1820–1977, in *The Invention of Tradition*, ed. Eric Hobsbawm and Terence Ranger (Cambridge: Cambridge University Press, 1983), 101–64.
71 @mry4354 comment, 'Lord Chamberlain Breaks Wand of Office and Places It on Queen's Coffin', *The Guardian News Youtube Channel*, 19 September 2022, https://youtu.be/NYTE49oi3xk?si=2Nyl6OlVGFeidRmI.
72 Jessica Warren, 'The King's Coronation Must Not Become a "Dumbed Down Woke-fest Celebration of So-Called Modern Britain" and Instead Remain a "Deeply Religious" Event, Senior Tory MP Says', *The Mail Online*, 17 November 2022, https://advance-lexis-com.library.smcvt.edu/api/document?collection=news&id=urn:contentItem:66WD-RW41-JBNF-W4JN-00000-00&context=1516831.
73 Richard Hardman, 'Is It Time to Abolish the Monarchy? – Recorded Live at the Cambridge Literary Festival', *New Statesman*, podcast audio, 8 May 2023, https://www.newstatesman.com/podcasts/new-statesman-podcast/2023/05/is-it-time-to-abolish-the-monarchy-recorded-live-at-the-cambridge-literary-festival.
74 Anderson, *Imagined Communities*, 24.
75 Walter Benjamin, quoted in Anderson, *Imagined Communities*, 24.
76 For example, 'Le couronnement du monarque britannique, cérémonie unique et grandiose', *Challenges*, 9 September 2022, https://www.challenges.fr/top-news/le-couronnement-du-monarque-britannique-ceremonie-unique-et-grandiose_827343.
77 Cele C. Otnes and Pauline Maclaran, *Royal Fever: The British Monarchy in Consumer Culture* (Oakland, CA: University of California, 2015), 295–6. Otnes and Maclaran argue that the re-branding began in 2013 with *Time* magazine's exclusive interview with Charles, which painted him as an environmentalist, preservationist, husband and father. Camilla's rehabilitation also occurred around this time with a playful

interview about the birthday presents she chooses for Charles. Also see Owens, *The Family Firm*, 387.
78   Sean Coughlan, 'Queen Backs Camilla to be Queen Consort on Jubilee', *BBC.com*, 6 February 2022, https://www.bbc.com/news/uk-60274816.
79   See, for instance, the obituary for Queen Alexandra which uses the terms interchangeably. 'Queen Alexandra', *The Times*, 21 November 1925.
80   'King Charles's Coronation Invitation Confirms Use of Title of "Queen Camilla"', *The Guardian*, 4 April 2023, https://www.theguardian.com/uk-news/2023/apr/04/camilla-to-be-crowned-queen-alongside-king-charles.
81   Sky News, 'King Charles III: A Modern Monarch', *King Charles III: A Modern Monarch*, 15 September 2022, *SkyNews.com*, video, 42:00, https://news.sky.com/video/king-charles-iii-a-modern-monarch-12695737.
82   Kiera O'Brien, 'The Official UK Top 50: King Charles Takes Crown Ahead of Jewell: The Little People, Big Dreams Series Title Focusing on the New Monarch Once Again Topped the Charts, but It Was a Slow Week for Book Sales', *The Bookseller*, no. 6019, 12 May 2023, 26; Gale Literature Resource Center, link.gale.com/apps/doc/A750194834/LitRC?u=vol_b92stm&sid=ebsco&xid=43426925.
83   Maria Isabel Sanchez Vegara, *King Charles* (London: Frances Lincoln Children's Books, 2023).
84   Impromptu interview/overheard conducted on 3 May 2023.
85   Impromptu interview/overheard conducted on 5 May 2023.
86   See Brian Cowan's arguments about early modern celebrity in 'Histories of Celebrity in Post-Revolutionary England', *Historical Social Research* 32 (2019): 83–98, especially 91.
87   Strong, *Coronation*, 364.
88   Ibid., 364; and Nairn, *Enchanted Glass*, 24–5.
89   Strong, *Coronation*, 363 and 365.
90   Ibid., 365.
91   'Monarchy Tracker', *YouGov*, 25–26 April 2023, YouGov_Monarchy_trackers.pdf.
92   Oli Smith, 'Monarchy Faces Breaking Point as Majority Public Support Could Collapse "Within Decade"', *Express Online*, 23 April 2023, https://www.express.co.uk/news/royal/1761538/Monarchy-Royal-Family-Charles-Coronation-polling.
93   For instance, Jon King, 'Labour Party Campaigners Urge Keir Starmer to Back a Referendum on the Monarchy', *The Mail Online*, 22 March 2023, https://www.express.co.uk/news/royal/1749200/labour-party-news-republic-referendum-monarchy; Gordon Rayner, 'Charles Hasn't Inherited People's Deference for the Late Queen; After Protesters Heckled the King This Week, Gordon Rayner Asks if Support for the Royals is Crumbling', *Daily Telegraph*, 15 March 2023, https://www.telegraph.co.uk/news/2023/03/15/republicanism-rise-scotland-driving-force/; and Zac Campbell, 'Who Are the "Not My King" Protesters Who Have Heckled Charles and Camilla? How Many of Them Are There? And What Do They Want?', *The Mail Online*, 6 April 2023, https://www.dailymail.co.uk/news/article-11946413/Who-Not-King-protesters-heckled-Charles-Camilla-want.html.
94   For instance, Alan Jehring, 'Even Most Republicans See No Benefit in Abolishing the Monarchy', *Mail on Sunday*, 2 May 2023.
95   r/AbolishTheMonarchy, *Reddit*, accessed 14 April 2024, https://www.reddit.com/r/AbolishTheMonarchy/.
96   r/Britain, *Reddit*, accessed 15 April 2024, https://www.reddit.com/r/Britain/.
97   r/RoyalFamily, *Reddit*, accessed 15 April 2024, https://www.reddit.com/r/royalfamily/. 'Sealioning is a type of trolling or harassment which consists of pursuing people with

persistent requests for evidence or repeated questions, while maintaining a pretense of civility. It may take the form of "incessant, bad-faith invitations to engage in debate." See r/Sealioning, *Reddit*, accessed 15 April 2024, https://www.reddit.com/r/Sealioning/.
98   r/monarchism, *Reddit*, accessed 15 April 2024, https://www.reddit.com/r/monarchism/.
99   cath_monarchist, 'A Question for Brazilian Monarchists', r/monarchism, *Reddit*, accessed 15 April 2024, https://www.reddit.com/r/monarchism/comments/1c3eraz/a_question_for_brazilian_monarchists/.
100 All follower data as of 19 September 2024.
101 See William Makis MD (@MakisMD), '@KensingtonRoyal If you had COVID-19 mRNA Vaccines, this would most likely be mRNA Induced Turbo Cancer. Please seek out competent doctors (outside of the UK medical establishment) who understand the phenomenon of mRNA induced Immune system damage and Turbo Cancer . . .', *X.com* (formerly Twitter), 22 March 2024, https://x.com/MakisMD/status/1771245440979124464.
102 Asa Briggs and Peter Burke, with Espen Ytreberg, *A Social History of the Media: From Gutenberg to Facebook*, 4th ed. (Cambridge: Polity Press, 2020), 321.
103 'Press release: British Social Attitudes to the Monarchy', *National Centre for Social Research*, 9 September 2022, https://natcen.ac.uk/news/british-social-attitudes-monarchy.
104 'Is the monarchy good or bad for Britain?', *YouGov*, accessed 17 April 2024, https://yougov.co.uk/topics/politics/trackers/is-the-monarchy-good-or-bad-for-britain.
105 'IPSOS: Attitudes to the Royal Family', *Ipsos.com*, September 2023, https://www.ipsos.com/sites/default/files/ct/news/documents/2023-10/Ipsos%20Sep%202023%20Political%20Monitor%20Charts_Royals_PUBLIC.pdf.
106 S7592, 'Coronation', Spring 2023, SxMOA2/1/127/3, Papers of the Mass Observation Project (SxMOA2), University of Sussex, Brighton, UK.
107 'Do You Think There Should or Should Not Be a Referendum on Whether or Not Britain Should Continue to Have a Monarchy?', *YouGov*, 4 May 2023, https://yougov.co.uk/topics/politics/survey-results/daily/2023/05/04/60f27/3.
108 Andrzej Olechnowicz, 'A Jealous Hatred: Royal Popularity and Social Inequality', in *The Monarchy and the British Nation, 1780 to the present*, ed. Andrzej Olechnowicz (Cambridge: Cambridge University Press, 2007), 300.
109 B7712, 'Coronation', Spring 2023, SxMOA2/1/127/3, Papers of the Mass Observation Project (SxMOA2), University of Sussex, Brighton, UK.
110 K7522, 'Coronation', Spring 2023, SxMOA2/1/127/3, Papers of the Mass Observation Project (SxMOA2), University of Sussex, Brighton, UK.
111 H6675, 'Coronation', Spring 2023, SxMOA2/1/127/3, Papers of the Mass Observation Project (SxMOA2), University of Sussex, Brighton, UK.
112 M4859, 'Coronation', Spring 2023, SxMOA2/1/127/3, Papers of the Mass Observation Project (SxMOA2), University of Sussex, Brighton, UK.
113 F32, 'Coronation', Spring 2023, SxMOA2/1/127/3, Papers of the Mass Observation Project (SxMOA2), University of Sussex, Brighton, UK.
114 Ibid.
115 Ibid.
116 Purcell and Courage, *Reflections on British Royalty*, 4–5; Olechnowicz, 'A Jealous Hatred', 292.
117 Dylan Difford, 'How Do Britons Feel about the Royals after Two Years of King Charles?', *YouGov*, 30 August 2024, https://yougov.co.uk/politics/articles/50427-how-do-britons-feel-about-the-royals-after-two-years-of-king-charles.

118 Ibid.
119 See YouGov's poll, 'Did You Attend a Coronation Celebration of Some Kind This Weekend?', where 79 per cent answered 'no'. 'Did You Attend a Coronation Celebration of Some Kind This Weekend', *YouGov*, 9 May 2023, https://yougov.co.uk/topics/politics/survey-results/daily/2023/05/09/162ef/3.
120 Jake Kanter, '"Bridgerton" Star Adjoa Andoh's Criticism of "Terribly White" Royal Family Escapes Probe After Becoming Most Complained About TV Moment of 2023', *Deadline*, 5 June 2023, https://deadline.com/2023/06/itv-adjoa-andoh-terribly-white-royal-family-ofcom-investigation-complaints-1235408511/.
121 Isobel Lewis, 'Queen Charlotte's Adjoa Andoh: "I'm Vibrant, Sexual, Have Appetite – Why Would My Stories Not Be Interesting?"', *The Independent*, 4 May 2023, https://www.independent.co.uk/arts-entertainment/tv/features/adjoa-andoh-interview-queen-charlotte-bridgerton-b2331619.html.
122 Greg Morrison, 'Making Sense of History: Adjoa Andoh on Richard II', shakespearesglobe.com, 12 September 2019, https://www.shakespearesglobe.com/discover/blogs-and-features/2019/09/12/making-sense-of-history/.
123 PA Media, 'Ofcom Will Not Take Action Against ITV over "Terribly White" Remark at Coronation', *The Guardian*, 5 June 2023, https://www.theguardian.com/media/2023/jun/05/ofcom-drops-action-against-itv-for-terribly-white-remark-at-coronation.
124 Ernst Renan, 'What Is a Nation?' quoted in Norman Davies, *Europe: A History* (New York: Harper Perennial, 1998), 813. See also Ernst Renan, *What Is a Nation? And Other Political Writings*, trans. and ed. MFN Giglioli (New York: Columbia University Press, 2018), chapter 9.
125 Davies, *Europe: A History*, 835.
126 Robin Wall Kimmerer, *Braiding Sweetgrass: Indigenous Wisdom, Scientific Knowledge and the Teachings of Plants* (Minneapolis: Milkweed Editions, 2013), x.

Chapter 2

1 Lucy D. Curzon, *Mass-Observation and Visual Culture: Depicting Everyday Lives in Britain* (London: Routledge, 2017), 146. Ian Walker refers to Jennings' photomontage as a manifestation of the 'tactics of looking away from the main event of the day'. See Ian Walker, *So Exotic, So Homemade: Surrealism, Englishness and Documentary Photography* (Manchester: Manchester University Press, 2007), 103.
2 Jennings's image of 12 May 1937 was not published until after his death. Likely, it first appeared in print in a 1982 volume edited by Jennings's daughter, Marie-Louise. See Mary-Lou Jennings, ed., *Humphrey Jennings: Film-maker/Painter/Poet* (London: BFI, 1982), 16.
3 Stuart Hall, 'The social eye of *Picture Post*', *Working Papers in Cultural Studies* 2 (1972): 83.
4 Tom Harrisson did create photo-essays for *The Geographical Magazine* and *Picture Post*, however. But it was not until the publication of *Britain Revisited* in 1961 that images were used in an MO publication. These include photographs taken in Bolton by Humphrey Spender and Michael Wickham, and reproductions of drawings and collages by Julian Trevelyan. See Lucy D. Curzon, 'Another Place in Time: Documenting Blackpool for Mass Observation in the 1930s', *History of Photography* 25, no. 3 (2011): 313–26; Lucy D. Curzon, *Visual Culture and Mass-Observation:*

Depicting Everyday Lives in Britain (London: Routledge, 2017), 18–49; and Annebella Pollen, 'Subjective Cameras and Ekphrastic Writing: The Present and Absent Photograph in Mass Observation', in *The Historical Contexts and Contemporary Uses of Mass Observation: 1930s to the Present*, ed. Lucy D. Curzon and Benjamin Jones (London: Bloomsbury Academic, 2025), 107–27.

5   Deborah Frizzell, *Humphrey Spender's Humanist Landscapes: Photo-documents, 1932–42* (New Haven, CT: Yale Centre for British Art/Yale University Press, 1997), 29; and Jeremy Mulford and Humphrey Spender, 'Interview', in *Worktown People: Photographs from Northern England, 1937/38*, ed. Jeremy Mulford (Bristol: Falling Wall Press, 1983), 21.

6   But more than twenty years later (for *Britain Revisited*), it was possible to publish images without fear of MO's operations being compromised. Tom Harrisson, 'Looking at Thirties Life: The Eye and the Camera', SxMOA32/11/7/5, Mass Observation Archive (SxMOA), University of Sussex, Brighton, UK.

7   Curzon, *Mass-Observation and Visual Culture*, 37–45.

8   Roland Barthes, *Camera Lucida: Reflections on Photography*, trans. Richard Howard (New York: Hill and Wang, 1981); Annette Kuhn, *Family Secrets: Acts of Memory and Imagination* (London: Verso, 2002); and John Tagg, *The Burden of Representation: Essays on Photographies and Histories* (Minneapolis: University of Minnesota Press, 1993).

9   Roland Barthes, 'The Photographic Message', in *A Barthes Reader*, ed. Susan Sontag (New York: Hill and Wang, 1982), 196.

10 John Tagg, *The Disciplinary Frame: Photographic Truths and the Capture of Meaning* (Minneapolis: University of Minnesota Press, 2009), xix.

11 Ibid., xxxvii.

Chapter 3

1   Annebella Pollen, 'Research Methodology in Mass Observation Past and Present: "Scientifically, about as Valuable as a Chimpanzee's Tea Party at the Zoo"?', *History Workshop Journal* 75 (2013): 213.

2   Dorothy Sheridan, Brian Street, and David Bloome, *Writing Ourselves: Mass-Observation and Literacy Practices* (Cresskill, NJ: Hampton Press Inc., 2000), 79.

3   Pollen, 'Research Methodology in Mass Observation Past and Present', 214.

4   Cited in ibid.

5   Ibid.

6   Mark Abrams, *Social Surveys and Social Action* (London: Heinemann, 1951), 112.

7   For more information see Lucy D. Curzon and Benjamin Jones, 'Historical Contexts or Contemporary Uses? Mass Observation and the Politics of Continuity', in *The Historical Contexts and Contemporary Uses of Mass-Observation: 1930s to the Present*, ed. Lucy D. Curzon and Benjamin Jones (London: Bloomsbury Academic, 2024), 1–24.

8   Paul Addison, 'Angus Calder (1942–2008)', *History Workshop Journal* 70 (October 2010): 300.

9   Addison adds, 'At that distant date ninety-five percent of the literature that we now have on the history of twentieth-century Britain did not exist'. Ibid.

10 Ibid.

11 In the preface to the second edition (1971) of *The People's War*, Calder responded to criticisms with his statement that the 'biasses and shortcomings [of the Observers] are so evident that it should be easy to allow for them. I stick to my idea that they are probably the richest source of material available to the social historian of the period'. See Angus Calder, *The People's War*, 2nd ed. (London: Panther, 1971), 2.

12 Dorothy Sheridan, 'Reviewing Mass-Observation: The Archive and Its Researchers Thirty Years on', *FQS Forum: Qualitative Social Research* 1, no. 3 (December 2000), paragraph 3.

13 Dorothy Sheridan offers a more comprehensive list of publications that followed Calder's and Addison's and adds that for 'every book, there have been five to ten articles, theses, research papers, TV or radio programmes and student essays and subjects on a wide range of themes'. Sheridan, 'Reviewing Mass-Observation', footnote 1 and paragraph 4.

14 MOP was first called 'The Inflation Project', then 'MO in the 1980s', and then 'MO in the 1980s and 1990s'. The name 'Mass Observation Project' was used formally after 2000. See 'Description of the 1980s Mass Observation Directives', *Mass Observation – Observing the 80s*, accessed 25 June 2024, https://blogs.sussex.ac.uk/observingthe80s/files/2014/01/DS_Directive_Summary_29_Feb1.pdf.

15 In the wake of Tom Harrisson's death, Ziegler – a biographer and historian – recruited a small panel of Mass Observers (with the help of Dorothy Sheridan) to chart popular reactions to Elizabeth II's Jubilee in 1977. Some of the data he collected was used in his 1978 publication, *The Crown and the People* (Collins Publishing).

16 Sheridan, Street, and Bloome, *Writing Ourselves*, 47.

17 Ibid., 45.

18 Ibid.

19 Ibid., 46.

20 James Hinton, *Seven Lives from Mass Observation* (Oxford: Oxford University Press, 2016), 1.

21 Ibid.

22 My italics. Susan D. Pennybacker, 'Mass Observation Redux', *History Workshop Journal* 64 (Autumn 2007): 418.

23 Penny Summerfield, *Histories of the Self: Personal Narratives and Historical Practice* (London: Routledge, 2019), 152.

24 Khaleda Brophy-Harmer, '"An Anthropology of Whites"? Race, Diversity and Mass Observation', 21 November 2023, *Youtube*, video, 21:51, https://www.youtube.com/watch?v=M8phA5ktSwI.

25 Michael Rustin cited in Hinton, *Seven Lives from Mass Observation*, 6.

26 See, for example, James Hinton, *Nine Wartime Lives: Mass-Observation and the Making of the Modern Self* (Oxford: Oxford University Press, 2011); Hinton, *Seven Lives from Mass Observation*; Lucy Noakes, *War and the British: Gender and National Identity, 1939–91* (London: Bloomsbury Academic, 1998); and Claire Langhamer, *The English in Love: The Intimate Story of an Emotional Revolution* (Oxford: Oxford University Press, 2013).

27 Hinton, *Seven Lives from Mass Observation*, 6.

28 Jennifer J. Purcell and Dorothy Sheridan, 'Voices from the Archive', in *Mass-Observation: Text, Context and Analysis of the Pioneering Pamphlet and Movement*, ed. Jennifer J. Purcell (London: Bloomsbury Academic, 2023), 124.

29 Rose Lindsey, 'Using Mass Observation as a Source of Qualitative Secondary Data for Interdisciplinary Longitudinal Research on Voluntary Action', in *Researching Voluntary Action: Innovations and Challenges*, ed. Eddy Hogg and Jon Dean (Bristol: Policy Press, 2022), 84–95.
30 Liz Moore and Emma Uprichard, 'The Materiality of Method: The Case of the Mass Observation Archive', *Sociological Research Online* 19, no. 3 (2014): 12.
31 Rachel Hurdley, 'Uncivilizing Sociology: How Mass Observation Can Free the Discipline', in *Mass-Observation: Text, Context and Analysis of the Pioneering Pamphlet and Movement*, ed. Jennifer J. Purcell (London: Bloomsbury Academic, 2023), 92.
32 Key texts in this area include Lucy D. Curzon, *Mass-Observation and Visual Culture: Depicting Everyday Lives in Britain* (London: Routledge, 2017); James Hinton, *The Mass Observers: A History, 1937–1949* (Oxford: Oxford University Press, 2013); Ben Highmore, 'Mass-Observation: A Science of Everyday Life', in *Everyday Life and Cultural Theory* (London: Routledge, 2002), 75–112; Nick Hubble, *Mass-Observation and Everyday Life: Culture, History, Theory* (London: Palgrave, 2006); Tony Kushner, *We Europeans? Mass-Observation, 'Race', and British Identity in Twentieth-Century Britain* (Farnham, Surrey: Ashgate, 2004); and Jeffrey Richards and Dorothy Sheridan, eds., *Mass-Observation at the Movies* (2007; reprint, London: Routledge, 2014).
33 Laura Clancy, 'Queen's Day – TV's Day: The British Monarchy and the Media Industries', *Contemporary British History* 22, no. 3 (2019): 427–50; Hubble, *Mass-Observation and Everyday Life*; Ben Jones, *The Working Class in Mid-Twentieth Century England: Community, Identity and Social Memory* (Manchester: Manchester University Press, 2012); Anne-Marie Kramer, 'Kinship, Affinity and Connectedness: Exploring the Role of Genealogy in Personal Lives', *Sociology* 45, no. 3 (2011): 379–95; Langhamer, *The English in Love*; Ross McKibbin, 'Mass-Observation in the Mall', *London Review of Books* 19, no. 2 (2 October 1997), https://www.lrb.co.uk/the-paper/v19/n19/ross-mckibbin/mass-observation-in-the-mall; James Thomas, 'From People Power to Mass Hysteria: Media and Popular Reactions to the Death of Princess Diana', *International Journal of Cultural Studies* 11, no. 3 (2008): 362–76; and Ina Zweiniger-Bargeilowska, 'Royal Death and Living Memorials: The Funerals and Commemoration of George V and George VI, 1936–1952', *Historical Research* 89, no. 243 (February 2016): 158–75.
34 Lucy Robinson quoted in 'How Have Our Views on Royalty Evolved since the 1980s'?, *BBC Radio 4 News Today*, last revised 30 May 2012, http://news.bbc.co.uk/today/hi/today/newsid_9724000/9724892.stm.
35 Jennifer J. Purcell and Fiona Courage's edited collection, *Reflections on British Royalty: Mass Observation and the Monarchy, 1937–2022* (2024), is the only sustained study on Mass Observation and the British Royal Family. Other scholars, however, have used Mass Observation materials to examine the Royal Family as a historical phenomenon. See Michael Billig, *Talking of the Royal Family* (London: Routledge, 1991); Laura Clancy, *Running the Family Firm: How the Monarchy Manages Its Image and Our Money* (Manchester: Manchester University Press, 2021); and Edward Owens, *The Family Firm: Monarchy and the British Public, 1932–53* (London: University of London Press, 2019).
36 McKibbin, 'Mass-Observation in the Mall', np.
37 Ibid.
38 Clancy, *Running the Family Firm*, 3–4.

39 Matthew Glencross, Judith Rowbotham, and Michael D. Kandiah, 'Introduction', in *The Windsor Dynasty 1910 to the Present: 'Long to Reign Over Us'?*, ed. Mathew Glencross, Judith Rowbotham, and Michael D. Kandiah (London: Palgrave Macmillan, 2016), 1.
40 Ibid.2.
41 Andrzej Olechnowicz, 'The Monarchy', in *The Oxford Handbook of Modern British Political History, 1800–2000*, ed. David Brown, Robert Crowcroft, and Gordon Pentland (Oxford: Oxford University Press, 2018), 205.
42 Jennifer J. Purcell, 'Tales We Tell Ourselves: The Endurance of British Monarchy in the 21st Century', in *Mass Observing the Coronation of Charles III: Monarchy, Spectable and Experience*, ed. Jennifer J. Purcell and Lucy Curzon with Fiona Courage (London: Bloomsbury Academic, 2025), 38–9, and 46.
43 Edward Shils and Michael Young, 'The Meaning of the Coronation', *The Sociological Review* 1, no. 2 (1953): 80.
44 Andrzej Olechnowicz, 'Historians and the Modern British Monarchy', in *The Monarchy and the British Nation: 1780 to the Present*, ed. Andrzej Olechnowicz (Cambridge: Cambridge University Press, 2007), 9.
45 Media coverage of the marriage of Hugh Grosvenor, 7th Duke of Westminster, to Olivia Henson in Chester Cathedral on 7 June 2024 is a case in point. It focused on Grosvenor's close relationship to the Prince of Wales and the Duke of Sussex (given that William played the role of usher, and Harry ostensibly turned down his invitation in order not to detract attention from Grosvenor and Henson). Few stories paid more than passing attention to the fact that the Duke of Westminster is the wealthiest person under forty in the UK (with £12.8 billion in assets) who owns more than 50 per cent of London's Mayfair and a huge portion of Belgravia. See Janine Henni, 'Britain's Most Eligible Bachelor, the Duke of Westminster, Is Getting Married – and It's Like a Modern Bridgerton', *People.com*, 4 June 2024. https://people.com/duke-of-westminster-wedding-modern-day-bridgerton-inside-royal-ties-8657936.
46 Clancy, *Running the Family Firm*, 7 and 9–11.
47 Purcell, 'Tales We Tell Ourselves: The Endurance of British Monarchy in the 21st Century', 40.
48 Cited in Jennifer J. Purcell and Fiona Courage, eds., *Reflections on British Royalty: Mass-Observation and the Monarchy 1937–2022* (Bloomsbury Academic: London, 2024), 146.
49 Ibid., 196.
50 M3055, 'Coronation', Spring 2023, SxMOA2/1/127/3, Papers of the Mass Observation Project (SxMOA2), University of Sussex, Brighton, UK.
51 Purcell, 'Tales We Tell Ourselves: The Endurance of British Monarchy in the 21st Century', 35–9.
52 Laura Clancy and Hannah Yelin, 'Monarchy Is a Feminist Issue: Andrew, Meghan and #MeToo Era Monarchy', *Women's Studies International Forum* 84 (2021): 1.
53 See Michael Billig, 'Identifying with "Them"', in *Talking of the Royal Family* (1992; reprint, London: Routledge, 1998), 86–115.
54 Ed Owens, *After Elizabeth: Can the Monarchy Save Itself?* (London: Bloomsbury, 2023), 10.
55 D6950, 'Coronation', Spring 2023, SxMOA2/1/127/3, Papers of the Mass Observation Project (SxMOA2), University of Sussex, Brighton, UK.
56 Walter Bagehot cited in Owens, *After Elizabeth*, 31.

57 The sources on this topic are many and varied. For examples, see Laura Clancy, '"Queen of Scots": The Monarch's Body and National Identities in the 2014 Scottish Independence Referendum', *European Journal of Cultural Studies* 23, no. 3 (2023): 495–512; J.S. Ellis, *Investiture: Royal Ceremony and National Identity in Wales, 1911–1969* (Cardiff: University of Wales Press, 2008); David McCrone, 'Unmasking Britannia: The Rise and Fall of British National Identity', *Nations and Nationalism* 3, no. 4 (December 1997): 579–96; Tom Nairn, *The Break-Up of Britain: Crisis and Neo-Nationalism* (1977; reprint, London: Verso, 1981); and *The Enchanted Glass*; and Olechnowicz, *The Monarchy and the British Nation: 1780 to the Present*.

58 Penny Summerfield, *Histories of the Self: Personal Narratives and Historical Practice* (London: Routledge, 2019), 6.

59 Ibid., 7.

60 Carolyn K. Steedman's book, *Landscape for a Good Woman*, is one of the most influential 'autobiographical' volumes in terms of recent approaches to modern British history. See Carolyn K. Steedman, *Landscape for a Good Woman: A Story of Two Lives* (New Brunswick, NJ: Rutgers University Press, 1987). See also Annette Kuhn, *Family Secrets: Acts of Memory and Imagination* (1995; reprint, London: Verso, 2002); Allison Light, *Common People: In Pursuit of My Ancestors* (Chicago, IL: University of Chicago Press, 2014); and Janet Wolff, *Austerity Baby* (Manchester: Manchester University Press, 2017).

61 Jason Arday, 'Dismantling Power and Privilege through Reflexivity: Negotiating Normative Whiteness, the Eurocentric Curriculum, and Racial Micro-Aggressions within the Academy', *Whiteness & Education* 3, no. 2 (2028): 141–61; Benjamin Blaisdell, Syntia Santos Dietz, and Christy Howard, 'The Secret Hurt: Exposing the Visceral Nature of Whiteness in the Academy', *Educational Studies* 58, no. 4 (2022): 474–94; Azeezat Johnson, 'An Academic Witness: White Supremacy Within and Beyond Academia', in *The Fire Now: Anti-Racist Scholarship in Times of Explicit Racial Violence*, ed. Azeezat Johnson, Remi Joseph-Salisbury, and Beth Kamunge (London: Zed Books, 2018), 15–25; and Leslie C. Sotomayor, 'Who's Curating?: Situating Autohistorias-Teorías in the Archives', *Artizein: Arts and Teaching Journal* 5, no. 1 (2020): 129–40.

62 Hinton, *Nine Wartime Lives*, 4.

63 Emma Casey, Fiona Courage, and Nick Hubble, 'Special Section Introduction: Mass Observation as Method', *Sociological Research Online* 19, no. 3 (2014): 17.

64 For example, panellists 'speak back' to the Directive authors, suggesting how boring or how interesting they found the Directive; how well (or how poorly) the Directive maps to their own experiences; or their need to 're-write' the Directive altogether and respond in a way that makes sense to them. Perhaps most importantly, however, they often address their awareness of the fact that they speak from specific contexts and thus the information they provide is only ever partial (i.e. they do not assume a universal voice but rather understand – implicitly – that the voices of others are equally formative). Anne-Marie Kramer, 'The Observers and the Observed: The "Dual Vision" of the Mass Observation Project', *Sociological Research Online* 19, no. 3 (2014): 3.1 and 4.3.

65 Also insightful regarding panellists' engagement with the archive in a self-reflexive way is Lucy Robinson's 'Perforating Even and Narrative, Experience and Analysis: Beyond the Retro Eighties', in *The Historical Contexts and Contemporary Uses of*

Mass-Observation: 1930s to the Present, ed. Lucy D. Curzon and Benjamin Jones (London: Bloomsbury Academic, 2024), 185–213.
66 Hurdley, 'Uncivilizing Sociology', 71–2.
67 Ibid., 74.
68 Robinson, 'Perforating Even and Narrative, Experience and Analysis', 205.
69 'Ofcom Will Not Take Action against ITV over "Terribly White" Remark at Coronation', *The Guardian*, 5 June 2023, https://www.theguardian.com/media/2023/jun/05/ofcom-drops-action-against-itv-for-terribly-white-remark-at-coronation.
70 See Brittney Cooper, *Eloquent Rage: A Black Feminist Discovers Her Superpower* (New York: St. Martin's Press, 2018).

Chapter 4

1 Ross McKibben, *Classes and Cultures: England 1918–1951* (Oxford: Oxford University Press, 1998), 15.
2 See special issue on 'Mass Observation: Poetics and Science', *New Formations*, no. 44 (2001).

Chapter 8

1 *Daily Telegraph*, 12 May 1937, cited in Humphrey Jennings and Charles Madge, *May the Twelfth: Mass-Observation Day-Surveys by over Two Hundred Observers* (London: Faber & Faber, 1937), 81.
2 Jennings and Madge, *May the Twelfth*, 104 and 139.
3 'The Coronation on TV', *The Guardian*, 6 May 2023, https://www.theguardian.com/uk-news/2023/may/06/the-coronation-latest-instalment-of-britains-longest-running-costume-drama-is-a-bit-of-a-damp-squib.
4 Benedict Anderson, *Imagined Communities: Reflections on the Origin and Spread of Nationalism* (London, Verso, 1983).
5 *The Times*, 12 May 1937, cited in Jennings and Madge, *May the Twelfth*, 84.
6 A YouGov poll of 3 May 2023 recorded 62 per cent of those polled supported a monarchy, while 25 per cent wanted an elected Head of State. 'Where Does the Population Stand on the Monarchy Ahead of the Coronation?', *YouGov*, 3 May 2023, https://yougov.co.uk/society/articles/45654-where-does-public-opinion-stand-monarchy-ahead-cor?redirect_from=%2Ftopics%2Fsociety%2Farticles-reports%2F2023%2F05%2F03%2Fwhere-does-public-opinion-stand-monarchy-ahead-cor.
7 Jennings and Madge, *May the Twelfth*, 246.
8 Jennings and Madge, *May the Twelfth*, 221–2.
9 *Edinburgh Evening News*, 5 March 1937, cited in Madge and Jennings, *May the Twelfth*, 35–6.
10 Both cited in Jennings and Madge, *May the Twelfth*, 37 and 41.
11 *Daily Express*, 27 April 1937, cited in Madge and Jennings, *May the Twelfth*, 35.
12 'The Guardian View on Coronation Day: A Mix of Serious and Absurd', *The Guardian*, 7 May 2023, https://www.theguardian.com/commentisfree/2023/may/07/the-guardian-view-on-coronation-day-a-mix-of-serious-and-absurd.

13 Jennings and Madge, *May the Twelfth*, 217.
14 Ibid., 192.
15 'King Charles Axes Royal Tradition to Invite 850 British Heroes to His Coronation', *Daily Mirror*, 8 April 2023, https://www.mirror.co.uk/news/royals/king-charles-axes-royal-tradition-29658846.amp.
16 'Oath of Allegiance Wording Changed for Coronation', *BBC News*, 6 May 2023, https://www.bbc.co.uk/news/uk-65507434.

Chapter 9

1 Annette Kuhn, *Family Secrets: Acts of Memory and Imagination* (1995; reprint, London: Verso, 2002), 70–99.
2 Ibid., 81.
3 Ibid.
4 Ibid., 80.
5 Humphrey Jennings and Charles Madge, eds., *May the Twelfth: Mass Observation Day-Surveys 1937 by over Two Hundred Observers* (1937; reprint, London: Faber and Faber, 2009), 120.
6 Ibid., 274.
7 Ibid., 306.
8 Andrew Marr et al., 'How the Death of the Queen will Change Britain: The New Statesman Podcast', 9 September 2022, *YouTube*, video, 30:90. https://youtu.be/W4xMvBHlfFA?si=7uRsZqRbzIMUk9Cd.
9 See, for example, Kelly Hartog, 'Americans Don't Get What Queen Elizabeth Meant to Brits Like Me. I Wish They Did', *nbcnews.com*, 8 September 2022, https://www.nbcnews.com/think/opinion/queen-elizabeth-ii-die-feels-passing-grandmother-rcna46921.
10 This is, of course, an echo of the title of Joan W. Scott's groundbreaking essay, 'Gender: A Useful Category of Historical Analysis', *The American Historical Review* 91, no. 9 (December 1986): 1053–75.
11 Alison Landsberg, *Prosthetic Memory: The Transformation of American Remembrance in the Age of Mass Culture* (New York: Columbia University Press, 2004).
12 Anne-Marie Kramer, 'Mediatizing Memory: History, Affect and Identity in *Who Do You Think You Are?*', *European Journal of Cultural Studies* 14, no. 4 (2011): 437.
13 Ibid.
14 Ian Johns cited in ibid., 440.
15 Michael Billig, *Talking of the Royal Family* (London: Routledge, 1991), 86–115; and Laura Clancy, *Running the Family Firm: How the Monarchy Manages Its Image and Our Money* (Manchester: Manchester University Press, 2021), 1–22.
16 Kramer, 'Mediatizing Memory', 437.

Chapter 10

1 Michael Young and Edward Shils, 'The Meaning of the Coronation', *Sociological Review* 1 (1953): 63.
2 Andrzj Olechnowicz, 'Britain's "Quasi-Magical" Monarchy in the Mid-Twentieth Century?', in *Classes, Culture, and Politics: Essays on British History for Ross McKibbin*,

ed. Clare V.J. Griffiths, James J. Nott, and William Whyte (Oxford: Oxford University Press, 2011), 70, 81–3.
3 Jack London, *The People of the Abyss* (New York: The MacMillan Company, 1903), 140–1, 143–4.
4 Stephen Turner and Edward Kissi, '"The Heart Has Its Reasons": Elizabeth II and the Post-Colonial Response', *Journal of Classical Sociology* 23, no. 1 (2023): 145.
5 Humphrey Jennings and Charles Madge, eds., *May the Twelfth: Mass-Observation Day-Surveys 1937 by over Two Hundred Observers* (London: Faber & Faber, 1937), 59.
6 Fred I. Greenstein et al., 'The Child's Conception of the Queen and the Prime Minister', *British Journal of Political Science* 4, no. 3 (1974): 257–87; and Sir Arthur Bryant, 'The Queen and the Monarchy', in *Silver Jubilee: Queen Elizabeth II, 1952–1977* (London: Elm House, 1977), 11–14.

Chapter 11

1 GESARA Show, '2023-04-19, GESARA Show 114 – Wednesday', 21 April 2023, *Rumble*, video, 2:30:30, https://rumble.com/v2jlec4-2023-04-19-gesara-show-114-wednesday.html. This example is representative of views that are consistent with the sovereign citizenship and QAnon movements and financial schemes tied to far-right conspiracy theories about globalists, magicians and child predators who are supposed to have had their hands in almost every historical event. The monarchy figures prominently in these intertwined narratives.
2 Anna Barry, 'Charles Won't "Rule" – "Biggest Shake-up for the Monarchy in 248 Years" Astrologer Claims', *Express*, 20 January 2023, https://www.express.co.uk/life-style/life/1722950/king-charles-coronation-camilla-astrology-predictions-exclusive; Mared Gruffyd, 'King Charles's Reign "Won't be Long" as Crown "May be Passed onto William" Psychic Claims', *Express*, 25 February 2023, https://www.express.co.uk/life-style/life/1737697/king-charles-reign-coronotion-predictions-psychic-astrology-2023. After Charles III's Coronation, similar predictions continued – for instance: GB News, 'King Charles may ABDICATE after FIVE YEARS Predicts Psychic Sally Morgan', 13 May 2023, *YouTube*, video, 9:01, https://www.youtube.com/watch?v=XJHMcDNrCrs.
3 Amy Walters and Olivia Dunnett, 'Royal "Superfans" Who Predicted Death of Queen and Philip Reveal Danger of Coronation', *Express*, 5 May 2023, https://www.express.co.uk/news/royal/1766550/king-charles-coronation-prediction-danger-dxus.
4 GESARA Show, '2023-05-10, GESARA Talk Show 120 – Wednesday', 12 May 2023, *Rumble*, video, 2:42:26, https://rumble.com/v2ngx3w-2023-05-10-gesara-talk-show-120-wednesday.html.
5 Abigail O'Leary, 'Coronation Guest Accused of Coming in Disguise to Steal Crown Jewels Speaks Out', *Mirror Online*, 10 May 2023, https://www.mirror.co.uk/news/royals/coronation-guest-accused-coming-in-29939925.
6 Jessica Adams, 'How Astrology Shows an Invalid Coronation', *Blog*, 13 June 2023, https://www.jessicaadams.com/2023/06/13/blog/how-astrology-shows-an-invalid-coronation/#:~:text=When%20Mercury%20appears%20to%20go,set%20his%20coronation%20for%20another.
7 Humphrey Jennings and Charles Madge, eds., *May the Twelfth: Mass Observation Day Surveys 1937 by over Two Hundred Observers* (1937; reprint, London: Faber and Faber, 2009).

8   Ibid., 29.
9   Ibid., 304–5.
10 Mass Observation, *Britain,* arranged and written by Charles Madge and Tom Harrisson (1939; reprint, London: Faber and Faber, 2009), 25–6.
11 Arnold van Gennep, *The Rites of Passage,* trans. Monika B. Vizedom and Gabrielle L. Caffee (1909; reprint, Chicago: University of Chicago Press, 1960).
12 Peter L. Berger, *The Sacred Canopy: Elements of a Sociological Theory of Religion* (1967; reprint, New York: Anchor Books, 1990).
13 Jennings and Madge, *May the Twelfth,* 3.

Chapter 12

1   Andre Rhoden-Paul, 'King Charles III's Coronation Watched by More Than 18 Million Viewers', *BBC News,* 7 May 2023, https://www.bbc.co.uk/news/uk-65518360.
2   Tom Morton, 'Coronation: 12 Pictures of Portsmouth Area Schools Marking the Event', *The News,* 6 May 2023, https://www.portsmouth.co.uk/education/-4133264.
3   For examples, please see, 'Coronation Issue', *Radio Times Magazine,* 6 May 2023.
4   Kirk W. Fuoss, 'Lynching Performances, Theatres of Violence', *Text and Performance Quarterly* 19, no. 1 (1999): 1–37.
5   Kirsten McStay, 'ITV This Morning Viewers "Turn Off" Minutes into Show Following Same Complaint', *Daily Record,* 3 May 2023, https://www.dailyrecord.co.uk/entertainment/celebrity/itv-morning-viewers-turn-off-29876445.
6   James Connolly, 'On the Visit of King George V to Dublin' (1910), transcribed by *The James Connolly Society* in 1997, *Marxists Internet Library,* accessed 6 May 2024, https://www.marxists.org/archive/connolly/1911/xx/visitkng.htm.
7   Ibid.
8   Ibid.
9   Georgie Wemyss, *The Invisible Empire: White Discourse, Tolerance and Belonging* (Oxfordshire: Routledge, 2009), 4–6, 12–16.
10 Robin DiAngelo, *White Fragility: Why It's So Hard for White People to Talk About Racism* (Boston: Beacon Press, 2018), 112.
11 Wemyss, *The Invisible Empire,* 12, 4–28, 128–33.
12 Ibid., 6; and Michel-Rolph Trouillot, *Silencing the Past: Power and the Production of History* (Boston, MA: Beacon, 1995), 27.
13 DiAngelo, *White Fragility,* 2.
14 Ibid.; and Nels Abbey, 'Brilliant Floella Benjamin and a Not-Very-Gospel Coronation Choir. Is This as "Diverse" as Britain Gets?', *The Guardian,* 7 May 2023, https://www.theguardian.com/commentisfree/2023/may/07/floella-benjamin-gospel-coronation-choir-diverse-britain-equality.
15 Wendy Brown, *Regulating Aversion: Tolerance in the Age of Identity and Empire* (Princeton, NJ: Princeton University Press, 2008), 25–47; Ghassan Hage, *White Nation: Fantasies of White Supremacy in a Multicultural Society* (London and New York: Routledge 2000), 85–101; and Wemyss, *The Invisible Empire,* 132–3.
16 Nicole Vassell, 'Bridgerton Star Adjoa Andoh Explains Her "Terribly White" Coronation Balcony Remark', *The Independent,* 10 May 2023, https://www

.independent.co.uk/arts-entertainment/tv/news/bridgerton-adjoa-andoh-terribly-white-coronation-b2336017.html.
17 PA Media, 'Ofcom Will Not Take Action against ITV over "Terribly White" Remark at Coronation', *The Guardian*, 10 May 2023, https://www.theguardian.com/media/2023/jun/05/ofcom-drops-action-against-itv-for-terribly-white-remark-at-coronation?CMP=share_btn_url.
18 Ben Chapman, 'Meghan Markle "Will be Delighted" as Woke Comment Sparks Race Row, Claims ex-MP', *GB News*, 11 May 2023, https://www.gbnews.com/royal/meghan-markle-adjoa-anodh-royal-latest-royal-race; Talk TV, '"It's Not Illegal to Be WHITE!" Piers Morgan Defends Royal Family's "White Balcony"', 9 May 2023, *Youtube*, video, 7:21, https://www.youtube.com/watch?v=EDXuXA7gIDc; and Cady Lang, 'The Core Message of Meghan and Harry's Oprah Interview: Racism Drove Us from the Royal Family', *Time*, 8 March 2021, https://time.com/5944613/meghan-markle-oprah-racism.
19 Vassell, 'Bridgerton Star Adjoa Andoh Explains Her "Terribly White" Coronation Balcony Remark'.
20 Ellie Lorizzo, 'Adjoa Andoh's Coronation Remark Is Most Complained About Moment of 2023 – Ofcom', *The Independent*, 10 May 2023, https://www.independent.co.uk/news/uk/adjoa-andoh-ofcom-charles-iii-buckingham-palace-bridgerton-b2336294.html.
21 DiAngelo, *White Fragility*, 2.
22 Barbara Rosenwein, 'Worrying About Emotions in History', *The American Historical Review* 107, no. 3 (2002): 821–45, 839.
23 Please see Gillian Brockell, 'The Koh-I-Noor and Cullinan Diamonds: British Crown Jewels Have Fraught History', *The Washington Post*, 5 May 2023, https://www.washingtonpost.com/history/2023/05/05/crown-jewels-coronation-cullinan-diamonds/; and Boris Gorelik, 'The Cullinan Diamond and Its True Story', *Jewellery Studies: the Journal of The Society of Jewellery Historians* 23 (Spring 2015): 3–11.
24 Alana Lentin, *Why Race Still Matters* (Cambridge: Polity Press, 2020), 52; GB News, '"Terribly White"?! What an Appalling Thing to Say!' Laurence Fox on Rampant Identity Politics', 12 May 2023, *Youtube*, video, 3:08, https://www.youtube.com/watch?v=0PEnu7-sTi4; TalkTV, '"Am I Too White?" Kevin O'Sullivan Seethes as Royal Family Described as "Terribly White"', 11 May 2023, *Youtube*, video, 2:43, https://www.youtube.com/watch?v=EDXuXA7gIDc; and Talk TV, '"It's Not Illegal to Be WHITE!" Piers Morgan Defends Royal Family's "White Balcony"'.
25 Lentin, *Why Race Still Matters*, 52–92.
26 Cedric J. Robinson, *Forgeries of Memory and Meaning: Blacks and Regimes of Race in American Theatre and Film before World War II* (Chapel Hill: University of North Carolina Press, 2012), 7.
27 Ibid., xii.
28 Stuart Hall, 'Race, the Floating Signifier (Transcript)', *The Education Foundation* (1997): 2, 6.
29 Ibid., 8; and Robinson, *Forgeries of Memory and Meaning*, xii–xiii.
30 Rosenwein, 'Worrying About Emotions in History', 842–5.
31 Sara Ahmed, *The Cultural Politics of Emotion* (Edinburgh: Edinburgh University Press, 2014), 194, 1–12.
32 Charles Madge and Tom Harrisson, *Mass-Observation* (London: Muller, 1937), 30.
33 Nick Clarke, ed., *Everyday Life in the Covid-19 Pandemic: Mass-Observation's 12th May Diaries* (London: Bloomsbury Academic, 2024), 257–82.

Chapter 13

1. Ellie Iorizzo, 'Star-studded Coronation Concert Viewing Figures Revealed', *The Independent*, 8 May 2023, https://www.independent.co.uk/arts-entertainment/tv/news/coronation-concert-tv-audience-viewing-figures-b2334831.html; and Laura Parkin, 'He Stole the Show', *The Mail Online*, 7 May 2023, Nexis Uni, https://advance-lexis-com.libdata.lib.ua.edu/api/document?collection=news&id=urn%3acontentItem%3a6862-2G41-JBNF-W27W-00000-00&context=1519360&identityprofileid=S8R4K355325.
2. Roisin O'Connor, 'Coronation Concert Review', *The Independent*, 7 May 2023, Nexis Uni, https://advance-lexis-com.libdata.lib.ua.edu/api/document?collection=news&id=urn%3acontentItem%3a685Y-76R1-JBNF-W105-00000-00&context=1519360&identityprofileid=S8R4K355325; Alexis Petridis, 'Coronation Concert Review', *The Guardian*, 7 May 2023, Nexis Uni, https://advance-lexis-com.libdata.lib.ua.edu/api/document?collection=news&id=urn%3acontentItem%3a6862-2JH1-DY4H-K28D-00000-00&context=1519360&identityprofileid=S8R4K355325; Ludovic Hunter-Tilney, 'Coronation Concert Review', *Financial Times*, 8 May 2023, Nexis Uni, https://advance-lexis-com.libdata.lib.ua.edu/api/document?collection=news&id=urn%3acontentItem%3a6863-46N1-F039-602J-00000-00&context=1519360&identityprofileid=S8R4K355325; and '"The Coronation Concert" Was a Sorry Sales Pitch for a Brand New King', *Variety*, 8 May 2023, Nexis Uni, https://advance-lexis-com.libdata.lib.ua.edu/api/document?collection=news&id=urn%3acontentItem%3a6861-X6T1-JB0P-B3SM-00000-00&context=1519360&identityprofileid=S8R4K355325.https://advance-lexis-com.libdata.lib.ua.edu/api/document?collection=news&id=urn%3acontentItem%3a685Y-76R1-JBNF-W105-00000-00&context=1519360&identityprofileid=S8R4K355325.
3. Will Hodgkinson, 'The Coronation Concert Review', *The Times*, 8 May 2023, Nexis Uni, https://advance-lexis-com.libdata.lib.ua.edu/api/document?collection=news&id=urn%3acontentItem%3a6861-DTB1-JBNF-W1R4-00000-00&context=1519360&identityprofileid=S8R4K355325.
4. BBC Studios, 'The Coronation Concert', BBC Select, BritBox, Apple TV, 2023.
5. Heather Wiebe, '"Now and England": Britten's "Gloriana" and the New Elizabethans', *Cambridge Opera Journal* 17, no. 2 (2005): 141–72.
6. Matthias Range, *Music and Ceremonial at British Coronations: From James I to Elizabeth II* (New York: Cambridge University Press, 2012), 21.
7. Caitlin Moran, 'Caitlin Moran's Celebrity Watch', *The Times*, 3 March 2023, Lexis Uni, https://advance-lexis-com.libdata.lib.ua.edu/api/document?collection=news&id=urn%3acontentItem%3a67P0-B6Y1-DYTY-C2J8-00000-00&context=1519360&identityprofileid=S8R4K355325; and Daniel Bird and Sam Elliott-Gibbs, 'A-List Celebrities Who Said NO to King Charles' Coronation Concert', *Mirror*, 6 March 2023, Lexis Uni, https://advance-lexis-com.libdata.lib.ua.edu/api/document?collection=news&id=urn%3acontentItem%3a67PP-1G31-JBNF-W3FH-00000-00&context=1519360&identityprofileid=S8R4K355325.
8. Hunter-Tilney, 'Coronation Concert Review'.
9. Victoria Ward, 'King Charles Puts Refugees and NHS at Heart of Diverse Coronation', *Telegraph*, 21 January 2023, Nexis Uni, https://advance-lexis-com.libdata.lib.ua.edu/api/document?collection=news&id=urn%3acontentItem%3a67PP-1G31-JBNF-W3FH-00000-00&context=1519360&identityprofileid=S8R4K355325.

10 Esther Morgan Ellis and Kay Norton, 'Introduction: Singing as Community, Singing into Community, and Growing the Singing Community', in *The Oxford Handbook of Community Singing*, ed. Esther Morgan Ellis and Kay Norton (New York: Oxford University Press, 2024); 'Meghan Markle Urged to Avoid Stealing Limelight from King Charles' Coronation', *Click Mag*, Updated 1 July 2023, https://news.411ug.com/songs/meghan-markle-urged-to-avoid-stealing-limelight-from-king-charles-coronation/music; and Sophia Alexandra Hall, 'What is the Coronation Choir and Who Is Singing in It?', *Classical FM*, 7 May 2023, https://www.classicfm.com/discover-music/king-coronation-choir-who-are-singers/.

11 Angela Epstein, 'PLEASE Don't Go Woke with the Coronation, Charles!', *Express Online*, 26 April 2023, Lexis Uni, https://advance-lexis-com.libdata.lib.ua.edu/api/document?collection=news&id=urn%3acontentItem%3a683J-WPP1-DY4H-K1SB-00000-00&context=1519360&identityprofileid=S8R4K355325.

12 Hall Rachel and Amelia Gentleman, '"Perfect Storm": Royals Misjudged Caribbean Tour, Say Critics', *The Guardian*, 25 March 2022, https://www.theguardian.com/uk-news/2022/mar/25/william-and-kate-caribbean-tour-slavery-reparations-royals; and Evan Dyer, 'The Queen's Death May Cause Many Old Commonwealth Ties to Unravel', *CBC News*, 15 September 2022, https://www.cbc.ca/news/politics/queen-elizabeth-commonwealth-1.6583152.

13 Pelumi Salako, 'Joy, Rebuke for Nigeria's Tiwa Savage over Charles' Coronation', *Al Jazeera*, 5 May 2023, https://www.aljazeera.com/news/2023/5/5/joy-rebuke-for-nigerias-tiwa-savage-over-charles-coronation.

14 Ward, 'King Charles Puts Refugees and NHS at Heart'.

15 Kirsten Grant, 'King Charles Coronation Concert: When Is It and Who Is Performing?', *The Telegraph*, 6 April 2023, Lexis Uni, https://advance-lexis-com.libdata.lib.ua.edu/api/document?collection=news&id=urn%3acontentItem%3a67Y8-56H1-JBNF-W1K8-00000-00&context=1519360&identityprofileid=S8R4K355325.

16 David Scott Diffrient, 'Backup Singers, Celebrity Culture, and Civil Rights: Racializing Space and Spatializing Race in *20 Feet from Stardom*', *Black Camera* 8, no. 2 (2017): 25–49. https://doi.org/10.2979/blackcamera.8.2.02.

17 BBC Studios, 'The Coronation Concert'.

18 Steven Feld, 'A Sweet Lullaby for World Music', in *Globalization*, ed. Arjun Appadurai (Durham, NC: Duke University Press, 2001), 189–216.

19 Trevor R. Nelson, 'Hearing Global Britishness on the BBC's *Commonwealth of Song* (1953–1961)', *Twentieth-Century Music* 19, no. 2 (2022): 311–41.

20 'Our History', *The Commonwealth*, accessed 27 October 2023, https://thecommonwealth.org/history.

SELECTED BIBLIOGRAPHY

Unpublished sources

Papers of the Mass Observation Archive (SxMOA), University of Sussex, Brighton, UK.
Papers of the Mass Observation Project (SxMOA2), University of Sussex, Brighton, UK.

Published sources

Abrams, Mark. *Social Surveys and Social Action*. London: Heinemann, 1951.
Addison, Paul. 'Angus Calder (1942-2008)'. *History Workshop Journal* 70 (October 2010): 299–304.
Ahmed, Sara. *The Cultural Politics of Emotion*. Edinburgh: Edinburgh University Press, 2014.
Anderson, Benedict. *Imagined Communities: Reflections on the Origins and Spread of Nationalism*. London: Verso, 1983.
Arday, Jason. 'Dismantling Power and Privilege through Reflexivity: Negotiating Normative Whiteness, the Eurocentric Curriculum, and Racial Micro-Aggressions within the Academy'. *Whiteness & Education* 3, no. 2 (2028): 141–61.
Barthes, Roland. *Camera Lucida: Reflections on Photography*, translated by Richard Howard. New York: Hill and Wang, 1981.
Barthes, Roland. 'The Photographic Message'. In *A Barthes Reader*, edited by Susan Sontag, 194–210. New York: Hill and Wang, 1982.
Berger, Peter L. *The Sacred Canopy: Elements of a Sociological Theory of Religion*. 1967. Reprint, New York: Anchor Books, 1990.
Billig, Michael. *Talking of the Royal Family*. London: Taylor and Francis, 1991.
Blaisdell, Benjamin, Syntia Santos Dietz, and Christy Howard. 'The Secret Hurt: Exposing the Visceral Nature of Whiteness in the Academy'. *Educational Studies* 58, no. 4 (2022): 474–94.
Boorstin, Daniel. *The Image: A Guide to Pseudo-Events in America*. New York: Vintage, 2012.
Borman, Tracy. *Crown and Sceptre: A New History of the British Monarchy from William the Conqueror to Elizabeth II*. New York: Atlantic Monthly Press, 2021.
Briggs, Asa and Peter Burke, with Espen Ytreberg. *A Social History of the Media: From Gutenberg to Facebook*, 4th ed. Cambridge: Polity Press, 2020.
Brophy-Harmer, Khaleda. '"An Anthropology of Whites"? Race, Diversity and Mass Observation'. *Youtube* video, 21:51, 21 November 2023. https://www.youtube.com/watch?v=M8phA5ktSwI.
Brown, Wendy. *Regulating Aversion: Tolerance in the Age of Identity and Empire*. Princeton, NJ: Princeton University Press, 2008.
Bryant, Arthur. 'The Queen and the Monarchy'. In *Silver Jubilee: Queen Elizabeth II, 1952-1977*. London: Elm House, 1977.

Buchan, John. *The People's King, George V: A Narrative of Twenty-Five Years*. Boston: Houghton Mifflin, 1935.
Calder, Angus. *The People's War*, 2nd ed. London: Panther, 1971.
Cannadine, David. 'The Context, Performance and Meaning of Ritual: The British Monarchy and the "Invention of Tradition", c. 1820-1977'. In *The Invention of Tradition*, edited by Eric Hobsbawm and Terence Ranger, 101–64. Cambridge: Cambridge University Press, 1983.
Casey, Emma, Fiona Courage and Nick Hubble. 'Special Section Introduction: Mass Observation as Method'. *Sociological Research Online* 19, no. 3 (2014): 129–35.
Clancy, Laura. 'Queen's Day—TV's Day: The British Monarchy and the Media Industries'. *Contemporary British History* 22, no. 3 (2019): 427–50.
Clancy, Laura. *Running the Family Firm: How the Monarchy Manages Its Image and Our Money*. Manchester: Manchester University Press, 2021.
Clancy, Laura. '"Queen of Scots": The Monarch's Body and National Identities in the 2014 Scottish Independence Referendum'. *European Journal of Cultural Studies* 23, no. 3 (2023): 495–512.
Clancy, Laura and Hannah Yelin. 'Monarchy is a Feminist Issue: Andrew, Meghan and #MeToo Era Monarchy'. *Women's Studies International Forum* 84 (2021): 102435. https://doi.org/10.1016/j.wsif.2020.102436.
Clarke, Nick, ed. *Everyday Life in the Covid-19 Pandemic: Mass-Observation's 12th May Diaries*. London: Bloomsbury Academic, 2024.
Cooper, Brittney. *Eloquent Rage: A Black Feminist Discovers her Superpower*. New York: St. Martin's Press, 2018.
Coupe, Laurence. 'Myth without Mystery: The Project of Robert Segal'. *Religious Studies Review* 29, no. 1 (2003): 3–17.
Cowan, Brian. 'Histories of Celebrity in Post-Revolutionary England'. *Historical Social Research* 32 (2019): 83–98.
Cressy, David. *Bonfires and Bells: National Memory and the Protestant Calendar in Elizabethan and Stuart England*. Berkeley, CA: University of California Press, 1989.
Curzon, Lucy D. 'Another Place in Time: Documenting Blackpool for Mass Observation in the 1930s'. *History of Photography* 25, no. 3 (2011): 313–26.
Curzon, Lucy D. *Mass-Observation and Visual Culture: Depicting Everyday Lives in Britain*. London: Routledge, 2017.
Curzon, Lucy D. and Benjamin Jones. 'Historical Contexts or Contemporary Uses? Mass Observation and the Politics of Continuity'. In *The Historical Contexts and Contemporary Uses of Mass Observation*, edited by Lucy D. Curzon and Benjamin Jones, 1–24. London: Bloomsbury Academic, 2025.
Davies, Norman. *Europe: A History*. New York: Harper Perennial, 1998.
DiAngelo, Robin. *White Fragility : Why It's So Hard for White People to Talk About Racism*. Boston: Beacon Press, 2018.
Diffrient, David Scott. 'Backup Singers, Celebrity Culture, and Civil Rights: Racializing Space and Spatializing Race in *20 Feet from Stardom*'. *Black Camera* 8, no. 2 (2017): 25–49. https://doi.org/10.2979/blackcamera.8.2.02.
Ellis, J.S. *Investiture: Royal Ceremony and National Identity in Wales, 1911-1969*. Cardiff: University of Wales Press, 2008.
Ellis, Esther Morgan and Kay Norton. 'Introduction: Singing as Community, Singing into Community, and Growing the Singing Community'. In *The Oxford Handbook of Community Singing*, edited by Esther Morgan Ellis and Kay Norton, xxi–xxviii. New York: Oxford University Press, 2024.

Feld, Steven. 'A Sweet Lullaby for World Music'. In *Globalization*, edited by Arjun Appadurai, 189–216. Durham, NC: Duke University Press, 2001.

Frizzell, Deborah. *Humphrey Spender's Humanist Landscapes: Photo-Documents, 1932-42*. New Haven, CT: Yale Centre for British Art/Yale University Press, 1997.

Fuoss, Kirk W. 'Lynching Performances, Theatres of Violence'. *Text and Performance Quarterly* 19, no. 1 (1999): 1–37.

German, Lindsey and John Rees. *A People's History of London*. London: Verso, 2012.

Glencross, Matthew, Judith Rowbotham, and Michael D. Kandiah, 'Introduction'. In *The Windsor Dynasty 1910 to the Present: 'Long to Reign Over Us'?*, edited by Mathew Glencross, Judith Rowbotham, and Michael D. Kandiah. London: Palgrave Macmillan, 2016.

Greenstein, Fred I. et al. 'The Child's Conception of the Queen and the Prime Minister'. *British Journal of Political Science* 4, no. 3 (1974): 257–87.

Hage, Ghassan. *White Nation: Fantasies of White Supremacy in a Multicultural Society*. London and New York: Routledge, 2000.

Hall, Stuart. 'The Social Eye of *Picture Post*'. *Working Papers in Cultural Studies* 2 (1972): 71–120.

Hall, Stuart. 'Race, the Floating Signifier (Transcript)'. *Media Education Foundation* (1997): 359–73.

Harrisson, Tom. *Britain Revisited*. London: Victor Gollancz, 1961.

Highmore, Ben. *Everyday Life and Cultural Theory: An Introduction*. London: Routledge, 2002.

Hinton, James. *Nine Wartime Lives: Mass-Observation and the Making of the Modern Self*. Oxford: Oxford University Press, 2011.

Hinton, James. *The Mass Observers: A History, 1937-1949*. Oxford: Oxford University Press, 2013.

Hinton, James. *Seven Lives from Mass Observation*. Oxford: Oxford University Press, 2016.

Hubble, Nick. *Mass-Observation and Everyday Life: Culture, History, Theory*. London: Palgrave, 2006.

Hurdley, Rachel. 'Uncivilizing Sociology: How Mass Observation Can Free the Discipline'. In *Mass-Observation: Text, Context and Analysis of the Pioneering Pamphlet and Movement*, edited by Jennifer J. Purcell, 69–98. London: Bloomsbury Academic, 2023.

Jennings, Humphrey and Charles Madge, eds. *May the Twelfth: Mass Observation Day-Surveys 1937 by over Two Hundred Observers*. 1937. Reprint, London: Faber and Faber, 2009.

Jennings, Mary-Lou, ed. *Humphrey Jennings: Film-maker/Painter/Poet*. London: BFI, 1982.

Johnson, Azeezat. 'An Academic Witness: White Supremacy Within and Beyond Academia'. In *The Fire Now: Anti-Racist Scholarship in Times of Explicit Racial Violence*, edited by Azeezat Johnson, Remi Joseph-Salisbury, and Beth Kamunge, 15–25. London: Zed Books, 2018.

Jones, Ben. *The Working Class in Mid-twentieth Century England: Community, Identity and Social Memory* Manchester: Manchester University Press, 2012.

Keay, Anna. *The Magnificent Monarch: Charles II and the Ceremonies of Power*. London: Continuum, 2008.

Kimmerer, Robin Wall. *Braiding Sweetgrass: Indigenous Wisdom, Scientific Knowledge and the Teachings of Plants*. Minneapolis, MN: Milkweed Editions, 2015.

Kramer, Anne-Marie. 'Kinship, Affinity and Connectedness: Exploring the Role of Genealogy in Personal Lives'. *Sociology* 45, no. 3 (2011): 379–95.

Kramer, Anne-Marie. 'Mediatizing Memory: History, Affect and Identity in *Who Do You Think You Are?*'. *European Journal of Cultural Studies* 14, no. 4 (2011): 428–45.

Kramer, Anne-Marie. 'The Observers and the Observed: The "Dual Vision" of the Mass Observation Project'. *Sociological Research Online* 19, no. 3 (2014): 226–36.

Kuhn, Annette. *Family Secrets: Acts of Memory and Imagination*. London: Verso, 2002.

Kushner, Tony. *We Europeans? Mass-Observation, 'Race', and British Identity in Twentieth-Century Britain*. Farnham, Surrey: Ashgate, 2004.

Landsburg, Alison. *Prosthetic Memory: The Transformation of American Remembrance in the Age of Mass Culture*. New York: Columbia University Press, 2004.

Langhamer, Claire. *The English in Love: The Intimate Story of an Emotional Revolution*. Oxford: Oxford University Press, 2013.

Lentin, Alana *Why Race Still Matters*. Cambridge: Polity Press, 2020.

Light, Allison. *Common People: In Pursuit of My Ancestors*. Chicago: University of Chicago Press, 2014.

Lindsey, Rose. 'Using Mass Observation as a Source of Qualitative Secondary Data for Interdisciplinary Longitudinal Research on Voluntary Action'. In *Researching Voluntary Action: Innovations and Challenges*, edited by Eddy Hogg and Jon Dean, 84–95. Bristol: Policy Press, 2022.

Malinowski, Bronislaw. *Myth in Primitive Psychology*. New York: WW Norton, 1926.

Mass Observation. *Britain*. Harmondsworth: Penguin, 1939.

May, Rollo. *The Cry for Myth*. New York: Delta, 1991.

Mayall, Laura. 'The Prince of Wales versus Clark Gable: Anglophone Celebrity and Citizenship between the Wars'. *Cultural and Social History* 4, no. 4 (2007): 529–43.

Mayne, Emily. 'Shows of Joy and Malice: Performance, the Star Chamber, and the Celebration of James I's Coronation in Norwich in 1603'. *Early Theatre* 23, no. 20 (December 2020): 169–82.

McCrone, David. 'Unmasking Britannia: The Rise and Fall of British National Identity'. *Nations and Nationalism* 3, no. 4 (December 1997): 579–96.

McKibbin, Ross. 'Mass-Observation in the Mall'. *London Review of Books* 19, no. 2 (2 October 1997). https://www.lrb.co.uk/the-paper/v19/n19/ross-mckibbin/mass-observation-in-the-mall.

Moore, Liz and Emma Uprichard. 'The Materiality of Method: The Case of the Mass Observation Archive'. *Sociological Research Online*, 19, no. 3 (2014): 136–46.

Morgan, David. 'The Crown and the Crowd: Sublimations of Monarchy in Georgian Satirical Prints'. *European Comic Art* 9 no. 1 (Spring 2016): 63–87.

Mortimore, Roger. 'Measuring British Public Opinion on the Monarchy and the Royal Family'. In *The Windsor Dynasty: 1910 to the Present, 'Long to Reign Over Us?'*, edited by Matthew Glencross, Judith Rowbotham and Michael D. Kandiah, 135–6. London: Palgrave Macmillan, 2016.

Muggeridge, Malcolm. 'The Royal Soap Opera'. *New Statesman*. 1955. Reprint, 30 May 2012. https://www.newstatesman.com/politics/2012/05/royal-soap-opera.

Mulford, Jeremy and Humphrey Spender. 'Interview'. In *Worktown People: Photographs from Northern England, 1937/38*, edited by Jeremy Mulford. Bristol: Falling Wall Press, 1983.

Nairn, Tom. *The Break-Up of Britain: Crisis and Neo-Nationalism*. 1977. Reprint, London: Verso, 1981.

Nairn, Tom. *The Enchanted Glass: Britain and Its Monarchy*, 3rd ed. London: Verso, 2011.

Nelson, Trevor R. 'Hearing Global Britishness on the BBC's *Commonwealth of Song* (1953–1961)'. *Twentieth-Century Music* 19, no. 2 (2022): 311–41.

Noakes, Lucy. *War and the British: Gender and National Identity, 1939-91.* London: Bloomsbury Academic, 1998.

Olechnowicz, Andrzej. 'Introduction'. In *The Monarchy and the British Nation: 1780 to the Present*, edited by Andrzej Olechnowicz. Cambridge: Cambridge University Press, 2007.

Olechnowicz, Andrzej. 'Historians and the Modern British Monarchy'. In *The Monarchy and the British Nation: 1780 to the Present*, edited by Andrzej Olechnowicz, 6–44. Cambridge: Cambridge University Press, 2007.

Olechnowicz, Andrejz. 'Britain's "Quasi-Magical" Monarchy in the Mid-Twentieth Century?'. In *Classes, Culture, and Politics: Essays on British History for Ross McKibbin*, edited by Clare V.J. Griffiths, James J. Nott, and William Whyte, 70–84. Oxford: Oxford University Press, 2011.

Otnes, Cele C. and Pauline Maclaran. *Royal Fever: The British Monarchy in Consumer Culture.* Berkeley: University of California Press, 2015.

Owens, Edward. *The Family Firm: Monarchy, Mass Media and the British Public, 1932-1953.* London: University of London Press, 2019.

Owens, Ed [Edward]. *After Elizabeth: Can the Monarchy Save Itself?* London: Bloomsbury, 2023.

Pearson, John. *The Ultimate Family: The Making of the Royal House of Windsor.* London: Bloomsbury Readers, 2016. https://www.google.com/books/edition/The_Ultimate _Family/EuacWNk3oTwC?hl=en&gbpv=1.

Pennybacker, Susan D. 'Mass Observation Redux'. *History Workshop Journal* 64 (Autumn 2007): 411–19.

Plunkett, John. *Queen Victoria: First Media Monarch.* Oxford: Oxford University Press, 2003.

Pollen, Annebella. 'Research Methodology in Mass Observation Past and Present: "Scientifically, About as Valuable as a Chimpanzee's Tea Party at the Zoo"?'. *History Workshop Journal* 75, no. 1 (2013): 213–35.

Pollen, Annebella. 'Subjective Cameras and Ekphrastic Writing: The Present and Absent Photograph in Mass Observation'. In *The Historical Contexts and Contemporary Uses of Mass Observation: 1930s to the Present*, edited by Lucy D. Curzon and Benjamin Jones, 107–27. London: Bloomsbury Academic, 2025.

Purcell, Jennifer J., ed. *Mass-Observation: Text, Context and Analysis of the Pioneering Pamphlet and Movement.* London: Bloomsbury Academic, 2023.

Purcell, Jennifer J. and Fiona Courage, eds. *Reflections on British Royalty: Mass Observation and the Monarchy, 1937-2022.* London: Bloomsbury Academic, 2024.

Purcell, Jennifer J. and Dorothy Sheridan. 'Voices from the Archive'. In *Mass-Observation: Text, Context and Analysis of the Pioneering Pamphlet and Movement*, edited by Jennifer J. Purcell, 118–35. London: Bloomsbury Academic, 2023.

Range, Matthias. *Music and Ceremonial at British Coronations: From James I to Elizabeth II.* New York: Cambridge University Press, 2012.

Richards, Jeffrey and Dorothy Sheridan, eds. *Mass-Observation at the Movies.* 2007. Reprint, London: Routledge, 2014.

Robinson, Cedric J. *Forgeries of Memory and Meaning: Blacks and Regimes of Race in American Theatre and Film before World War II.* Chapel Hill: Univeristy of North Carolina Press, 2012.

Robinson, Lucy. 'Perforating Event and Narrative, Experience and Analysis: Beyond the Retro Eighties'. In *The Historical Contexts and Contemporary Uses of Mass Observation:*

1930s to the Present, edited by Lucy D. Curzon and Benjamin Jones, 185–213. London: Bloomsbury Academic, 2025.

Rosenwein, Barbara. 'Worrying About Emotions in History'. *The American Historical Review* 107, no. 3 (2002): 821–45.

Scott, Joan W. 'Gender: A Useful Category of Historical Analysis'. *The American Historical Review* 91, no. 9 (December 1986): 1053–75.

Segal, Robert. *Myth: A Very Short Introduction*. Oxford: Oxford University Press, 2004.

Sheridan, Dorothy. 'Writing for….Questions of Representation/Representativeness, Authorship, and Audience'. In *Ordinary People Writing: The Lancaster and Sussex Writing Research Projects*, edited by David Barton, David Bloome, Dorothy Sheridan, and Brian Street, 17–23. Lancaster: The Lancaster and Sussex Writing Centre for Language in Social Life Working Paper Series, 1993.

Sheridan, Dorothy. 'Reviewing Mass-Observation: The Archive and its Researchers Thirty Years on'. *FQS Forum: Qualitative Social Research* 1, no. 3 (December 2000).

Sheridan, Dorothy, David Barton, Brian Street, and David Bloome. *Writing Ourselves: Mass-Observation and Literacy Practices*. Cresskill, NJ: Hampton Press Inc., 2000.

Shils, Edward and Michael Young. 'The Meaning of the Coronation'. *The Sociological Review* 1, no. 2 (1953): 63–81.

Sotomayor, Leslie C. 'Who's Curating?: Situating Autohistorias-Teorías in the Archives'. *Artizein: Arts and Teaching Journal* 5, no. 1 (2020): 129–40.

Steedman, Carolyn K. *Landscape for a Good Woman: A Story of Two Lives*. New Brunswick, NJ: Rutgers University Press, 1987.

Strong, Roy. *Coronation: From the 8th to the 21st Century*. London: Harper Perennial, 2005.

Summerfield, Penny. *Histories of the Self: Personal Narratives and Historical Practice*. London: Routledge, 2019.

Tagg, John. *The Burden of Representation: Essays on Photographies and Histories*. Minneapolis: University of Minnesota Press, 1993.

Tagg, John. *The Disciplinary Frame: Photographic Truths and the Capture of Meaning*. Minneapolis: University of Minnesota Press, 2009.

Thomas, James. 'From People Power to Mass Hysteria: Media and Popular Reactions to the Death of Princess Diana'. *International Journal of Cultural Studies* 11, no. 3 (2008): 362–76.

Trouillot, Michel-Rolph. *Silencing the Past: Power and the Production of History*. Boston, MA: Beacon, 1995.

Turner, Stephen and Edward Kissi. '"The Heart Has Its Reasons": Elizabeth II and the Post-Colonial Response'. *Journal of Classical Sociology* 23, no. 1 (2023): 142–8. https://doi.org/10.1177/1468795X221138108.

van Gennep, Arnold. *The Rites of Passage*, translated by Monika B. Vizedom and Gabrielle L. Caffee. 1909. Reprint, University of Chicago: Chicago Press, 1960.

Vegara, Maria Isabel Sanchez. *King Charles*. London: Frances Lincoln Children's Books, 2023.

Walker, Ian. *So Exotic, So Homemade: Surrealism, Englishness and Documentary Photography*. Manchester: Manchester University Press, 2007.

Wemyss, Georgie. *The Invisible Empire: White Discourse, Tolerance and Belonging*. Oxfordshire: Routledge, 2009.

Williamson, Philip. 'The Monarchy and Public Values, 1910-1953'. In *The Monarchy and the British Nation: 1780 to the Present*, edited by Andrzej Olechnowicz, 223–57. Cambridge: Cambridge University Press, 2007.

Wolff, Janet. *Austerity Baby*. Manchester: Manchester University Press, 2017.
Ziegler, Philip. *The Crown and the People*. London: Collins Publishing, 1979.
Zweiniger-Bargeilowska, Ina. 'Royal Death and Living Memorials: The Funerals and Commemoration of George V and George VI, 1936-1952'. *Historical Research* 89, no. 243 (February 2016): 158–75.

INDEX

Note: Page number followed by 'n' indicates note numbers.

Abdication Crisis   1, 41, 162
Aberystwyth   142
Abrams, Mark   121
academia   121–9
Addison, Paul   121
adultery   71, 73, 115–16, 122, 177
AIDS   7, 70, 176
Algeria   15–16
Alsace   146
Alzheimer's Disease   177
Andalucia   105
Anderson, Benedict   35
Andoh, Adjoa   51–3, 57, 166–7
Andrew, Prince   17, 23, 25, 70–1, 112, 176
Animal Rising   162
Anne, Princess   12, 17, 23–5, 38, 112–13, 116
anointing   22, 25, 28, 42–3, 108, 112, 135–7, 153
Anti-Monarchism   24, 27, 47–9, 56, 59–60, 64–5, 104, 107, 109, 115, 173, 175
Archbishop of Canterbury   17, 42–3, 104–5, 135, 142, 174, 177
A Queen is Crowned (film)   135
Arthur, King   65
ASDA   12, 65
astrology   161
Auschwitz   147
austerity   20, 104
Australia   15, 46, 116, 124, 170
Azores   129, 157–8

Baade, Christina   129
Bagehot, Walter   39, 126
Baker, Norman   75
Balding, Clare   116

Balfour, Michael   121
Balmoral   139
banal monarchism   35, 49
bank holiday   20, 61, 63, 68, 102–3, 105, 108, 111, 117, 151, 176
Barrow-in-Furness   177
Barthes, Roland   78
BBC   3, 13, 16–17, 22, 33, 58–9, 71, 73–4, 111, 116, 145, 154, 158, 166, 169–71, 177
Belfast   22, 24, 107
Belgium   48
Belize   170
Berlusconi, Silvio   58
Bernstein, Leonard   169
Big Help Out   61, 70, 104, 110, 173, 175–6, 180
Big Lunch   35, 57, 177
Billig, Michael   38, 40, 125, 155
Birmingham   1, 34, 41, 121, 150–1
Blackheath   149
Blitz   3
Bloome, David   120, 122
Boer War   52
Bolton   14
bombings   3, 142
Bond, James   145
Boorstin, Daniel   38
Brazil   48
Brexit   4, 51, 150, 162, 169, 171
Briggs, Asa   121
Bristol   52, 174
British Communist Party   150
British Empire   34, 52, 60, 77, 120, 137, 153, 158, 163, 166, 171
British Legion   105
British Social Attitudes (BSA) survey   49
Brixton   15, 86

Index

Broken Britain 4, 51
Brophy-Harmer, Khaleda 122, 129, 165
Brown, Wendy 166
Buckingham Palace 21, 24, 31–2, 45, 58, 64, 75, 125, 134, 149, 177
bunting 13–14, 19, 21, 28, 35, 50, 57–8, 66–8, 73, 75, 102, 109–11, 150, 173–4, 177, *see also* Coronations, and decorations
Burley, Kay 111

Caernarfon Castle 141
Calder, Angus 121, 195 n.11
Cambridge 150
Camilla, Queen 3, 14–16, 22–5, 28, 32, 48, 50, 57, 62–4, 67–8, 71, 75, 113, 116–17, 124, 161, 170, 173, 175, 177–8, 181
   and age 13, 18
   and comparison with Diana 4, 23
   and influence over Charles 5
   and Queen Consort 44, 46, 61, 72
   and rehabilitation of image 5, 44, 73, 111, 191 n.77
campers 3, 14, 45, 91–2
Canada 15, 34, 47, 93, 124, 154, 157–8
Cannadine, David 41
Casino Royale (novel) 145
Catherine, Princess of Wales 17, 29, 39, 48, 57, 61, 76, 106, 125, 170, 174
celebrity 1, 31, 38–9, 41, 46, 57, 76, 120, 124, 137–8, 155, 173–4, 181
Celtic (Football club) 103
Chamberlain, Austen (Sir) 41
Channel 4 12, 25, 113
Charles I 33
Charles II 33, 43
Charles III 3–4, 12–14, 16–19, 22–8, 31–2, 34, 38, 42, 45–6, 51–3, 58–70, 89, 102–17, 124, 136–7, 152, 154, 159, 161, 166, 170–7, 180–2
   and age 13–14, 18, 22–3, 50, 57, 71–2, 107
   and environmentalism 13, 23–4, 44–5, 60–1, 66, 70, 102, 111
   and political opinions of 179
   as Prince Charles 31, 44, 61, 110
   and body 129, 137–9
   investiture as Prince of Wales 141–3
   Prince's Trust (Charity) 45, 52, 70, 72, 108, 110, 179
   and Princess Diana 2, 4, 23, 45, 71, 116, 138, 176–7
   and 'Tampongate' 44, 177
   and public image 137–8
   and rehabilitation of image 5, 44–6
   and relationship with Camilla 23, 28, 45, 48, 61, 71, 75, 116–17, 161, 177
   and right to be king 4–5, 14, 45, 177
   and Wales 141–2
   and wealth of 50, 110, 124, 177, 179
Chichester 8, 14, 45, 79–80, 89
children 3, 12–13, 19, 26, 28–9, 31, 34, 45, 57, 59–60, 67, 69, 71–2, 102, 107, 111–12, 125, 149, 151, 154, 165, 167, 173–4, 176, 178
   and keepsakes 57, 72, 75, 145, 154
choirs 13, 22, 107, 169–71
chores 61, 71, 174
Christianity 26, 135, *see also* religion and Church of England
Christie, John 145
Church of England 42, 60, 64, 105–6, 126, 135, 174, 180
Citizen Kane (film) 142
Clancy, Laura 124–5, 155
class 37, 41, 46–7, 53, 60, 64, 68, 77, 104, 122–3, 125, 128, 151, 158
colonialism 15, 30, 60, 127, 129, 153, 170–1, 180, *see also* imperialism
Commonwealth 3, 15, 34, 46–7, 52, 124, 158, 169–71
Connolly, James 165
Conservative party (Tories) 4, 13, 20, 51, 56, 60, 63, 180
Cornwall 29, 107, 126
Coronation Concert 18, 73, 110, 129, 169–72
Coronations
   and ambivalence 5, 14, 28–9, 46, 49–51, 62, 65, 70–1, 124, 155, 158, 170

Index

and avoidance   20, 26–7, 50, 56, 63, 67, 74, 106, 109, 111, 173–5, 186
and celebrations   13, 19–21, 23, 28, 33–4, 45, 57, 59–60, 65, 67, 74, 102–4, 106, 109–10, 173–5, 181
and commentary   24–5, 33, 42, 51–3, 64, 112, 114, 150, 166
and commercialization   2, 12–13, 45, 65, 81, 85, 181
and coronation service   2, 13, 16–18, 21–2, 25–6, 28–9, 32, 41–4, 46, 52, 56, 58–61, 63–7, 72–4, 103, 107–9, 111–12, 114, 117, 135–7, 139, 142, 149, 152, 158, 162, 166, 170, 173–4, 180, 182
and cost of   2, 14, 19–21, 27–9, 49–50, 56–7, 61, 63–4, 66–7, 69, 71, 73–5, 103–4, 106, 110, 113, 134, 151, 173, 175, 179–81
and decorations   2, 8, 12–15, 19, 31, 34–5, 50, 58–9, 66, 79–80, 86–7, 91, 99, 105–6, 111, 117, 142, 149–50, 165, 174–5, 177
of Elizabeth I   33
of Elizabeth II (*see* Elizabeth II, Coronation)
and food   3, 12–13, 17, 21, 23, 29, 57, 59, 62, 65–7, 73, 85, 107, 111, 117, 165, 181
of George IV   33
of George V   165
of George VI   2, 4, 32, 34, 68, 77, 119, 123, 126, 149–50, 153, 161
and historical significance   16, 19, 21–2, 24, 26, 29, 34, 43, 50, 56–9, 61, 63, 65, 68, 71, 75, 104, 108–11, 113, 173, 180
and music   18, 22, 28, 33–4, 57, 61, 64, 72, 107, 112, 114, 151, 158–9, 169–70, 172
and mystery   41–4, 46, 63, 66, 112, 129, 135–6
and pageantry   13, 41, 56–8, 61, 67, 102, 107, 142, 147, 150, 179
and personal recollections   3, 12, 23, 26, 58, 67–8, 72–5, 107, 112, 145, 147, 153, 177

planning of   12, 28, 34–5, 57, 65–6, 73, 102, 106, 117, 151–2, 163, 169, 175, 177–8
and pomp   16, 21–2, 27, 30, 56–7, 63–4, 66–7, 77, 108, 137, 141, 152, 173–4
and processions   2–3, 17, 22–3, 26, 31–5, 59, 63–4, 77, 111, 137, 149, 154, 162, 165, 178
and religion   26, 43, 52, 64, 72, 74, 135
and representation   2, 51–2, 57, 60, 64, 72, 74, 103, 107, 152, 159, 165–7, 169–71, 178
and school celebrations   3, 13, 23, 26, 57, 59, 73, 165, 167
and souvenirs   2, 13, 57, 65, 72, 75, 145, 154, 159
and spectacle   1–2, 20, 22, 25–6, 32, 61, 65, 67–8, 113, 128, 165–6, 169, 173, 179
and televising of   2–3, 6, 12–13, 16, 18–19, 21–2, 24–7, 29, 31–2, 51–2, 58–9, 61, 63–9, 73–4, 102, 104–6, 109, 111–13, 116, 119, 136, 139, 142, 145, 153, 157–8, 166, 173–4, 180
'uncoronation'   161
and volunteering   19, 62–3, 104, 170, 173
cost of living crisis   4, 26, 49, 56, 63, 66–7, 74, 104–5, 110–11, 128, 150, 162, 169, 179
Covid-19   4, 48, 56, 72, 105, 116, 134, 157, 178
Cromwell, Oliver   43
Crown estate   29, 107
Crown, The (television programme)   15, 44, 124
Crownations   33–4
crowning   17, 26, 29, 32, 43, 67, 69, 74, 114, 117, 162
Curzon, Lucy   129, 154–5

deference   3, 104, 149–50
democracy   19–20, 43, 65–6, 78, 109, 135, 150, 152, 170
Denmark   60
Deslandes, Paul   129, 137, 139

Devon 50
Diana, Princess 4, 14, 44, 63, 70–1, 96, 116, 175, 178, 181
 and death of 4, 6, 45, 70, 123–4, 161
 and Prince Charles 2, 23, 45, 122, 137–9, 176–7
DiAngeo, Robin 166
Dilke, Charles 41
Dimbleby, Jonathan 116
Disney 57, 71, 169
divorce 1, 4, 38, 45, 117, 138, 161, 177
documentary 2, 38, 45, 78, 123, 125, 171
Downey, Robert Jr. 46
dreams 79, 126, 133–6
drinking 24–5, 64, 151, 158, 177
Duchy of Cornwall 29, 107, 126
Duchy of Lancaster 19, 29, 126

Eden Project 117
Edinburgh 65, 151
Edward I 42, 135, 141
Edward II 33
Edward, Duke of Edinburgh 17, 38
Edward the Confessor 42–3, 72
Edward VII 135, 141, 158
Edward VIII 1, 4, 117, 141, 161–2
 as Duke of Windsor 2
Edwards, Huw 116
elections 15–16, 20, 60, 159
Elizabeth, Queen Mother 75, 125, 138, 150
Elizabeth I 22, 33, 120
Elizabeth II 2–3, 17, 27, 38, 44, 50, 61, 64, 68, 70–3, 102, 106, 108, 110, 117, 133, 135, 138, 141, 143, 154, 175–7, 180
 and coronation 2, 16, 22–3, 28, 32, 50, 56–7, 59, 61, 67–9, 71–3, 75, 109–10, 112, 122, 125–6, 134–5, 142, 145, 149, 153, 158, 169, 171, 177–9
 and death of 14, 18, 20, 22, 26, 39–40, 42–5, 56–7, 64, 74–5, 109, 114–15, 129, 133–4, 141, 150, 154–5, 162, 175, 177, 180–1
 and jubilees 2, 19–20, 26, 28, 35–6, 45, 68, 74, 104, 125, 134, 159, 177, 180
 and 'New Elizabethan Age' 4, 134, 172

Elizabeth of York 33
Ellis, Catherine 129, 157–9
emotions 4–6, 16–18, 21, 23, 26, 37, 39–40, 42, 44, 46, 51, 63, 67, 112, 122–4, 127, 129, 134, 139, 146–7, 155, 158, 162–3, 165–7, 178, 181
enchantment 135, 149
environmentalism 14, 18, 24, 29, 31, 44–5, 52, 59–60, 66, 70, 102, 110–11, 137
Ethiopia 176
Europe 4, 43–4, 73–4, 124, 150, 158
European Union 150
Eurovision contest 17, 74
everyday, the 5, 7, 34–5, 40, 78, 120, 123–5, 152–3, 163, 166–7

fairy tales 24, 45, 72
fascism 4, 162
fashion 23, 26, 31, 37, 58, 65, 68, 73, 96, 109, 112, 114, 138–9, 151, 153, 171, 174, 181
femininity 138, 163
Ferrier, Kathleen 145
fireworks 33
First World War 150, 173
Fisher, Geoffrey 135, *see also* Archbishop of Canterbury
flags 12–14, 19, 23–4, 28–9, 31, 34–5, 52, 58, 63, 67, 87, 96, 99, 105–6, 111, 117, 142, 149, 165, 169, 174–5, 177–9
food banks 19, 28, 63, 69, 179, 184
football 14, 70, 103
Francis, Martin 129, 133
Freemasons 174
French Resistance 147

Game of Thrones (television programme) 39, 69, 180
gardening 22, 27, 106
Gawthorpe 28
gender 53, 72, 122, 127, 137–9
George, Prince 17
George IV 33
George V 37, 41, 141, 158, 165
George VI 2, 4, 32, 34, 41, 68, 77, 119, 123, 126, 134, 149–50, 153, 161

Germany   146–7, 159
Glencross, Matthew   124
Globe, the   52
graffiti   35–7, 50–1, 142
Granada   105
Grant, Hugh   46
Grant, Patrick   58
Greece   108
Green Park   31, 33, 87, 134
Grim Reaper   115, 161
Grosvenor Square   134

Hage, Ghassan   166
Hall, Stuart   78, 162
Handel, George Friderik   170
Harris, Leonard   2
Harrisson, Tom   2, 4, 8, 78, 119–20, 135, 167
Harry, Duke of Sussex   15–18, 22–3, 25, 48, 66, 70–1, 111, 116–17, 139, 162, 176–8
Hartley, L. P.   145
Hayward Gallery   27
Henry VII   32
Hinton, James   2, 6, 122, 127
HM Prisons   8, 21, 26, 64, 178
holiday (travel)   56, 61, 67, 108, 170
Holocaust   146–7, 155
homelessness   27, 178
Hong Kong   60
Hubble, Nick   129, 142–3
Hurdley, Rachel   123, 127–8
Huxley, Julian   119
Hyde Park   15, 31–3, 77, 97, 99

Ibiza   169
imagined community   35–6, 40, 48, 51–3
imperialism   34, 47, 52–3, 60, 77, 120, 137, 152–3, 158, 163, 166, 171
inequality   20, 24, 104, 125, 166
Instagram   29, 66, 70, 108
Ipsos Mori (market research company)   49
Isle of Man   126, 177
Isle of Portland   21
Isle of Skye   126
Isle of Wight   26, 64
It's a Royal Knockout (game show)   38
ITV   51–2, 111, 116, 165–6

Jamaica   170
Jenkins, Karl (Sir)   114, 161
Jennings, Humphrey   2, 8, 77, 123, 135, 151, 167
Jeremy Kyle Show (talk show)   116
Jerusalem   112
John, Elton   170
Johnson, Boris   60, 66, 68, 74
Jordan   48
Just Stop Oil   116, 161–2

Kandiah, Michael   124
Keep, the   35, 37
Kent   14, 40, 159
Kimmerer, Robin Wall   53
King Charles (children's book)   45
Kissi, Edward   158
Kramer, Anne-Marie   127, 155
Kuhn, Annette   78, 153–5

Labour Party   47
Lancashire   154
Lancing   14
Landsberg, Alison   155
Langhamer, Claire   129
Last, Nella   135
Leeds   28
Leith, Dame Prue   111
Leith   65, 151
Lindsey, Rose   123
Liverpool   59, 74, 141–2
London   3–4, 8, 12, 17, 19, 27, 32–3, 35–6, 63, 68, 70–1, 74, 77, 125, 134, 137, 145, 147, 149–52, 154, 157, 173–4, 178, 181
London, Jack   158
Lucas, Caroline   109

Macron, Emmanuel   58
Madge, Charles   1–2, 5–6, 8, 121, 123, 135, 149, 167
Madrid   105
Mair, Kimberly   129
Malinowski, Bronislaw   119, 190 n.61
Mall, the   3, 14, 16, 21, 45, 77, 91–3, 96, 178
Manchester   145, 147, 151
Mann, Thomas   41
Manuel II   158

Index

Marble Arch 149
Margaret, Princess 117
Markle, Meghan Duchess of Sussex 15–18, 23, 45, 48, 114, 125, 128, 161, 166, 169, 176
Marr, Andrew 154–5
Marxism 128, 154, 167
Mary I 139
masculinity 129, 137–9
Mass-Observation 1–2, 5–9, 77–9, 111, 119–23, 125–9, 134, 149–54, 161, 167
 anthropology of ourselves 1, 120
 Archive 35, 37, 119, 121, 127–8
 and Day Surveys 1, 8–9
 and diaries 126, 150
 and Directives 2–3, 6–8, 49, 75, 122–3, 127, 155
 and File Reports 2
 First Year's Work, 1937-8 119
 May the Twelfth: Mass-Observation Day Surveys 1937 by over Two Hundred Observers 1–2, 6, 77–8, 119, 123, 150, 158, 161–2
 and monarchy 2, 5
Mass Observation Project 2, 121–2, 128, 188 n.24, 196 n.14
Masters, Brian 133
Matilda 33
Matthews, Stanley 3
Maxton, James 41
May, Rollo 40
McKibbin, Ross 123–4, 136
media 1–3, 5–6, 14–15, 28, 35–7, 39, 42–4, 46–9, 51–3, 56, 59, 66, 71, 88, 108, 111, 116, 118, 122–3, 125, 128, 134, 138, 152, 155, 157, 162, 166–7, 170, 176, *see also* social media
memes 30, 65
Metz (France) 146–7
Milburn, Martina Dame 45
military 26, 45, 58, 110, 113, 138, 159, 161, 181
Minogue, Kylie 170
Mitchison, Naomi 135
monarchy 3, 6, 16, 21, 32, 35, 41, 48, 57, 61, 63–4, 72, 105, 107, 113, 119–20, 123–9, 135–7, 141, 154–5, 158–9, 162, 169, 174, 180
 and abolishment of 14, 21, 40, 47–8, 60, 64, 69, 71, 104, 108, 173
 and celebrity 38–9
 and Commonwealth 15, 46–7, 158
 and community (or unifier) 14–15
 constitutional 36, 39–40, 66
 and cost of 15, 20, 21, 60, 104, 108, 110
 and elitism 68
 and the everyday 34–5, 40
 and future of 14, 46–9, 51, 58–60, 62, 65, 69–70, 73, 135, 143, 163, 171, 174
 and image management 37–8, 137–8
 and indifference 62
 and the media 6, 36–8, 43
 and modernity 141, 159
 and myth 40–1, 50
 and national identity 15, 35, 39–44, 49–51, 108, 125–6
 and opinion polling 2, 6, 49, 51, 104
 and philanthropy 45, 52, 70, 72, 108, 110, 179
 and racism 128, 166
 and relevance 5, 19, 46, 51, 65, 70, 74, 103, 110, 128
 and religion 43, 135
 and ritual 41–3
 and role of 14–15, 19, 46
 and scandal 38–9, 51
 and social media 47–8
 and tourism 61, 108, 173
 and wealth 18, 20
Moor, Liz 123
Mordaunt, Penny 13, 21, 61, 65, 106, 113–14, 181
Morpurgo, Michael (Sir) 111
Moscow 116
Mountbatten, Earl Louis 75
Mt. Everest 3, 71, 145
Mudiad Amddiffyn Cymru (Movement to Defend Wales) 142
Muggeridge, Malcolm 38
multiculturalism 53, 72, 135, 169–70

music, *see* Coronation Concert; Coronations, music
myth 1, 18, 40–2, 44, 47, 49–51, 53, 66, 123, 126, 134, 136

Nairn, Tom 39, 41
National Health Service (NHS) 20, 27, 51, 63, 102–3, 170, 179
national identity 6, 40, 49–51, 119, 123, 125–6, 149
  and the British 13, 15, 22, 36, 40, 52, 66, 107, 126, 149, 166
nationalism 35, 49–50, 53, 71
Nazis 6, 146
Nelson, Trevor R. 129
New Brunswick 34, 53
newspapers 27, 36, 38, 61, 114, 119, 142, 150, 165
Nigeria 15–16, 170
Noakes, Lucy 129
Norfolk 34, 133–4
Northern Ireland 22, 24, 107, 126, 142, 145, 174
nostalgia 3, 166
Not My King 68, 70, 116

oath of allegiance 12, 18, 25, 60, 62, 64–6, 103–4, 129, 142, 152, 174
Ofcom 52, 166
Olechnowicz, Andrzej 34, 49, 124–5
Olivier, Laurence 135
olympics 70
Oswestry 13
Owens, Edward 37, 126
ox roasts 34, 151
Oyelowo, David 45

para-social relationships 39
Paris 147
parliament 40–1, 95, 141
Pennybacker, Susan 122
pensioners 31, 176
People's Coronation 152
performance web 166–7
Perley, Imelda 34, 53
Perry, Katy 170, 178
personal identity 5, 8, 39–41, 50, 110, 123, 166–7

Philip, Duke of Edinburgh 2, 35, 70, 104, 116, 176
photography 8, 26, 31, 37–9, 48, 68, 77–99, 102, 115, 137–8, 146–7, 153, 157, 173, 176, 194 n.4
Picture Post (magazine) 78
Plaid Cymru 141
Pocock, David 122
police 14–15, 21, 24, 29, 60, 77, 115–16
politicians 15–16, 31, 109–10, 145
politics 4, 15–20, 26, 29, 41, 46, 51, 63, 66, 68, 70, 105, 110–11, 116, 119, 122–4, 141, 150, 154, 159, 162–3
popular memory 153
Portugal 157–8
postbox toppers 19, 35, 92
poverty 4, 20, 111
Private Eye (magazine) 69, 84
privilege 24, 30, 41, 56, 60, 69–70, 75, 104, 106, 139, 150, 154, 166–7, 173, 176
propaganda 109, 111, 121, 180
protest 20, 24, 45, 50, 60, 63, 67, 70, 94, 106, 110–11, 115–16, 141
psychics 161
Public Order Bill 162
pubs 25, 61, 63–4, 103, 105
Purcell, Jennifer J. 124–5
Putin, Vladimir 58

Qatar 75

race 51–3, 58, 127–9, 165–7
radio 6, 27–9, 33, 37–8, 61, 112, 114, 119, 123, 133, 154, 166–7, 171
rationing 3, 57, 69, 145
recipes 17, 66, 73, 111
Red Arrows 17, 24, 74
referendum 28, 47, 49, 142, 150
regalia 18, 22, 26, 34, 41, 43, 141, 159, 181
religion 2, 43, 47, 52–3, 72, 74, 108, 123, 135, 174, 180
Renan, Ernst 53
Republic UK (organization) 46–7, 70, 104, 109, 116, 162
republicanism 14, 39–41, 43, 46–51, 62, 65, 67–8, 70–1, 73, 75, 104–5, 108–9, 116, 150, 162, 170–1, 173–4, 177, 181

Richard II 22
Richard II (play) 52
Ritchie, Lionel 170, 178
ritual 1–2, 26, 29–30, 41–3, 46, 56, 58, 61, 72, 77, 112, 119–20, 129, 135–7, 139, 149, 152, 161–3, 165, 173, 181
Robinson, Cedric 167
Robinson, Lucy 7–8, 128, 199 n.65
Rowbotham, Judith 124
royal body 39, 137–9
Royal Family 3, 5, 20, 27, 29–30, 37–8, 40, 42–3, 47–50, 56–7, 61, 64, 67, 70–1, 73–5, 103, 107–9, 113–14, 117, 120, 122–6, 129, 133, 155, 157, 166, 173–4, 180–1
    and cost 69, 75, 174
    and deaths 2, 6, 26, 39–40, 42, 44, 64–5, 70, 73–4, 104–5, 123–4, 129, 134, 141, 154–5, 161, 176, 178, 180
    and dreams 79, 133–6
    and image management 38, 110
    and scandal 75, 102, 116
    and soap opera 39, 67, 113
    and weddings 2, 64, 73, 75, 106, 122, 137–8, 154, 161, 174
Royal Family, The (documentary film) 38, 125
Royal National Lifeboat Institution 170
Royal Variety Performance 169
rumour 2, 39, 116, 126, 129, 161–3

Sainsbury's 181
Salisbury 8, 92
Sandringham 133–4
São Miguel 157
Saudi Arabia 75
scandal 1–3, 38–9, 75, 176
Scotland 15, 25, 47, 51, 56, 67–8, 73, 107, 126, 134, 138–9, 142, 151, 170
Scottish National Party (SNP) 47
Second World War 52, 57, 69, 72, 119, 121, 123, 138, 171
self, the 2, 5, 40, 53, 127–8
Sex Pistols 159, 177
sexuality 122, 137–8
Shakespeare, William 21–2, 52, 169

Sheridan, Dorothy 7, 120, 122–3, 195 n.13
Shils, Edward 125, 158
Shoreham-by-Sea 102
Simon, John Sir 41
Simpson, Wallis 1, 161
Sky News 111, 116
slavery 52, 60, 155, 170
Smith, Graham 47
social consciousness 1, 2, 5, 167
social media (blog, forum, internet) 6, 37, 39, 46–8, 51, 61, 107–8, 114, 119, 167, 176
    Facebook 107
    Instagram 29, 66, 70, 108
    Reddit 47
    TikTok 111, 114
    WhatsApp 8, 12, 22, 64, 181
    X (Twitter) 24, 47–8, 65, 112, 115, 181
    YouTube 28, 42, 52
Soho 91, 145
Somerset 14
Sophie, Duchess of Edinburgh 17, 25
South Bank (London) 27, 134
Southampton 14
Spain 31, 105–6
Spitting Image (television programme) 113
St James Park 32
St Vincent and Grenadines 178
Starmer, Keir 47
Stone of Scone 25
Street, Brian 120
street parties 3, 12, 19, 24, 26, 57, 62–3, 65–6, 68, 102–3, 105, 107, 109, 111, 117, 143, 174, 177, 181
Streisand Effect 115
Strong, Roy 41, 46
Sudan 176
Sulzberger, C. L. 3–4
Summerfield, Penny 121–2
Sussex, University of 6, 121–2, 127

Tagg, John 78–9
Teddy Boy 145
television 2–4, 6, 12–13, 16, 18–19, 21–7, 29, 32, 37–8, 58–9, 61, 63–7, 69, 71, 73–4, 102, 104–6,

109, 111–13, 119, 123–4, 136, 138, 142, 145, 153–4, 157–8, 165, 173–4, 178, 180
Tennyson, Lord Alfred 51
Thompson, Major Johnny 114
Tonga, Queen of 12
Tories, *see* Conservative party
Toronto 157
tourism 27, 31–2, 61, 79, 107–8, 134, 173–4, 179
Townsend Affair 2, 117
Transport for London 15, 90, 125, 134
Trump, Donald 60, 66
Truro 107
Truss, Liz 68
Tudors 21, 139
Twickenham 158

Ukraine 4, 17
United States 4, 14–15, 40, 60, 66, 68, 71, 74, 109, 115, 124, 134, 161, 169, 170, 176–7, 189 n.29, 190 n.54
Uprichard, Emma 123

Victoria 34, 36–7, 51, 120, 137
Virtual Commonwealth Choir 170–1
visual narrative 77–9
volunteerism 19, 61–3, 70, 104, 110, 122, 170, 173, 175–6, 180

Waitrose 79
Wakefield 28
Wales 25, 45, 126, 141–3
walking 24, 27, 56, 65–6, 106
Walney Island 177
weather 3, 12–13, 19, 21, 24, 27–8, 31–2, 50, 66, 102, 126, 129, 149, 157, 175, 177
Webber, Andrew Lloyd 170

Welby, Justin 17–18, 26, 42–3, 104–5, 117, 135, 142, 174, *see also* Archbishop of Canterbury
Wemyss, Georgie 166
West Side Story 169
Westminster Abbey 13, 21–2, 26, 28–9, 32–3, 43, 51, 63–4, 67, 73–5, 77, 88, 94, 104, 107, 111, 113–15, 134–5, 142, 150, 152, 157, 161, 166, 180
Westminster Hall 134
WH Smith 34, 45
whiteness 52, 57, 122, 127, 129, 165–7
Who Do You Think You Are? (television programme) 155
William I 33–4
William, Prince of Wales 17–18, 73, 105, 112–13, 116, 125, 141, 170, 174–5, 178, 181, 198 n.45
and passing over Charles as King 4–5, 14, 45, 57, 107, 175, 180, 182
Windsor 73, 138, 169
Windsor, House of 18, 33, 37, 44, 66, 120, 123–6, 171
Windsors, The (television programme) 12, 25, 67, 113
Winwood, Steve 171
Wolastoqey Nation 34, 53
Wolf, Naomi 115
Wolff, Janet 129, 145–7
World Cup 70

Yeovil 14
Yes Cymru 142
Yorkshire 3, 27, 106, 174
YouGov 28, 49, 51, 193 n.117, 200 n.6
Young, Michael 125, 158

'Zadok the Priest' (choral anthem) 18, 32, 74
Ziegler, Philip 2, 122